For Peter Fawbert
A warrior and a survivor

Damien Lewis

OPERATION RELENTLESS

THE WORLD'S MOST-WANTED CRIMINAL
THE ELITE FORCES HUNT TO CATCH HIM

Quercus

First published in Great Britain in 2017 by

Quercus Editions Ltd
Carmelite House
50 Victoria Embankment
London EC4Y 0DZ

An Hachette UK company

A CIP catalogue record for this book is available
from the British Library

HB ISBN 978 1 84866 539 2
TPB ISBN 978 1 84866 543 9
Ebook ISBN 978 1 84866 540 8

PICTURE CREDITS
(numbered in order of appearance)

1 – Mike Snow
2, 17 – USAF
3 – Vladimir Melnik
4, 9, 16, 19, 20 – DEA exhibits
5, 7, 8 - Andrew Chittock
6 - Reuters
9 – DEA
10 – Reuters/Jose Gomez
11 – Reuters/Jaime Saldarriaga
12 – AP/Fernando Vergara
13 – Reading Eagle
14 – Alamy/SPUTNIK
15 – Getty/Luis Robayo
18 - Snow/Sagastume

10 9 8 7 6 5 4 3

Text designed and typeset by CC Book Production
Printed and bound in Great Britain by Clays Ltd. St Ives plc

Once the wings go on they never come off . . . They fuse to the soul through adversity, fear and adrenalin, and no one who has ever worn them with pride, integrity and guts can ever sleep through the call of the wild . . .

When a good flier retires . . . we wonder if he knows what he is leaving behind . . . We know that after a lifetime of camaraderie that few experience . . . there is a fellowship that lasts long after the flight suits are hung up in the back of the closet. We know that even if he throws them away, they will be on him every step that remains in his life. We know that the very bearing of the man speaks of what he was and in his heart still is.

Because we flew, we envy no man on earth.

Author unknown

Life is very much a matter of luck and the odds in favour of success are in no way enhanced by extreme caution.

Erich Topf

ACKNOWLEDGEMENTS

I am grateful to the following for their efforts and assistance in enabling me to tell this story:

Annabel Merullo, my literary agent for this book at PFD. My film agent, Luke Speed, at Curtis Brown. All at my publisher Quercus, and especially my editor, Richard Milner, Ben Brock (editorial), Charlotte Fry (editorial), Dave Murphy (sales), Bethan Ferguson (marketing) and Patrick Carpenter (cover design).

Freelance editor and fellow author Josh Ireland. Lucy Dundas and Digby Halsby at Flint PR. My UK researcher, Simon Fowler. My US researcher, Sim Smiley; thank you for all your sterling efforts. Dawn Dearden, Senior Public Information Officer for the US Attorney's Office for the Southern District of New York. Caroline Walton, author of books on Russia and the USSR, who acted as my Russian translator. David Lewis, who acted as my French translator.

Michael Braun, former DEA Assistant Administrator and Chief of Operations, and now General Manager at SAVA Workforce Solutions. Lord Peter Hain, who as a government minister spearheaded the British efforts to capture Viktor Bout, for his comments and insight. Lee Wolosky, who during his time at the NSC led the US hunt for Viktor Bout. General Sir David Richards for his comments on the Sierra Leone conflict and permission to use them herein. Author and sometime Bout confidant, Gerald Posner, for the timely discussions and insight. Former SAS man and TV adventurer, Bear Grylls. Matt Potter, author of *Outlaws Inc.*, a superlative book about the global airfreight business and the arms trade. Saul David, friend, fellow author and commentator on all matters military. Paul and Anne Sherratt, for the Curaçao visit and the excellent input, as always.

I am also indebted to those authors and others that have previously dealt with some of the topics addressed in this book. In alphabetical order they are: Douglas Farah and Stephen Braun (*Merchant Of Death*); Andrew Feinstein (*The Shadow World: Inside the Global Arms Trade*); Peter Hain (*Outside In*); Alexander Mishchenko (*Escape From Kandahar*); Matt Potter (*Outlaws Inc.*); Tony Gerber and Maxi Pozdorovkin (the documentary film *The Notorious Mr. Bout*).

I am enormously grateful for the cooperation, assistance and hospitality extended to me by Mike Snow, Margaret Snow and Carlos Sagastume.

Finally, my heartfelt thanks, once again, to Eva, David, Damien Jr and Sianna, for putting up with me during the time spent writing.

It can't have been easy.

AUTHOR'S NOTE

During the writing of this book I have been granted access to DEA (Drug Enforcement Agency) transcripts and recordings, and to the records of the court case that resulted from Operation Relentless. The scenes and dialogue as portrayed in this book are largely based upon those recordings and transcripts, augmented by the personal testimonies of those involved.

Transcripts have been used verbatim, complete with verbal errors, grammatical errors and incorrect spelling. To note all these 'errors' in the customary fashion – [sic] – would be too repetitive and burdensome and I have refrained from doing so. At times, the dialogue may appear a little stilted and disjointed, but this is how people tend to converse, especially when they are not speaking in their first language. For clarity, use of ellipses generally denotes a break, where I have edited conversations to ease the sense and flow.

The only scene germane to Operation Relentless for which there exist almost no DEA transcripts is that of Andrew Smulian's meeting with Viktor Bout in Moscow. Smulian spoke at length about this meeting under oath at Bout's trial, and also under cross-examination. I have worked on the assumption that what he said under oath in a US court of law is true and accurate. My rendering of this part of the story is also based upon the testimony of the DEA team as to what Smulian told them, immediately following his Moscow visit.

The DEA carried out in-depth forensic analysis of Viktor Bout's laptop computer, which was seized during the Operation Relentless takedown. I have had access to that analysis as it was presented at Bout's trial. Elements of this story that concern the computer and online activity of the protagonist(s) are based upon that forensic analysis, which is remarkably detailed and revelatory.

I have also had access to the plethora of trial documents, and the appeal documents, resulting from Bout's court hearings. While this book chiefly tells the story of the hunt for, and capture of, Viktor Bout, I have endeavoured to tell a fair and balanced story from the side of the hunted. However, I did not find some aspects of Bout's defence credible. The verdict at his trial would seem to suggest that the jury came to a similar conclusion.

A number of the Confidential Sources – DEA undercover agents – who testified at Viktor Bout's trial did so using aliases, for security reasons. Likewise I have been asked to use aliases in this book. I have also, where requested, altered some minor biographical details, to further protect identities and for security reasons. This includes changing a number of individuals' names, specifically at their request or at the request of the agencies for which they work.

In papers filed by Bout's lawyers in the US Courts, the Mike Snow written about in this book has been accused of being an agent in the employ of MI6, Britain's Secret Intelligence Service, as has fellow Britain Andrew Smulian, also written about in these pages. No credible evidence is presented to support these claims and I have no reason to believe that either individual served with Her Majesty's Secret Intelligence Service.

As a general rule, I have referred to the Operation Relentless members via the names that their teammates used for them: Christian names or nicknames.

Two major conflicts in recent history have dominated news headlines: the wars in Iraq and Afghanistan. However, this same period has witnessed other, equally devastating wars, which flew largely below the radar in terms of Western consciousness. In Angola, Rwanda, the Congo, Sudan and Sierra Leone these 'second level' conflicts rumbled on largely unnoticed by the outside world, yet claiming a far greater loss of life than both the Iraq and Afghan wars combined. In the Congo alone some five million are estimated to have died. These conflicts were perpetuated in large part by the clandestine flow of weaponry to these parts of the world.

This is the story of how one of the men most implicated in that illicit trade – the Russian arms trafficker and businessman, Viktor Bout, also known as 'The Merchant of Death' – was brought to justice. It is the story of the undercover operatives who went into harm's way to track him down – a cast of maverick adventurers, former soldiers, agents and informants who succeeded where all others had failed. It deals, therefore, in part with those 'forgotten' modern wars that have convulsed the continent of Africa.

CAST OF CHARACTERS

MICHAEL SNOW: former British soldier and bush pilot, recruited by the DEA as a confidential source on Operation Relentless. Known to all as Mike or The Bear.

JOSEPH REILLY: British pilot long versed in operating in Africa, and Mike Snow's sometimes co-pilot. Known to all as Joe.

CARLOS SAGASTUME: former Guatemalan military G2 intelligence officer, turned longtime DEA confidential source. Known to all variously as Carlos, El Mexicano and the King of Sting.

RICARDO JARDENO: former Colombian military officer, turned DEA confidential source, known to all on the Operation Relentless team as Ricardo and El Comandante.

PIERRE VILLARD: French former bush pilot turned aircraft dealer and DEA confidential source, known to all as Pierre.

WILLIAM BROWN: former US Marine (reserves) and one of the two main DEA Agents on Operation Relentless, known to all as Wim or Dutch.

ROBERT ZACHARIASIEWICZ: former US Navy and one of the two main DEA agents on Operation Relentless, known to all as Zach or Polski.

LOUIS MILIONE: former actor and the DEA's Supervising Agent on Operation Relentless, known to all as Lou.

RÓMULO RAMIREZ: former Venezuelan Air Force pilot turned drugs trafficker and money-launderer.

LOUIS STAVROS: US citizen of Greek extraction who works as an undercover source for the DEA, on financial and money-laundering operations.

ANDREW SMULIAN: British-born former South African Air Force officer and bush pilot, known to all as Andrew or Babu (Swahili for grandfather).

MIKHAIL BELOZEROSKY: Viktor Bout's longstanding Russian bodyguard.

VIKTOR BOUT: former Russian Air Force and alleged Soviet intelligence officer, turned global airfreight operator, known by a number of nicknames and aliases.

CHAPTER ONE

HIGHVELD EAST OF JOHANNESBURG, SOUTH AFRICA, MAY 1995

He came to with a start. His limbs were stiff and cramped with the cold. For a brief moment he tried to work out what had woken him. Then he heard it: the squawk of radio static reverberating around the bare and echoing hold.

With bleary eyes Mike Snow checked his alarm clock: 3.15 a.m. Who in the name of God was calling at this time? Of one thing he felt certain: it couldn't be good news. He was still weak from a bout of malaria, and he wasn't feeling on top of the world.

Mike had slept the night in the aircraft. It was a crazy thing to have done, but he'd just felt too tired to drive home after a long day working on the engines. An icy wind whistled through the open-sided hangar, rattling the tin-sheet roofing. It was one of those bitter nights for which the South African highveld – the high-level inland plateau – is famous.

He swung his legs off the fold-up camp bed. His throat felt parched, his eyes smarted and he was frozen to the bone. He forced himself to focus on the caller: 'Can you send a taxi to Northgate ASAP?' the voice intoned.

The message was from the UNITA representative then living

in South Africa, UNITA – the National Union for the Total Independence of Angola – being a US-backed guerrilla movement fighting the leftist government of Angola, an oil- and diamond-rich nation set on the west coast of Africa.

The message was code for: 'Depart for Charlie Two right away'.

Charlie Two was a rich alluvial diamond mine set amidst the rugged folds of the Kwango River valley, in north-eastern Angola. The Kwango River's diamonds were UNITA's chief source of revenue right then, but for Mike it was a punishing eight-hour flight away.

For a moment he considered replying: 'Taxi out of order.' But he didn't want to ruin his reputation for prompt and reliable service. Instead, he replied: 'Will be there shortly.'

He sat on the bed, head pounding and throat rasping. He couldn't remember the last time he'd felt this bad. *Coffee. He needed coffee.* He sent a second message, this to his co-pilot: 'I cannot sleep'. Standard code for: 'Get yourselves here; we have a flight.'

That done, he wrapped his sleeping bag tighter around himself and shuffled out of the aircraft, reaching for the camping stove.

The hangar lay on the edge of a dirt airstrip that had once served a remote farmstead, both of which were now long abandoned. It was still perfectly usable, if freezing cold and unwelcoming at this time of the year. The early highveld winter had proved harsh: frost had already burned the thick bush grass an anaemic yellow.

From the far corner Mike heard bodies stirring. Kema and Zorro, his trusty Congolese flight mechanics.

A figure made his way through the darkness. 'Bonjour, boss. Do we have work?'

Mike nodded. The way he was feeling right now, he wouldn't be up for speaking much until Kema had made him several cups of his signature strong black coffee. Snow could be blunt-spoken and abrasive, and he was known to rub people up the wrong way, but his Congolese aircrew were fiercely loyal, as he was to them. Wherever Snow went across strife-torn Africa, Kema and Zorro followed.

Kema squatted, reaching for the percolator. 'I will make café,' he announced, quietly.

Zorro joined him, lighting the Petromax paraffin lantern and setting it on its hook. They settled back to watch the coffee brew, chatting softly in Swahili – their native tongue – while Mike contemplated the journey ahead.

The wind gusted, setting the lantern swinging and sending ghostly shadows dancing through the hangar. Somehow, he found the hiss of the burner and the familiar smell of kerosene fumes comforting. Despite the state that he was in, he felt sure they'd be all right. Joe Reilly, his first officer, had just had three days' solid rest. He was sure to be raring to go.

Mike, a former SAS soldier turned bush pilot, known to all as 'The Bear', was short, squat, shaven-headed and massively barrel-chested, with rugged, weather-beaten features. Everyone presumed it was his physique that had earned him his nickname. It wasn't. As a child he'd been something of a rebel without a cause. When he was twelve, he'd been given a cast-off rabbit-skin coat by his father, who'd worn it to fend off the cold when serving as an electrician in the RAF during World War Two.

Mike had cut the sleeves off, turning it into a body-warmer. He'd taken to wearing it the wrong way around, with the fur on the outside. One day he'd gone to visit a schoolmate. His friend was out, but when the kid got home his father had told him: 'One of your mates called. He was wearing this coat with the fur on the outside. Made him look like a bear.' After that, he'd been 'The Bear' ever since.

Mike's teachers had told him that he'd 'never amount to anything'. Repeatedly. At age sixteen he'd gone for a stint in the Merchant Navy, then tried for SAS selection, largely to prove them wrong. After a decade or more in elite soldiering he'd struck out for Africa. Having earned his SAS wings in Britain, he'd gone on to win his pilot's wings in South Africa, and flying had become his passion. It had proved a crazy, highwire ride for the past two decades – a long blast of adrenalin-fuelled adventure.

No doubt, tonight's mission promised more of the same.

The snarl of Joe Reilly's flame-red Ducati announced his arrival. He swept into the hangar dressed like an Eskimo, trussed up against the bitter cold. A stocky redhead with close-cropped hair, fellow-Brit Reilly was Mike's long-time co-pilot. A bundle of energy, he made a beeline for the mug proffered by Kema, and with one hand supping coffee and the other stripping off his biking gear he began firing questions at Mike.

Mike told him the little that he knew about the coming flight: their destination, plus the call in the middle of the night signifying that it had to be urgent. Joe had checked on the weather conditions: they'd have a good tailwind at between twelve and seventeen thousand feet, though it would be minus sixteen degrees outside.

'It's going to be one cold flight, that's for sure,' he added.

Mike stared into his coffee mug. 'I'm not looking forward to it, to be honest. But we need the money.'

4

By now the coffee pot was drained dry, and Mike was feeling marginally better. There were three hours until sunrise, in which time they needed to get airborne and well on their way.

Mike got to his feet. He eyed Joe. Dressed in his thick sheep-skin flying-jacket he looked more like a Second World War fighter pilot than any modern-day sanctions-busting adventurer, which considering the age of the aircraft they were flying was somehow rather apposite.

'Let's do it,' Mike growled, his thick north-east of England tones overlain by a South African accent, the legacy of the years spent living in the country.

He clambered into the aircraft. In his mid-forties, his limbs weren't quite as nimble as they used to be. Still, he figured he had a good few years flying left in him.

Joe set off on a pushbike to place storm lanterns at the far end of the runway. Mike needed a reference point to aim for in the darkness. Kema and Zorro hooked up the aircraft's tow bar to Mike's 4x4, and dragged it out of the hangar.

Joe returned, and stood where Mike could see him, giving the thumbs up: *start engines*. Mike felt the aircraft rocking in the wind as he flipped the magnetos for engine one: it coughed into life almost instantly. Those three days on maintenance had been time well spent.

The roar of the lone engine shook the entire airframe, as all fourteen cylinders began to fire smoothly. Mike had his eyes glued to the oil and fuel gauges. Once those had stabilized he fired-up number two engine. He raised his eyes to Kema and Zorro and gave the signal to remove the chocks from the wheels.

They darted beneath the wings, reappearing moments later

chocks in hand. Struggling against the back-blast from the props, they rushed around to the rear and handed the chocks inside, before squeezing through the cargo door that battered against them in the wash.

Several minutes later and with oil temperatures 'in the green' – the safe operational zone – Mike taxied on to the runway. He lined up, nose into the teeth of the wind. The buffeting tugged at the flight controls, making column and rudder pedals judder back and forth, as he fought to keep hold of them.

Joe glanced at Mike from the co-pilot's seat. 'The sooner we get airborne and out of this wind, the better.'

'Thirty inches manifold pressure,' Mike ordered.

'Thirty inches,' Joe confirmed, nudging the throttles forward. 'All temps and pressures in the green.'

Mike reached out his hand and eased the throttles to take-off power, keeping his eyes glued to the two marker lanterns twinkling in the darkness up ahead. He felt Joe tap his hand, to indicate they were at max power, and he released the brakes. As the aircraft surged forwards, Mike felt that familiar buzz of being poised to take to the skies.

'Forty knots, temps and pressures all in the green,' Joe intoned. Then, as they gathered speed: 'V1! Rotate!'

Moments later Mike felt the wheels lifting free of the dirt strip. It had taken a bare few seconds and six hundred feet for this ageing war-bird to claw her way into the stormy skies.

You didn't find many DC3s flying commercial operations outside of Africa these days. The military cargo version had proved one of the most iconic aircraft of the Second World War, but it had been quickly superseded by more modern airframes. Yet its rugged construction, ease of maintenance and ability to land just about anywhere made it a regular in some of the remoter parts of Africa.

Mike loved the aircraft. Everything about it thrilled him, not least its classic lines. This morning, as they pulled away from the airstrip he could tell that she was flying beautifully.

At two hundred feet he levelled off. They would steer a course north through the hills, keeping low to avoid detection by the nearest radar station at Johannesburg's international airport. Joe spread a chart across his lap, showing the altitude and direction they needed to fly between each marked waypoint.

Some legs required Mike to lose altitude; others to climb to avoid a small hill or power cables. It had taken hours of daylight flying to plot this route, ensuring they could execute it in pitch darkness. Still, there was little room for error. One moment's lost concentration, one wrong move, and the DC3 would plough into the highveld.

As they thundered onwards the atmosphere was thick with tension. This was flying at its most challenging and there were no words spoken, except for the turn and altitude instructions from Joe and Mike's terse verifications. Two sets of eyes scanned the night, not that there was a great deal to be seen. Outside the glow of the flight deck it was a sea of inky black.

They pressed northwards towards the Magaliesberg Mountain range. Rising to some 6,000 feet, the Magaliesbergs formed a natural barrier where the highveld gave way to bushveld – lower-lying semi-tropical plains stretching north. The passage through the Magaliesbergs presented Mike his greatest challenge.

The twists and turns and heart-stopping plunges became ever more extreme as he threaded the DC3 along a thickly wooded pass between knife-cut peaks, the snarl of the engines reverberating off sheer rock walls. Mike kept one eye glued to the oil temperature and pressure gauges; the slightest change might signal danger, and in such terrain disaster could quickly follow.

He threw the DC3 through the last of the split-second manoeuvres, and they left the peaks of the Magaliesbergs behind them. Mike would have to stick to tree-top height until they reached the vast expanse of the Kalahari Desert, to avoid detection by the radar base at Botswana's capital, Gaborone – the next major airport on their flight path – but at least it was mostly flat terrain.

The first streaks of silver-blue rent the distant horizon. So far it had all been perfectly timed: all any observers on the ground might have seen was a flash of blue exhaust flames as the DC3 roared overhead, but no one would be able to identify the aircraft.

They pressed on for thirty minutes, flying at one hundred feet across flat grasslands dotted with acacia trees, before Mike figured they had to be well out of radar range.

He handed the controls to Joe. 'Configure to climb at fifty feet a minute, target altitude 12,000.'

It was a slow rate of climb, but deliberately so, to conserve fuel. Once they reached 12,000 feet they'd accelerate to the DC3's cruise speed of 200mph, for the air was thinner at altitude and made for faster flying.

Mike ducked through the doorway leading into the hold and was hit by a blast of freezing air. The aircraft's bare metal sides acted as a cold sink, sucking the chill through to the inside. Kema and Zorro were busy strapping down camp beds to lugs set in the floor.

Snow busied himself over the stove, frying bacon and brewing coffee to ward off the chill. They needed it: for every thousand feet of climb, the outside air temperature plummeted by three degrees centigrade. The men perched on the camp beds and ate and drank in silence, as the aircraft continued to gain altitude.

They were flying over one of the harshest lands in Africa – the 360,000-square-mile Kalahari Desert – where it is terribly tough to survive. Likewise, the African airfreight business was a cutthroat, dog-eat-dog affair. Mike had resorted to stripping out the DC3's heating system, to save weight. Removing it meant that more cargo could be carried. He'd replaced it with a simple but well-tested system: blankets, plus Second World War sheepskin flying jackets.

Mike felt confident they'd slipped through invisible to any radar. Once they crossed the border into Angola there would be few such worries, for that country possessed no radar facilities whatsoever. But the Angolan government did operate a Beech-craft King Air, a fast turboprop aircraft packed full of electronic warfare equipment. It could detect electromagnetic emissions from aero-engines at up to 26,000 feet, and would have little problem finding the DC3.

Mike had one card up his sleeve: the Beechcraft was flown by a pilot who was an old acquaintance of his. Mike had warned him that if he ever interfered with The Bear's operations, he should expect long and lasting retribution. The pilot has assured him that he'd turn a blind eye, for Mike was 'one of the boys'. In due course he'd even telephoned to warn Mike of Angolan Air Force operations in his area.

But Mike still didn't trust the guy entirely: once into Angolan airspace they'd need to keep a close watch on surrounding skies. As they alternately munched on bacon and took a sniff of oxygen – you needed it at such altitude – they chatted away about why they might have been called to Charlie Two at such short notice.

'Maybe Savimbi is sick and needs to get to hospital,' Zorro suggested.

'Nah,' Mike replied. 'If he's that sick they'd have called for the Learjet.'

Jonas Savimbi was the UNITA leader. A man of that importance and means would call for a fast executive jet were his life in any danger, not a relatively slow DC3.

'Yeah, I guess it's got to be something more ... interesting,' Zorro conceded. 'But what?'

They threw the question around for a while, but no one seemed to have any answers. They'd just have to see what transpired upon arrival at Charlie Two. They were making excellent progress and Mike figured they'd complete the entire flight within seven hours, a record for the DC3, which was normally laden with cargo.

Beer, cigarettes and whisky were the commonest loads, hence the need to keep below any radar cover. The deal with Savimbi was simple. His miners needed feeding and watering, and Mike had to show his purchase receipts upon delivery. He was allowed to make twenty-five per cent on top, to cover his expenses, but if he was ever caught messing with diamonds he was out.

One hundred miles out from Charlie Two the DC3 began its descent. Mike was back in the pilot's seat, and he was scanning the Angolan air traffic control frequencies. He'd detected no other aircraft, but there was always the chance that another operator was 'silent running', so they'd need to keep their eyes peeled.

Mike waited until he was executing his final turn, before making contact with UNITA's air traffic control. If the King Air pilot was out flying search patrols, he'd be monitoring the UNITA frequencies. He could warn ground or airborne units to intercept Mike's aircraft, but not when he was this close to landing. In active war zones like this, it was such precautions that kept you alive.

As he neared Charlie Two, Mike searched the long expanse of red dirt, checking for any recent deliveries. The real player when it came to jetting in supplies to UNITA was a somewhat mercurial Russian called Viktor Bout. Bout was former Russian military, reputedly former Russian intelligence, and a serious contender in the airfreight business. In contrast to Mike's lone DC3, Bout operated a fleet of gnarly Eastern European cargo planes, including dozens of giant Ilyushin and Antonov aircraft.

He had a reputation – hard won – of being able to fly just about anything anywhere. It was an open secret that he was shipping in weapons and victuals to both sides in Angola's civil war. The UNITA high command's attitude seemed to be 'better the devil you know', plus there was no one else with anything like the capacity, the connections or the clout of Viktor Bout.

Mike did what he did for a love of flying, of Africa and adventure. Bout, by contrast, was a skilful and clever businessman with truly global reach. He'd made millions – some said billions – of dollars from his airfreight operations, and his mantra was never to fly empty. He'd even furnished Savimbi with a training force for his fighters, led by Slava Grinche, a friend from Bout's military days, leading a force of Russian military veterans.

Mike and Bout knew each other, of course. Your paths couldn't fail to cross in this kind of business. Over the years the two men had developed a wary respect for each other, and it made sense for Mike to keep an eye on what the big guy in the airfreight business was up to. But he wasn't naive or deluded enough to ever consider himself a competitor. They were in totally different leagues.

Mike couldn't see anything strikingly new at Charlie Two in terms of deliveries. The touchdown went without a hitch, and he taxied to a standstill on a dirt airstrip fringed with thick bush. He powered down the engines and hurried aft to greet Americo, the UNITA Chef du Bas – the chief of operations at Charlie Two.

'Mark, Mark, how are you?' Americo asked, thrusting out a hand in greeting. He pronounced Snow's first name as 'Mark', Mike seemingly beyond him. 'We are so happy you could make it today.'

Mike shook his hand. 'Always happy to oblige, Americo. And how is everything right now?'

Americo rapidly dispensed with the pleasantries, leading Mike towards his headquarters. 'Come. I explain everything.'

Mike was doubly intrigued. Such directness was unusual with the UNITA crowd. Normally, there was plenty of time for swopping news and stories.

Americo's headquarters hardly warranted the name. It was a tin shack with a dirt floor about the size of a single garage. Inside it was furnished with a basic wooden desk, a gaudy red velour sofa and a fridge. That was about it. Americo waved Mike towards the sofa, and asked if he'd like tea or a soda.

'Tea please. I'm still cold from the flight.'

It was stiflingly hot here in the Kwango River valley, but Mike had yet to warm up. Americo ordered his batman to fetch tea, then settled behind his desk.

'Mark,' he announced, leaning forward, 'this is a very, very, very important job you have to do for the boss.'

Mike nodded his reply. The floor was uneven, and he noticed that the desk tended to wobble back and forth as Americo talked.

'You have to fly one of our Special Forces officers to South.'

'South' was coded slang for South Africa. 'You will fly him to a grid reference that he will give you, and there . . . he will parachute from your plane. Do you understand?'

Mike's mind was racing, as images of what he was being asked to do here flashed through his head: a lone UNITA parachutist leaping out over South African territory. For what possible purpose, he wondered? Mike was somewhat taken aback, but there was no sense in betraying that to Americo.

'Yes, sir, I understand,' Mike replied, evenly.

'Good. I'm curious. Have you ever done anything like this before?'

'Many times. When I was younger I flew a lot of skydivers.'

Americo smiled. 'Ah, Mark, that is very, very, very good.'

During his time in the military Mike had jumped out of a fair few aircraft himself. Indeed, it was that experience and watching the pilots fly the C130 Hercules that had first given him the idea that one day, he'd like to give this flying lark a go. But it wasn't until he'd reached Africa that he'd finally got the chance.

The tea arrived, and Americo told the batman to go and call the individual who was going to jump out of Mike's plane. A lean figure entered, dressed in a military-issue jumpsuit under a thick khaki parka. Strange attire for the hot and sticky Kwango River valley, but not for leaping out of a DC3 into the freezing blue. Mike noted the gaunt face and the obligatory 'thousand-yard stare' that most battle-hardened UNITA troops seemed to possess.

He offered a hand. 'I am Lieutenant James Bokk.'

'I'm Mike. Why don't you show me what you're intending.'

By way of answer Bokk pulled out a map and with a thin grass stalk pointed out the Drop Zone (DZ) where he wanted Mike to deliver him. 'This is the DZ. It will be lit with good lamps, so it should be easy to spot?'

'Let's hope so,' Mike affirmed. 'We can talk more once we're airborne. No point wasting any more time.'

Bokk went to fetch his gear. Mike bid farewell to Americo and made his way back to his aircraft. Joe had refuelled the DC3 from barrels of avgas stacked beside the strip, and was busy having a 'bush shower' – using a bucket with holes punched in the bottom slung from the port side propeller.

'We've got one VIP passenger going back to Jo'burg, for a special meeting,' Mike announced. 'Get done with your ablutions and let's get rolling.'

Kema and Zorro made do with throwing a bucket of water over their heads. The take-off went smoothly, and less than two hours after touching down they were heading back south at altitude.

Mike handed the controls to Joe, and went aft to speak to 'Skydiver', as he'd nicknamed Bokk in his head. Bokk handed Mike a scrap of paper with the scribbled latitude and longitude coordinates of the DZ.

'Are you good to drop me from 15,000?' he asked.

'Say that again?' Mike queried.

Jumping from 15,000 feet put this into the kind of territory that Mike had trained for, when serving with Special Forces. Sure enough, Bokk planned to execute a HALO – a High Altitude Low Opening jump. In a HALO you jumped at anything up to 30,000 feet, and plummeted to earth in a crazed freefall, triggering your chute at the last possible moment, which gave the enemy minimum time to target you while in the air.

'I can do 15,000, but it's not without its risks,' Mike told Bokk.

'I've got no way of knowing the wind speed at the DZ, and I can't exactly get on the air and ask anyone.'

Bokk pulled out a compact satellite phone from his backpack. 'I'll call the reception party at the DZ, and ask.'

Mike shrugged. 'I'll drop you from 15,000. But it's your funeral.'

They talked over the details of the jump some more, before Mike's curiosity got the better of him. Where had a UNITA Lieutenant learned to HALO, he asked. Bokk explained that a handful of UNITA high-fliers had received training from Brazil's Special Operations Brigade – their nearest equivalent to the SAS – and he was a veteran of dozens of HALO jumps.

Bokk's explanation had answered one of Mike's questions. But the big one – the elephant in the room as it were – remained: what exactly was Bokk's mission? He had hauled a massive rucksack into the DC3's hold, and Mike figured he had to be delivering some specialist kind of cargo. He just couldn't fathom what.

Bokk got his head down and was shortly in the land of nod. Mike studied his maps, matching up the coordinates of the DZ with what lay on the ground. Bokk and his people had planned the drop most carefully. The DZ lay within a vast conservation area, and there were no public roads or human settlements for miles around – no inquisitive eyes to spot the lights marking the DZ.

Over the years Mike had learned not to pry too much about the comings and goings he facilitated from places like Charlie Two, but with Skydiver he felt he had the right to probe a little. When Bokk stirred he popped the question: what was his mission for tonight?

Bokk explained that he was meeting with a general in the South African Defence Force. Mike didn't believe a word. If the

SADF top brass needed to talk to UNITA, they would hop on an aircraft and go to meet Savimbi. It was more likely an illicit diamond deal or cash transfer; eyeing Skydiver's bulging pack, Mike favoured the latter.

UNITA was paid in cash for its diamonds. US dollars, which could be traded on the black market in South Africa for up to twenty-five per cent more than the official exchange rate. It made good commercial sense to bring cash into the country undetected, but even by Mike's standards HALO-ing at night from 15,000 feet to a clandestine DZ was a little . . . extreme.

UNITA would only accept payment in cash for the diamonds they mined, for obvious reasons. Those dollars were in turn used to buy weaponry. Global arms dealers were only too happy to do business with them, and on occasions flights packed with weapons were traded direct for gemstones. Indeed, Viktor Bout was known to have a gemologist that he kept on a retainer, for flying into places like Charlie Two to value parcels of uncut stones.

Many times Mike and his crew had spotted the telltale tracks left by giant Russian Ilyushin IL-76 cargo aircraft – the 'Vodka Burner', to those in the trade – at UNITA airstrips. The massive four-engine jets could carry up to fifty tonnes of cargo, and they left a distinctive signature on the long dirt runways. UNITA kept its own gemologist on hand to ensure that the Russian arms dealers gave them a reasonable price on their wares.

The going rate was for UNITA to accept between three to six per cent below the prices paid on the bourses of Antwerp, Tel Aviv or Zurich, the main diamond-trading centres of the world. It might seem like a small margin, but with parcels of eight to twelve million dollars' worth of stones being handed over for a single aircraft's cargo, there was real money to be made.

Twenty minutes out from the DZ they removed the para-hatch from the DC3's main cargo door. A panel two metres high and one wide, it would be a tight squeeze for Skydiver. As Mike went forward to take control of the aircraft, Bokk was busy on his satphone, warning the reception party of his imminent arrival.

'Five minutes out,' Mike informed all, via the DC3's intercom.

'Jumper ready and has given thumbs-up,' came the reply from the hold.

At three miles out Mike spotted the lights blinking far below – an isolated L-shape marking the LZ (landing zone). He eased the throttles back, slowed to seventy-five knots and began the countdown: 'Twenty, nineteen, eighteen . . .' Far below the lights slipped out of view beneath the DC3's bulbous nose. 'Three, two, one, GO!'

In the DC3's rear the lone figure dropped into the empty darkness. Bokk's head-torch plummeted away from the DC3, as he accelerated into the freefall, before being swallowed into the black of the night.

He was a brave man for sure, Mike reflected.

CHAPTER TWO

SHARJAH AIRPORT, UNITED ARAB EMIRATES,
AUGUST 1995

Figures scurried about in the arid heat, using thick ropes to drag the chocks away from the Ilyushin's massive wheels. The giant aircraft squatted on the burning hot asphalt, her fuselage painted in the distinctive red, white and green of Airstan, a Russian-based airfreight company.

To one side lay the sun-blasted, featureless desert and scrub of the Emirate of Sharjah, situated just to the north of Dubai, and forming part of the United Arab Emirates. To the other stretched the single black runway and taxiways, plus the assorted hangars serving the dozens of airfreight companies operating out of Sharjah's busy global cargo hub.

Thankfully, the temperature inside the Ilyushin's massive air-conditioned cockpit was blissfully cool. Designed back in the sixties as a commercial freighter able to carry heavy cargoes to remote areas, the IL-76 had earned a reputation of being a bulletproof-reliable workhorse that was able to brave the most challenging of flight conditions.

In the left-hand seat, Commander Vladimir Sharpatov, a decorated former Soviet Air Force veteran, was preparing to get airborne. The Ilyushin's cavernous hold was crammed full of crates of shells and ammunition – including some three million AK-47 rounds – loaded aboard the aircraft in Tirana, the capital of the Eastern European country of Albania. Sharpatov was keen to get his cargo delivered to its destination, nine hundred miles east across the Gulf of Oman.

Commander Sharpatov and his crew had executed this flight many times before: this should be just another routine delivery.

Sharpatov began to taxi towards the runway. On his right sat Gazinur Khairullin, his co-pilot, and behind them in the cave-like rear were his flight crew – navigator Alexander Zdor, radio operator Yuri Vshivtsev and flight engineer Ashkad Abbyazov. The atmosphere was relaxed as they joked via the radio with their air-operations manager, situated in their Sharjah business headquarters.

Behind Sharpatov figures reached back and forth across the dimly lit space, flicking ranks of switches and adjusting illuminated dials. All in their thirties or forties, Sharpatov's six-person crew were veterans of this kind of work, and he had every confidence in them, just as he had in his aircraft.

As Sharpatov lined up the IL-76 on the runway, this unassuming, levelheaded man was keen to get under way. Sharpatov had three decades' experience as a pilot. He lived to fly, and his love of the profession hadn't dimmed much over the years. Shortly, the 152-foot long behemoth was powering along the runway, her four giant turbofan jet engines howling deafeningly as he eased them up to maximum take-off thrust.

The Ilyushin climbed to her cruise altitude of 30,000 feet, Sharpatov and crew settling back to enjoy the incredibly smooth and almost silent ride. They were dressed in the spotless white uniforms with golden epaulets of Rus Transavia Export, the aircraft's operator, a company run by the Russian entrepreneur and businessman Viktor Bout. Sharpatov had flown many such trips, and he found his boss to be a softly spoken, calm, but grittily determined man, and very business savvy. If you worked conscientiously for Bout, he was known to take very good care of his aircrews.

Sharjah International was perfectly situated for an airfreight business such as this, which covered the Middle East, Africa and south-central Asia. It was made all the more attractive in that the regulation and inspection regime at Sharjah was somewhat less rigorous than that at many other airports, to put it mildly.

Not that there was anything illegal about today's flight. The customer was the government of Afghanistan, then run by President Burhanuddin Rabbani. Locked in a bitter and bloody struggle for control of Afghanistan, Rabbani's forces had lost huge swaths of territory to the Taliban. This cargo of weaponry was desperately needed to repulse the Pakistani-backed religious militants.

Ironically, Rabbani – a former Mujahideen commander who had fought against the Russians during the 1970s and '80s – was now reliant upon a Russian businessman providing Eastern Bloc weaponry. At Rabbani's behest Bout's freighters had airlifted in hundreds of tonnes of arms sourced from Albania, Bulgaria and other former Soviet republics.

Or rather, such shipments were more often at the orders of Ahmed Shah Massoud, the legendary Mujahideen leader who was Rabbani's defence minister. Over the course of their dealings, Bout and Massoud had become good friends. Indeed, Bout believed that Massoud and Rabbani offered the only hope for

Afghanistan. Of Massoud he remarked, 'You could see the flame in his eyes.'

Privately, Massoud and others railed against the high prices that Bout charged for his services. But who else had the capacity and the connections – not to mention the appetite for risk – to fly such missions?

Commander Sharpatov's flight had been airborne for around an hour-and-three-quarters when a harsh alarm started blaring through the cockpit. It was the air-collision warning indicator. The seemingly inconceivable had happened: Sharpatov's plane had suffered a close brush with an unidentified aircraft.

There was precious little air traffic over war-torn Afghanistan, and Sharpatov and his crew could barely believe that this was happening. But before they could check whether the warning indicator was malfunctioning, they caught sight of the aircraft. The dart-like silhouette of a fast jet – military, undoubtedly – flashed past just above the Ilyushin's cockpit.

Sharpatov ordered his radio operator to check if the mystery aircraft was trying to make contact. As he did so, the jet eased down towards the Ilyushin's stern, then crept past its port wing, coming to rest just abeam of Sharpatov's position in the pilot's seat.

Commander Sharpatov eyed the unidentified warplane. With its rocket-like nose-cone set within a cylindrical air intake, before sharply raked wings and tail, it was unmistakable: it was a Soviet-era Mikoyan-Gurevich MiG-21 supersonic jet fighter. This one had to be a decade or more old, but Sharpatov didn't under-estimate its air-worthiness or potency as an attack aircraft.

After a little dial-twiddling, Sharpatov's radio operator was able to raise the MiG's pilot, only for him to order 'plane 842' to

land in Kandahar. By 'plane 842' he had to be referring to the Ilyushin – its tail number was 76842 – and 'Kandahar' had to mean
Kandahar International Airport, some two hundred miles short
of their intended destination, Bagram Airbase just outside Kabul.

More to the point, Kandahar was Taliban-controlled territory.
In a few short seconds the jovial atmosphere in the Ilyushin's
cockpit had evaporated.

Kandahar was the Taliban movement's spiritual heartland,
and the base from which they had launched an insurgency that
threatened to engulf the entire nation. Kandahar Airport was one
of the country's largest airbases, and doubtless where the MiG-21
now sitting on Sharpatov's wingtip hailed from.

Any order to land at Kandahar had to be resisted.

Sharpatov knew that neither his flight nor its cargo were
illegal. The Albanian authorities had signed a contract with the
Afghan regime to provide the weaponry. Bout was the carrier,
and Sharpatov had already made two such runs under this very
contract: the Taliban had no right to force them down.

Sharpatov challenged the pilot's reasons for ordering them to
make a forced landing. The answer came back that plane 842 was
flying over the territory of the 'Islamic Emirate of Afghanistan',
and that Sharpatov needed to land in Kandahar so they could
inspect his cargo.

'You've got no right to make us land,' Sharpatov retorted.

'You must land as instructed,' the MiG pilot shot back at him.
'It's an order. It's not a joke. You have to land. You don't have any
choice.'

For a long moment Sharpatov eyed his crew. What options did
they have? Most, like him, were familiar with the MiG's capabilities. They certainly couldn't outrun her, and their lumbering

transport plane was hardly going to outmanoeuvre the agile fighter. Plus the MiG boasted a 23mm cannon and heat-seeking missiles; shooting down the Ilyushin would be like hitting a barn door at ten paces.

As if to underline the threat the MiG's pilot executed another pass, streaking past breathtakingly close to the Ilyushin's cockpit and triggering the warning alarm again. Sharpatov had already ordered his radio operator to try to raise their Sharjah headquarters. Did the pilot really understand who he was dealing with? This was a Russian aircraft and a Russian crew, and to mess with them was tantamount to messing with the Russian state.

But maybe that was in part what this was about? Sharpatov didn't doubt that the Taliban wanted to inspect his cargo, and for 'inspect' you could substitute 'seize', as far as he was concerned. But were the Taliban also trying to force some kind of showdown with the Russian government, the old enemy?

In a sense it didn't much matter right now. The MiG was circling Sharpatov's aircraft, as if preparing to open fire.

'I have my orders. I'll shoot you down,' the MiG pilot warned.

Sharpatov had one last ruse to play. He argued that his aircraft had full fuel tanks and was too heavy to risk landing. It might explode upon impact, turning the airbase into a raging inferno. The MiG pilot was having none of it. He repeated his ultimatum. Either Sharpatov turned his aircraft on to a bearing for Kandahar International, or he would blast them out of the skies.

Sharpatov took a quick poll of his crew. Though shocked and appalled at the unimaginable turn of events, all were in agreement: it was either land, or die. They'd have to take their chances in Kandahar.

Reluctantly, Sharpatov turned his aircraft onto a bearing for

Kandahar International, and with the MiG in close escort he began his descent.

A short while later Sharpatov saw the blocky form of the Kandahar control tower looming out of a dusty, haze-enshrouded plain. To one side the crumpled brown folds of a range of mountains rose in the distance, while the McDonald's-like arches of the airport's main terminal building drew closer by the second.

Designed and built in the fifties by American architects with American money, Kandahar was meant to serve as a NATO-friendly airbase on the Soviet Union's doorstep. But the years of subsequent conflict had taken their toll. Apart from the odd shrivelled tree and the ranks of tin shacks, the airport looked brown, sun-blasted and bare.

Sharpatov had a horrible sinking feeling in his guts, as his wheels made contact with the grey concrete of the runway. He taxied to a halt, clouds of sand and dust billowing from under the Ilyushin's giant wings. A high chain-link fence fringed the runway, with a line of red-painted stones on the far side. Anyone with any experience of the Afghan war knew what that signified: they were placed there to mark the border of a minefield.

Sharpatov knew he had to show some leadership right now. He hurried aft to be the first down the ladder. Outside, there was a welcoming committee of sorts. A group of around a dozen presumably Taliban, dressed in baggy black trousers and Arabic-style scarves, swarmed around the aircraft.

The Ilyushin's captain stepped down to meet them, followed closely by his crew.

Each of the Taliban sported an AK-47, and the atmosphere was confrontational from the very start. Sharpatov demanded an explanation for their use of force against a Russian aircraft, but the more he sought answers, the more the aggression and animosity became palpable.

The standoff finally came to an end when he and his crew were bundled aboard an ancient-looking VW airport bus. As they were driven away from the runway, their Ilyushin was left where they'd parked her, isolated on one corner of a concrete apron fringed with scraggy brown grass and war debris.

The VW bus sped out of the airport, but not before the crowd that had gathered vented their anger and frustration on the vehicle, raining down blows from sticks and from fists, and from the butts of rifles. Word had spread about the new arrivals, and as Sharpatov and his crew were soon to realize, the sins of Russia's war in Afghanistan were about to be visited very personally on them all.

The bus barrelled through the dilapidated streets of Kandahar, heading towards the Governor's residence. Even as it did so, Taliban fighters were already breaking open the green wooden crates in the Ilyushin's hold, revealing their contents. Just as they'd hoped, Sharpatov's aircraft was chock-full of weaponry.

Upon the VW's arrival, the seven men were bundled out and thrust into Kandahar's version of hell: a dirt-floored compound open to the sky, with a sagging washing line strung across it, plus a couple of wire-framed garden chairs and some battered oil drums piled in one corner. On the walls above, guards toting AK-47s ratcheted back their cocking mechanisms menacingly, as if to open fire.

Sharpatov – a literature graduate – began noting everything in his diary. Just days into captivity, he wrote: 'In one week we have all become old men. The courtyard is forty-five paces long and there are two little cells. This is our home ... On the roof they keep pulling back the bolts of their machineguns. But the most depressing thing is the unknown. The life of each of us is worth no more than a bullet.'

As the aircrew struggled to come to terms with their new living quarters, none of them would have believed that they were to be imprisoned here for the next 378 days.

It would be a time of terrible privation, and it would end in the most unimaginable of ways.

CHAPTER THREE

KINSHASA, DEMOCRATIC REPUBLIC
OF THE CONGO, APRIL 2001

Five years on from delivering Skydiver without any undue blow-back, business was expanding for Mike Snow. He'd acquired some new aircraft and a new base from which to operate: Kinshasa, the capital of the Democratic Republic of the Congo, more commonly known as 'the Congo' to Mike and his ilk.

The Congo was Joseph Conrad's infamous 'Heart of Darkness', if you believed the hype. Mike didn't. He loved the place. Kinshasa was unique: a city full of energy and spirit, plus Belgian-inspired cuisine and culture. More to the point, the Congolese people were some of the kindest, or so Mike found them. Of course, being Congolese, Kema and Zorro were delighted to be based in their home country again, and to be near their loved ones.

Ever since colonial times the Congo had been repeatedly 'ragged, bagged and shagged', as Mike put it. Rich in resources – diamonds, precious metals and timber – the Congolese people had been robbed by everyone. But in spite of that they remained upbeat, vibrant and loyal to a fault, and they lived in hope.

This was embodied by their attitude to education: they would bust a gut to send their children to school, proud in their smart uniforms and never missing a day. Hope sprang eternal in the Congolese psyche, and that was what Mike so admired.

He also loved the sheer unpredictability of the place. Everything was 'fucked up', as he put it, so you had to think on your feet. He liked that. He liked the open spaces, lack of rules and the pioneering spirit. He couldn't stand the rigid constraints of Western societies. He didn't like tick to follow tock the whole time.

He'd been based in Kinshasa for three years now, and he'd become quite a figure in his own right. Famous or infamous, depending on how you viewed things. The Congo was the kind of place where Mike felt he could be something, and maybe do some good while he was there. Or so he hoped.

The Congolese climate did take some getting used to, though. It was sticky, hot and humid the entire time. In the 'cold' season it was thirty degrees; thirty-four the rest of the year. Thankfully, Mike's house perched on a hill set a thousand feet above the surrounding city, so it enjoyed a little cooling breeze.

Now into his early fifties, Mike figured he'd earned the right to a few of life's comforts. He'd hired Leon, a houseboy to look after him and his wife Margaret, a childhood sweetheart who'd followed him out to Africa. They would sit on the veranda of an evening gazing out over a city fringed with lush jungle.

'Leon!' Mike would call.

'Yes, Captain,' he would reply, in his French-accented English.

'Coffee, Leon.'

'Yes, Captain.'

Leon would materialize shortly with a tray laden with refreshments.

This was a dream job for Leon. It kept him and his extended

family in food and accommodation, and allowed him to pay his children's all-important school fees. As with Kema and Zorro – not to mention Mike's other Congolese crew – Leon had every confidence that the Captain would treat him well.

Mike's new aircraft – a pair of Canadair CL-44s, one of the world's largest commercial turboprops – had been rescued from an aircraft graveyard in North Carolina. They'd been lying there abandoned for seventeen years, most CL-44s having been retired from service in the seventies. Mike had purchased the two aircraft at scrap prices, no one ever imagining that he might intend to rebuild and *fly* them.

With a length of 136 feet and a cargo capacity of some 27 tonnes, the CL-44 had been a serious player in the airfreight business. It was never designed for landing on dirt strips carved out of the tropical bush, but experience had shown Mike that he could fly a CL-44 into just about anywhere, standing on his head and with his hair on fire.

With his CL-44s, Mike had formed Sky Master Freight Services. It was his ultimate riposte to Mr Foot, the form tutor who'd repeatedly told the young tearaway that he'd 'never amount to anything'. Mike figured he'd led an incredible life; he'd travelled the world as a merchant seaman; he'd soldiered in the SAS; and now he was running his own airline. Mike believed that no teacher should ever have spoken to a child as Mr Foot had done, and every day was about showing people like him just how wrong they had been.

It was 10 a.m. on 14 April 2001 when Mike took a phone call to alert him that his aircraft was loaded with 'general freight' and good to get airborne. As he drove to Kinshasa's N'Djilli Airport, he reflected upon how he'd heard that same refrain countless times before. He wondered what hurdles he'd have to leap this time before he took to the skies.

In a bid to curb the sneaking of contraband onto his flights, Mike had banned any loading at night, and it was mid-morning by the time they'd got the aircraft ready. A thought struck him in passing. Something of a history buff, he realized that it was the anniversary of the sinking of the *Titanic*, 89 years ago to the day. Mike wondered why that had come unbidden into his head.

He shrugged it off: there was flying to be done.

By 11.00 a.m. he was standing next to the sleek form of one of his CL-44s, checking the cargo-sheet and trying to ensure that the aircraft hadn't been too overloaded. Normally, any number of stowaways would somehow have made it onto the plane. They'd be crouched among the cargo crates, and all would need to be removed.

Nice people though they might be, the Congolese never seemed to understand that a badly overloaded aircraft was a dangerous aircraft. Mike was just in the middle of warning the airport's Chef du Bas, Gaston, that if there were too many stowaways it was very likely too late to get airborne, when all hell let loose.

A cataclysmic explosion ripped across the airport, the shock wave practically knocking Mike off his feet. He'd been standing in the shade beneath one of the CL-44's wings, and suddenly aviation fuel began to gush down from a ruptured fuel tank. At the same time Mike could hear heavy lumps of blasted metal crashing down onto the surrounding tarmac, deafeningly.

He dived for the cover of the main landing gear, as Gaston took to his heels. Then: *boom, boom, boom*. A further series of massive explosions rent the air, bleeding into one long continuous earth-shattering blast. As repeated shock waves tore over him, Mike felt the massive fuselage above rocking with the hits, twisted chunks of metal ricocheting everywhere.

The noise, the shaking of the ground and the shock waves were so all-consuming that it felt like being in the midst of an artillery barrage. As he tried to make himself as small as possible, to avoid being skewered by a lump of razor-edged steel, it dawned upon Mike that whatever was going on, he would be lucky to survive this one.

He didn't have a clue what was happening and there was no way for him to shoot back, for he had no idea who was attacking right now. He could only imagine that someone – the Congo was awash with various rebel factions – had dynamited the military's ammo dump, which lay just near by.

Mike smelled jet fuel thick and heady in his nostrils. Swivelling his head, he saw streams of it pouring out of numerous holes punched in the underside of the CL-44's wing. Luckily there was a slight camber to the asphalt, which meant that it was flowing away from him.

For fifteen minutes the explosions continued to tear apart the air, as Mike huddled in the cover of the CL-44's wheels. By the time the cataclysm seemed to have died down a little, he was still shaking.

A relative silence descended upon the airport. Mike crawled out from cover and glanced around. Of the dozen or so aircraft that he could see, not one appeared to be unscathed. All were peppered with shrapnel. Not a square foot of the runway seemed clear of debris: metal bolts, rivets, lumps of angle-iron and huge chunks of blasted machinery lay scattered along its length.

Kinshasa's main commercial airport had been transformed into a war zone. What in the name of God had happened?

He glanced in the other direction, to spy an Antonov An-12 – a four-engine Russian transport aircraft – on fire. A huge hole had been driven clean through its right wing, and it was gushing out fuel, which was feeding the roaring flames.

Where the fuel was creeping across the tarmac so the fire was following – and moving in the direction of the pool of fuel that was pouring out of his own aircraft. If the two streams should meet, flame would flash across and engulf everything around it.

Parked beneath the An-12's starboard wing was one of Mike's crew buses. Christ, was anyone inside, he wondered? He considered dashing across to check, but something told him that the worst was yet to come.

As he watched in horror a part of the An-12's wing burned through and crashed onto the bus's roof, crushing it under the weight of fiery debris. Moments later the bus itself burst into flames. Mike cursed despairingly. Where were Kema and Zorro?

He sensed a figure emerge from the CL-44's main door, and step onto the ladder. It was Joe Reilly, his co-pilot. 'What the fuck is going on?' Joe yelled.

Mike signalled for him to get down. 'Who the fuck d'you think you are, Sergeant Barnes? Get your head down before it gets blown off! Get into cover!'

In the iconic movie *Platoon*, the Platoon sergeant, Barnes – a hard-as-nails Vietnam veteran – utters the immortal line to one of his commanders: 'You wasted a lot of people with your fucked-up fire mission.' The scene of devastation at Kinshasa airport somehow reminded Mike of that.

No sooner had he uttered those words than the airport was rocked by a renewed barrage of blasts. Joe dashed into cover beside Mike.

'Where's the rest of the aircrew?' Mike demanded, above the snarl of the detonations.

'Shrapnel's gone right through the cockpit,' Joe yelled back. 'We took whatever cover we could.'

Mike gestured toward their nearest minibuses. 'That's where we're heading, all right?'

'Okay,' Joe confirmed, 'but wait one.'

He dashed back into the CL-44, returning with the flight engineer, plus Tarcis, one of Mike's star mechanics.

Mike waited for a break in the explosions, and then he was sprinting across the tarmac. 'Let's go!' he yelled.

He had to weave a path between the debris and the corpses. The dead were groundcrew mostly, who'd been caught in the open by the blasts. He noticed figures with their arms blown off and with their guts hanging out, but he had time for only one thought right now: *get to the bus.*

If this were a rebel assault, whoever was left alive here would be utterly defenceless once the rebel troops hit the airport. He needed to get to the military end of the airbase, to raise help. The bus was their route out of here. *Maybe.*

This being Africa, most vehicles were missing one or more of their vital parts. Often they had no starter motor, or not enough juice in their ancient batteries – so they needed to be bump-started. Not a drama in the normal scheme of things. A real pain, with the airport seemingly under some kind of massive assault.

Mike leapt aboard and slid behind the wheel. Thank God, the keys were in the ignition. As another explosion tore the air asunder, he bent his head in silent prayer and turned the key. Unbelievably, the vehicle started. At the noise of the engine coughing into life, some of the figures Mike had presumed were dead miraculously came to life, and made a dash for the bus.

With all aboard Mike rammed it into gear and stamped on the gas. As he did so he noticed what looked like a ten-year-old boy running alongside, with his kid sister held by the arm. He watched as the boy lifted her up and threw her on-board. Mike knew it made no sense – the risk was too great just to save the one life – but he slammed on the anchors. Realising Mike had stopped for him, the girl's brother dashed forward and threw himself aboard.

As he got the vehicle moving again Mike noticed that the little girl, who looked about eight years old, had a strip torn right across her scalp. The raw flesh had been scorched black. As they raced away from the explosions, more blasts shook the bus and shrapnel pinged into its sides.

Mike had to weave his way between crates of AK-47 ammunition scattered across the tarmac, plus smoking lumps of metal that had been torn from various airframes. It was utter chaos.

After a few minutes hard driving he'd left most of the fire and ruin behind. It seemed the civilian side of the airport was taking the main hammering. He reached the military end of the base, only to see an all-too-familiar sight in this part of Africa. Outside the barracks was a huge pile of discarded army boots.

When Congolese soldiers decided that they needed to take to their heels, they generally dispensed with their footwear, believing they'd be faster and more nimble barefoot. They ripped them off so they could really run. It was just how they did things in Africa.

Mike managed to locate a few Zimbabwean soldiers milling about nervously. They'd been drafted into the capital to help defend it against rebel attack. The Zimbabweans were trying to work out if this was a rebel assault, or whether the arms dump had somehow self-combusted.

From the far end of the base the explosions changed noticeably. A cache of 122mm Katyusha rockets began to go up. Normally unleashed on the battlefield from vehicle-mounted rocket launchers, with nothing to aim them properly dozens of these high-explosive projectiles spiralled into the air, like giant and very deadly fireworks.

It was as if the death and destruction was following Mike and his crew.

Mike told the Zimbabwean sergeant to go and find them some medical help. He returned with a pale-faced Finnish Red Cross worker, who had been checking out the welfare of prisoners-of-war held at the base. The Finn had some medical training and he'd brought with him a basic surgical kit.

Mike pointed out the small girl with the torn and scorched scalp. 'Start with her. But prepare yourself. There's scores of casualties and be ready for some rough stuff.'

Mike sought out the Zimbabwean force commander, for there were scores of wounded needing help. He found him kneeling in some cover and moaning repeatedly that he didn't want to die. Mike hauled him out. A captain, he looked to be in his mid-twenties, and it seemed that he'd been crying.

'What the fuck are you doing?' Mike bawled. 'And what the hell is going on?'

The captain shook his head. 'No, no, no ... no idea. Everything ... out of control. I don't want to die. I want to go home.'

Mike got his face in the captain's. 'You – stand – up. You get up

35

and show some leadership, 'cause your people are watching you. You do that, or I'll shoot you with your own pistol.'

In a way he felt sorry for the Zimbabwean captain, but now was not the time to indulge such sympathies. He forced the captain out of cover, and made him walk the sixty-odd yards across the barrack's compound, to set an example to his troops.

Next, he got on his mobile phone and called Margaret, just to let her know that he was safe. She would no doubt have heard word of the explosions and would be worried sick. She begged him to return home, but Mike knew that he had to stay and see this through. There was a great deal that would need to be sorted.

Mike and his crew started shuttling the wounded to the military end of the base. In no time, all the tyres of their vehicle had been punctured by shrapnel. One young woman had had her thigh muscle torn away and she was bleeding profusely, the footwell sloshing in blood. After making several evacuation runs driving on flat tyres, Mike and his crew returned to the business end of the airport to assess the damage.

The main apron was strewn with unexploded Katyusha rockets, broken ammo cases, shrapnel and . . . bodies. There were fewer blasts now, and what there were sounded like secondary explosions. If this had been a rebel attack, none of their fighters had yet seen fit to show themselves.

The An-12 that had been leaking fuel was now a roaring inferno. At any moment the fire threatened to engulf both of Mike's CL-44s. Typically, the airport's fire crew had fled, so Mike and his team made a beeline for the deserted fire station. They managed to get one of the fire trucks started, and figured out how to work the foam nozzle.

Mike released the handbrake and they roared off to deal with the burning Antonov. They'd clearly got something wrong with the foam-dispenser, for half of it ended up spewing out beneath the truck, but enough foam still hit the An-12 to douse the flames. After that they coaxed a second fire truck into action, and managed to douse another burning plane.

Mike's main worry now was his crew. He began to search, looking for Kema and Zorro, but there was no sign of them. He did discover three of his crew in the long grass. One, his electrician, had taken a lump of shrapnel in the top of his thigh. It must have severed the femoral artery, for the man had bled to death. All it would have taken to save him was a tourniquet, but it was too late for that now.

Another of Mike's crew had taken a huge chunk of shrapnel through his chest, which had blown his guts out. At least he would have died instantly. Of the stowaways on his plane, one had been a woman with a small baby. They'd managed to make the cover of Mike's ill-fated minibus: shortly thereafter it had been crushed under the Antonov's burning wing, and those inside had been scorched to ashes.

All around aircraft had been reduced to holed and smoking ruins. It turned out that there had been no rebel attack on the airport. With the Congo's long-running civil war dying down, huge quantities of ammunition and shells had been brought back from the front lines. Mike himself had flown several such cargoes in his CL-44s.

The munitions had been stored in hangars adjacent to the airport. Many of the aircrew had their wives and kids living at the airbase. They cooked up meals and slept in the hangars beside the ammo crates. Some had taken to brewing up their food on top of the metal cases, which made good cooking platforms.

One such case had ignited, triggering a long series of further detonations – around five hundred tonnes of shells, rockets and ammo going up in smoke – hence the impression that the airport had been under some kind of a massive rebel assault.

Having learned the truth of what had happened, Mike was reminded of an old phrase that often came to mind: 'TIA.' This is Africa. He loved it and yet at moments like this he hated it, all at the same time.

As there were no more lives to save, Mike began to survey the ruins of his own airfreight business. Of his two CL-44s, one was utterly wrecked. An explosion had blown a forklift truck into the air. It had landed on top of his CL-44, blasting a car-sized gash in its fuselage. The aircraft was also peppered with two hundred and seventy five other holes.

It might just be possible to repair his other plane, cannibalising the ruined one for the spare parts that it would need, but even so Mike felt sick to the stomach. His life savings were bound up in those aircraft, and it looked as if it might all have gone to waste. Of course, operating in this region and in this business, neither plane had been insured.

In Africa, a man's fortunes could turn practically in the blink of an eyelid. But frankly, Mike was alive, as were most of his crew, which was a blessing in itself. He just had to hope that his one aircraft – CL-44 flight 9Q-CTS – was salvageable.

That evening Mike returned home utterly shattered. One hundred and fifty people had lost their lives at the airport, ten of whom were his crew, and there were scores more injured. Thankfully, Kema and Zorro weren't among the victims, but for some reason the entire experience had Mike properly spooked.

He'd been just as scared when flying through a monumental

Congo thunderstorm, but at least then he'd had some measure of control; some say in whether he lived or died. For long periods at the airport he'd had zero idea what was going on and had felt utterly helpless. All those people torn to pieces and so needlessly: it was a stark reminder of just what the AK-47 rounds, shells, grenades and rockets stored at N'Djilli Airport were designed to do.

Mike was haunted by two images from the day's terrible events. One was the Zimbabwean captain crawling along the ground, crying that he didn't want to die. The other was the boy throwing his sister on to the crew bus, in an effort to save her. They were the opposite ends of the spectrum of human behaviour: craven cowardice and self-preservation, versus self-sacrifice to save a loved one.

He couldn't help but wonder whether at that boy's age, he would have had the foresight and guts to save his kid sister. He feared he would have simply run for his life. The scene of the boy lifting her into his bus was seared into Mike's mind. As he contemplated it, for some reason he began to cry.

He sat long into the night, contemplating the day's events and the fact of his own survival. He replayed the images of walking among the dead – men, women and children rendered into torn, lifeless corpses. This was the curse of the arms trade in Africa: time and again the weaponry ended up killing the innocent and vulnerable.

Originally, Mike had opted for SAS selection largely out of a thirst for action and adventure. His father had told him a little about the regiment and its wartime exploits, and he had been hooked. It had been 1972, and he'd trained over the rain-lashed

Brecon Beacons, in Wales, anticipating the long weeks of a cold, bitter test.

As it transpired, a significant chunk of selection had taken place overseas. The night before leaving they were issued with tropical kit, and so it was the SAS that had first taken Mike to Africa. They'd headed for Nanyuki Showground, a British military base in northern Kenya, and from there into the deep bush.

Used to trekking the Brecons in freezing rain, speed marching in Kenya proved red-hot. In the remote, sun-baked bush the recruits were gasping for breath, and there were elephants, lions, and buffalo seemingly at every turn.

Willy Mundell, the sergeant major taking selection, had told them: 'Don't be afraid of the animals. They're more afraid of you than you are of them. They won't bother you if you don't them.'

Mundell had been right, but what Mike hadn't appreciated was the attitude of many of those running selection. The DS – directing staff – actually seemed to want to be as objectionable as possible to the raw recruits. Mike was fit and strong, but it wasn't that that got him through: it was his resentment of the DS and how they lorded it over them.

What was the point in insulting and abusing recruits, Mike wondered? What did that prove? How did that help them find the best future SF operators? It was only sheer bloody-minded stubbornness that had got him through; that and a thirst for action and adventure.

Sure enough, he'd found plenty of both in the SAS, and thereafter serving as a bush pilot in Africa. But today's action was the kind that Mike could very much do without. A part of him wondered how many more death-defying close encounters a man had in him. Had he used up all of his nine lives? In truth, Mike just didn't know.

A few days later he made contact with the boy and his little sister whose images so haunted him. The girl had made a seemingly miraculous recovery and she didn't remember much from that terrible day. As for her brother, he remonstrated shyly when Mike told him that he was the real hero of the hour.

Mike decided that he would find the money to ensure they had their school-fees paid, at least for the foreseeable future. He didn't quite realize it yet, but the events at N'Djilli Airport had hugely altered his outlook on life.

He'd been through a living hell, and it would change him in the most unexpected of ways.

CHAPTER FOUR

KANDAHAR AIRPORT,
AFGHANISTAN, AUGUST 1996

At first Commander Sharpatov had rejected his captors' demands: no way was he willing to train the Taliban's wannabe 'pilots', using the Ilyushin parked on the apron as the chief teaching resource. He and his aircrew refused, although by now they knew full well what kind of response that might provoke.

Over the months of captivity the Russian aircrew had been subjected to beatings and mob justice. They were shown off to groups of belligerent locals, like animals in a zoo. Veterans from the war with the Soviet Red Army displayed their wounds and their stumps, yelling: 'This is what your soldiers did to us!'

Sharpatov and his crew were berated for being 'infidels'. Taliban doctors refused them medical treatment, because the Russians didn't speak Arabic and couldn't read the Koran. They were berated by Taliban religious leaders: Russia and the West believed that might was right, because they had the nuclear bomb, but they were morally bankrupt, and the Taliban would destroy them, just as ancient Rome had been destroyed.

They'd been permitted one small luxury – a radio, via which they could keep track of the media reports of their own fortunes.

Sharpatov had been surprised at how little progress negotiations were making. When the UN issued a resolution calling for the 'immediate and unconditional release' of the seven Russian airmen, the Taliban had countered by demanding that Russia release all Afghan prisoners of war.

Moscow had denied holding any such prisoners. A stalemate had ensued. Months had rolled by, in which there had been various warnings issued to the captives telling them to prepare for their release, but all had come to nothing.

Instead, the Taliban guards had hustled Sharpatov and his men from place to place, fearing an attempt might be made at a rescue. In truth, the Russian government had considered just such an operation, but dropping paratroopers into the heart of the Taliban's stronghold was seen as being too risky.

Sharpatov – who read *Jane Eyre* to kill the endless hours of imprisonment – noted everything in his diary. 'Each one is harder than the last,' he wrote of their days in captivity. 'The crew is losing heart, becoming depressed and sad . . . Life has thrown me a jar of scorpions. I feel like running out of the door and screaming at the top of my voice . . . I talk to them all about escape.'

By now Sharpatov and his crew sported massive, greying beards – under the Taliban's rule it was a crime for any man to shave – and wore stained and ragged clothes. As time dragged interminably, the Russians turned on each other. Sharpatov was the main focus of the crew's ire: he should never have agreed to make the flight, they argued. Sharpatov countered that none of them had been forced to fly.

The lack of progress in freeing the captives was all the more disturbing considering who had become involved. The Russian

Foreign Ministry had sent Zamir Kabulov, a veteran of Afghan and Central Asian diplomacy, to negotiate on the men's behalf. Kabulov had flown into Kandahar, and met the man who spoke for Mullah Omar, the Taliban's supreme leader.

But the negotiations had proved confrontational and unfriendly from the start. The Taliban seemed convinced that Bout's arms flights were a front for a Russian Secret Service operation, rather than the enterprise of a freelance businessman running a highly profitable global airfreight company.

In due course US Senator Hank Brown – a Republican from Colorado – had intervened, acting as a mediator between the two sides. Senator Brown had scored a breakthrough, winning the Taliban's approval to allow the crew regular maintenance visits to their aircraft, without which the Ilyushin would rapidly fall into disrepair.

Of course, Viktor Bout himself had also become involved, shuttling back and forth between Sharjah and Kandahar, and meeting with Mullah Omar, the Taliban's supreme leader. But still his aircrew had remained in captivity. The fact that Bout had been unable to break the logjam surprised them. They had every faith in their boss. He was after all the world's leading postman, an extraordinary individual who could deliver just about anything, anywhere.

Bout had piercing blue eyes creased with laughter lines, set above a droopy brown moustache, and he was blessed – or cursed – with a typically dour, deadpan Russian sense of humour. Some people got it. Liked it. Others didn't. Whichever way you reacted pretty much determined your impression of the man.

Resolutely professional, and well attuned to foreign cultures, he had rightly earned a reputation for getting rich by getting things done. A millionaire by the age of twenty-five, by now Bout had thirty planes at his disposal and by his own admission had earned himself 'an empire', yet still he liked to fly very much below the radar. He was private, discreet and shied away from any form of publicity.

Outside of the close circle of those who dealt in the airfreight and arms business, he was practically unknown. Of course, the capture of his aircraft and crew by the Taliban had attracted some unwelcome publicity, but Bout had skilfully managed to duck most of it.

A global fixer filled with an innate wanderlust, he had recently gone to live in Sharjah, along with his Russian wife and their young daughter. Speaking half a dozen different languages, Bout had shown himself to have an ability to relate to those of other faiths and cultures. If anyone could build bridges with the Taliban, Viktor Bout should have been able to.

But all negotiations seemed to have run into the sand, prompting Sharpatov's decision to comply with the Taliban's demands to start training their would-be pilots. He and his crew had begun to believe that only *they* could engineer their own escape, and the key to that might well lie in the most unlikely of places – the hulking great aircraft that had led to their capture.

Sharpatov's change of mind was driven in part by this realization, but there were other factors. Foremost were the threats the Taliban had made against him and his crew's loved ones. Recently a care mission had been granted access to the airmen, led by Sergey Kudinov, of Russia's Emergency Control Mission, (EMERCOM), part of Moscow's Ministry for Emergency Situations.

Kudinov had found the crewmen malnourished and riddled

with hepatitis, and his medical team had done their best to treat their ailments. But the worst was their state of mind. 'They were in a terrible state of depression,' Kudinov remarked. 'Awful. Many were simply in despair . . . It was hard to see, to believe, the conditions, the hell, that nightmare in which they lived.'

To the aircrew's joy, Kudinov had brought with him a sack of mail from their families. But it was from those letters that the Taliban claimed to have discovered the home addresses of some of the airmen. Threats had been made: train the Taliban pilots, or your families will suffer.

It was then that Sharpatov had cottoned on to something: by agreeing to the Taliban's demands for training, he and his men could maybe prepare their aircraft as a potential means of escape. It would also give them a chance to gather intelligence at the airport – checking out its routines, defences and weaknesses, and crucially the Taliban guards' prayer times.

The Islamic holy day is Friday. Strictly speaking the true believer should observe five prayers, including Fajr, the dawn prayer, Dhuhr, the noon prayer, and Maghrib, the prayer at sunset. In keeping with their religious zeal, few Taliban were inclined to miss out on the Friday prayer ritual.

At the start of their fifty-fourth week in captivity, Sharpatov and his crew discovered that month's aircraft maintenance slot coincided with Friday prayers. Viktor Bout had asked his friend, Ahmed Shah Massoud, the Afghan government's defence minister, to help engineer the Russian aircrew's escape. On Friday 16 August 1996, had there been some form of inside assistance, to enable the Muslim holy day and the Ilyushin's maintenance day to somehow coincide?

It certainly seemed that way. Today was extraordinary on

another level, too: it was one of the few occasions on which the Taliban permitted all seven Russian airmen to visit their aircraft. Prior to that there had been other opportunities that had promised escape, but Sharpatov and his men had been adamant: either all would make the escape attempt or none would.

Prior to this Sharpatov and his crew had planned things exhaustively, and discussed at length the risks involved. They'd sketched out the airport's gun-emplacements, planning how their take-off route might best avoid exposure to hostile fire, plus they'd used the previous 'maintenance' visits to prepare the Ilyushin for flight.

Normally, Taliban guards stayed with them on the aircraft as they went about their work. That August Friday, seven young men armed with Kalashnikovs duly accompanied the seven Russians to the airport. But by the approach of Asr, the afternoon prayer, three attempts to start the aircraft's giant engines had apparently failed, and the guards were getting frustrated and bored.

The plaintive cry from the Muezzin calling the faithful to prayer rang across Kandahar, echoing around the hot and dusty airfield. After a brief discussion among themselves, four of the guards peeled away. Three junior Taliban remained, killing time in the shade of the Ilyushin's cavernous hold.

It was now that the Russian airmen's detailed planning came into play. Routine maintenance had always involved starting the Ilyushin's engines, and letting them run for a time, which in turn served to charge the aircraft's on-board batteries, which could be used to start its Auxiliary Power Unit (APU).

With a poker face, Sharpatov strolled towards the cockpit and lowered himself into the pilot's seat. He slipped on his headphones and began to call out instructions calmly to his crew. Nothing unusual there: they'd made sure to do this previously, when carrying out their 'routine' maintenance work. But today Sharpatov was determined to make a break for it. If they got shot up or crashed in the process, so be it.

'Run the generator,' Sharpatov commanded.

'Yes, sir.'

Sharpatov and his co-pilot, Gazinur Khairullin, began flipping switches on the flight consoles set before them.

'Activate APU,' Sharpatov ordered.

Behind him, figures flitted about the cockpit, responding to his commands. 'APU activated.'

'Start engines one-two-three-four, in that order,' Sharpatov instructed.

'Engine one ready,' the Flight Engineer confirmed.

With Kandahar Airport sitting at an altitude of 1,900 metres the air was too thin to start all four engines simultaneously, hence the need to fire them up in series. In the rear of the aircraft, the Taliban guards sat with their AK-47s slung across their knees, as yet unaware that the Russian aircrew was attempting anything untoward.

As flight preparations continued, Sharpatov sent his navigator and flight engineers into the hold, to prepare for the life-or-death struggle that was coming. It would be three on three, and none of the Russians was armed; they were relying on the element of surprise.

'Start engine two,' Sharpatov ordered, as his hands flicked across the controls.

'Engine two ready,' co-pilot Khairullin confirmed.

Sharpatov ordered engine three started. He told his radio operator to call the control tower, and ask for permission to taxi around the apron, just as they had during previous maintenance sessions. The radio operator tried. No one at the control tower was answering.

Well then, Sharpatov told himself, *you pray, we fly!*

'Engine three ready,' Khairullin informed him, before confirming that engine four had also been successfully started.

'Begin taxiing,' Sharpatov announced.

He reached out with his right hand and eased the throttles forward, releasing the brakes at the same time. The noise of the engines gradually rose in pitch and volume, as the massive form of the Ilyushin began to inch across the apron.

As the Ilyushin gathered speed, those in the hold studied the faces of the Taliban guards. One complained that the aircraft felt like it was moving. He glanced forward, but the bulky forms of the two Russian engineers were wedged in the doorway, blocking the view into the cockpit.

'We're not,' flight engineer Ryazanov assured him. 'It's a big plane. It's just the vibrations of the engines.'

In the cockpit, they had their own problems. From the co-pilot's seat, Khairullin had spotted two Taliban vehicles heading onto the concrete strip, in an effort to intercept the Ilyushin. One was the minibus that had brought them to the airport, the other a heavy Russian Ural military truck. They were racing to block the runway.

'Two vehicles heading towards us!' Khairullin hissed.

The Ilyushin gathered speed, thundering towards the pair of Taliban vehicles speeding to intercept her. The minibus had overtaken the Ural, and it seemed to be heading down the aircraft's very throat. Like a man possessed, the driver raced towards a cataclysmic collision.

'Take-off status,' Sharpatov growled, grim determination showing in the line of his jaw.

'Stand-by for take-off,' his co-pilot announced, as he called out the ground-speed. 'One-hundred and twenty . . . One-hundred and forty. One-hundred and sixty . . .'

Those in the cockpit heard the muffled sounds of cries and blows ring out from the rear; the Taliban guards had finally realized that the aircraft was trying to get airborne. Six men wrestled for control of the assault rifles, and if the Taliban won they could still force Sharpatov to abandon take-off at gunpoint.

'He's preparing to shoot,' a voice warned Sharpatov, over the aircraft's intercom.

'Silence him!' Sharpatov ordered. He glanced at his radio operator. 'Go on! Help them!'

As the radio operator hurried aft, Khairullin continued counting out their speed: 'Two hundred. We're running out of strip!'

'We'll make it,' Sharpatov countered. There was a light head-wind, and he just prayed it would help get them airborne.

'Two-twenty,' Khairullin announced, breathlessly.

'Take-off,' mouthed Sharpatov.

At that moment the giant Ilyushin seemed to shudder along her length and shake free of the runway, the sagging wings trailing long plumes of dust as she burned across the bush at the far end of the strip, soaring over the outer fencing. They'd made it with bare seconds to spare, the minibus and Ural truck flashing past just feet beneath their wheels.

'Altitude two hundred,' Khairullin reported, 'velocity two-twenty.'

'Retract landing gear!' Sharpatov ordered.

From below, five sets of giant wheels folded into the aircraft, the covers swinging closed. Lights and warning alarms blared out from the flight console. The aircraft had lain idle for a year, under blistering Afghan sun, wind and sand. Sharpatov had problems with his elevators and rudder, his flight-speed indicator was malfunctioning and the altimeter was haywire.

He switched to his back-up systems, as the Ilyushin flashed across trenches, dug-out systems, barbed wire fencing and military installations. Their air speed had to be pushing 370kmh, but still Sharpatov kept the giant aircraft at 200 metres altitude, to hide her from any pursuers.

The IL-76 began to shake and vibrate horribly, as if it were a vehicle driving over cobblestones at speed. The giant airfreighter was never designed to fly at such velocity and low altitude: it was buffeted by shock waves from the ground. The air, thick with heat and dust, acted like a force field between the Ilyushin's underbelly and the ground, the entire fuselage clanking and groaning horribly.

Sharpatov's navigator crouched over his charts, calling out altitude and bearings, as Sharpatov brought the ponderous aircraft around. Flying at little more than rooftop height the Ilyushin turned towards the west, the heat blasted out by the howling engines throwing a shimmering haze across the backdrop of mountains.

From the Ilyushin's rear an AK-47 magazine was hurled into the cockpit, followed by the assault rifle itself. Clearly, Sharpatov's crew was getting the better of the Taliban guards. Sharpatov jammed the mag under his backside, and the AK-47 beneath one of his pedals. It would be hard for any guard to retrieve it from there.

Finally, a white-faced figure emerged from the hold. All three guards had been subdued, he reported. He needed rope to tie them up. Sharpatov pulled a length out of a storage compartment and flung it in the man's direction.

As they powered ahead, each man was acutely aware of the attack jets parked in their shelters at the military end of Kandahar Airport. The MiG-21 has a top speed of Mach 2.0, or 1,351.48mph. The question was: how long would it take the pilots to extract themselves from Friday prayers and get airborne? Sharpatov figured it would be a good twenty minutes, by which time it would require almost twice that time to catch up with the speeding IL-76.

And even if a MiG did manage to get airborne in time, how would it locate the low-flying Ilyushin? Even with its on-board radar, the MiG would very likely lose the airfreighter amid all the interference and chatter from the ground. As for the radar stations in Taliban territory and in neighbouring Pakistan, he'd need to keep low enough to avoid those.

Sharpatov's spirit was fired up. The words from a well-known Russian aviator flashed through his mind: 'The pilot stops being a pilot when he no longer flies the plane, but the plane flies him.' He nudged the giant aircraft further west, hugging the undulating dunes and throwing up a storm of sand in their passing.

A voice suddenly cut through the hiss of static on the radio. 'Ilyushin, Ilyushin, what is your number?'

Sharpatov could just imagine the pilot at the controls of his MiG: he was trying to flush out a response from the Russian crew. They retained absolute radio silence as the Ilyushin powered onwards towards the uncertain sanctuary of Iranian airspace, which lay 300 miles to the west.

In heading for Iran, Commander Sharpatov was taking a desperate gamble. He figured the Taliban pilots would fly search transects north of Kandahar, on the assumption that the Ilyushin would make direct for Russia. Heading west, he hoped to fox them. Iran and Russia were long-standing allies, and the Iranians were no friends of the Taliban, but there were no guarantees that the Iranians would permit him to enter their airspace.

The Taliban pilot made the same radio call several times, before Sharpatov put his aircraft into a steep climb. By the time they hit Iranian airspace, the Ilyushin had clawed her way to 30,000 feet, and Sharpatov ordered his radio operator to make contact with Tehran. If the Iranians refused them passage, they'd act as if they hadn't heard. If the Iranians ordered them to land, they'd issue a mayday: *This plane is hijacked. We cannot land. On course for Sharjah.*

Some ninety minutes later Sharpatov nursed his aircraft into a safe landing at Sharjah International. The Iranians had granted them permission to transit their airspace, and local news crews had already been alerted to the dramatic escape. The first figures to get escorted down the Ilyushin's ladder and into the arms of the waiting press were the stunned Taliban guards, now captives themselves.

They were hustled away unceremoniously by the Sharjah authorities. The seven airmen stumbled down the steps, hardly daring to believe that the nightmare was over; that they were truly free. One – his scraggy grey beard reaching to his chest, his hair long and unkempt – turned to the cameras.

'Two vehicles cut us off during take-off,' he exclaimed, wide-eyed with the emotion of the moment. 'We made it by one second! Right down the middle of the runway!'

That evening Viktor Bout held a party to celebrate their

escape. He liked to film most things that happened in his life, and he videoed the merriment. His escaped aircrew – freshly shaven and wearing clean clothes – drank and sang. At one point they formed a line with others of his crew, marching up and down carrying a red flag, and stomping their feet in time to the singing:

> We have a long march before us.
> Soldier, look ahead with joy.
> Our flag is blowing in the wind.
> And our captain leads the way.

That captain, of course, was Viktor Bout. He was just twenty-nine years old.

Sharpatov and his crew returned to a hero's welcome in Russia. But shortly thereafter rumours began to circulate among those in the know that perhaps Bout had played a greater role in their escape than had at first seemed the case. Even Bout's own statements appeared to suggest that he might have had deeper involvement.

'They didn't escape,' Bout would go on to tell the media. 'They were extracted.'

Gradually, a story emerged that the Taliban might have quietly 'assisted' the aircrew's escape, by turning a blind eye. But why might they have done so?

The answer, perhaps, lay in Bout's own activities. Even as his aircrew had been held hostage, the Russian businessman had started flying for the Taliban. Just as he had in Angola, he'd realized there was business to be done with both sides of the war.

His aircraft had jetted into Kandahar, ostensibly on captive-release negotiations, only to fly on to Jalalabad, a Taliban-held city in the east of the country. At first, they were packed full of consumer goods – TVs, fridges, clothes – plus food. But in time, Viktor Bout would also be accused of running arms to the Taliban.

From his Sharjah base Bout began to service airliners flown by the Taliban, once the militants had seized control of the country's national carrier, Ariana Afghan Airways. He was rumoured to have sold the Taliban a fleet of cargo aircraft, which were used to haul tonnes of weaponry into Afghanistan. Western officials estimated that Bout had done deals with the Taliban worth some $50 million. Moreover, they claimed that the aircraft Bout had supplied had hauled the Taliban's cash, narcotics and militant fighters back and forth to war.

Viktor Bout – the man who could deliver anything anywhere – was far too smart an individual to have knowingly done business with a militia that harboured Osama Bin Laden and Al Qaeda. Even so, it was not the most diplomatic of alliances to have forged. Bout was far too savvy to have knowingly put his head in the noose, but this was pre-9/11 and hindsight, as they say, is a very fine thing.

Bout had been born in 1967, in Dushanbe, the capital of Tajikistan, a nation that borders Afghanistan in the south and which then formed a part of the Soviet Union. The son of a mechanic father and a bookkeeper mother, he proved gifted at volleyball, and by his own account was popular with the girls. But his real talent lay in languages. He studied Esperanto – a universal world language – hoping that one day all humankind would speak the same tongue.

Having completed his schooling and his national service, Bout graduated to the Soviet military's Institute of Foreign Languages, in Moscow, a body long-suspected of being a training ground for the Soviet military intelligence service (the GRU). There he hoped to study French. Instead, he was placed on a ten-month intensive course in Portuguese, before being posted far from the Soviet Union.

It was 1987, Bout was twenty years old, and he was sent to the southern African country of Mozambique as part of the Russian military's presence there. It was Bout's first time out of the motherland. He fell in love with Africa – its wide-open skies, exotic wildlife, rich red soil and the sound of the drumbeats reverberating through the bush.

While there he met a Russian woman, Alla Protasva, at a function at the Soviet Embassy. She was the wife of a diplomat but the marriage wasn't going well. Three years later she and Bout were married, in Moscow. By then the Berlin Wall had come down, the Soviet Union was about to implode and everything was up for sale.

Bout left the military in 1991. He tried building a living from his and Alla's modest Moscow apartment. The former Soviet Union was opening up to business, and by trading foreign goods – beer, Coca-Cola, sweets – Bout began to make his first real money. Russia was undergoing unprecedented change, and he wanted to capture all of that on film, videoing everything almost as if it were a compulsion.

But over time he realized that all business in Moscow was a 'dirty kind of business'. In 1993 he left Russia and set up an airfreight company in Brussels. It began flying on behalf of the Angolan government, then embroiled in a decades-long civil war.

Smart and ambitious, Bout was contracted to fly one hundred hours per month. Business boomed, especially when he realized it was just as lucrative to fly for the other side.

By the time Bout was shuttling back and forth to Kandahar to negotiate the release of his seven airmen, he reportedly spoke Portuguese, English, French and Uzbek, along with several African languages. A year or so earlier he had teamed up with Peter Mirchev, a Bulgarian arms dealer, to source the weaponry sought by the Afghan government.

With the collapse of the Soviet Union the Bulgarians were desperate to market their arms, and Mirchev had become the nation's pre-eminent dealer. The demands of the Afghan regime were stupendous; they needed someone to arm the nation's military in the midst of a bloody civil war. When Bout approached Mirchev, he proved a fast learner. Together they turned the Bulgarian government's desire to sell and the Afghan government's urgent desire to buy into their very own money-printing machine.

Not long after his captured aircrew had returned to Russia, Viktor Bout celebrated his thirtieth birthday. As with most things, the partying was filmed. One of his friends had composed a little ditty. He sat at an electric organ and began to sing:

> Born thirty years ago today.
> Went to grade school, liked to play.
> Went to Angola many times.
> Sold all kinds of shady stuff.
> What's his name?
> Bout! Bout! Bout! Bout!

The rest of the partygoers hurrahed and stomped and sang along. As for Bout, he clapped his hands and smiled, clearly enjoying himself. But selling 'all kinds of shady stuff' to Angola was one thing. Doing so to the Taliban was quite another.

And with Viktor Bout, it would come back to haunt him.

CHAPTER FIVE

N'DJILLI AIRPORT, KINSHASA, THE CONGO, FEBRUARY 2002

After 1,500 man-hours of repair work, Mike Snow's CL-44 – 9Q-CTS – had been resurrected from the aircraft graveyard that was Kinshasa's blast-damaged N'Djilli Airport. Mike was back in business, shipping food to front-line positions, and flying wounded soldiers back again.

It was the morning of Sunday 6 February 2002 when Leon said he'd like to accompany him on that day's flight. Mike had taught his houseboy to fly straight and level, as a treat to say thank you for the way Leon looked after the Snow household. Leon's cuisine had become so renowned that Mike's friends had started to hire him out to cater for their dinner parties. Leon was keen. Work spelled money, and that meant he could pay his children's school fees.

Mike and Leon had grown close - so much so that one of Leon's four children had been named after Snow. He was a very grand sounding 'Michel Du Neige'. But Leon's request was still an odd one. Who would ever *volunteer* to fly in an aircraft that had been patched up after Kinshasa's version of World War Three? It was a Sunday, and Leon would normally be at church, but for some reason he seemed at a loose end.

Mike proceeded to round up his trusted crew: Kema and Zorro, plus his mechanic, Honoré, a pygmy who hailed from the eastern jungles of the Congo, and a handful of others. Today's job was a round flight to Mbuji-Mayi, in the east of the Congo. On the outward leg he'd be empty of cargo. As Mbuji-Mayi lay in Kasai-Oriental Province, which was a major producer of commercial-grade diamonds, Mike figured that would make up his return cargo.

Mbuji-Mayi was no big deal, as far as Mike was concerned. The Congo's third city, it lay some six hundred miles to the east of Kinshasa, deep in the country's isolated interior, an hour-and-a-half away by CL-44. On today's flight Colonel George Kibongi of the Congo Air Force would be accompanying them, a guy Mike knew well.

Mike was grateful for the Colonel's presence. He knew there would be scores of Congolese intent on gaining a free passage to Kinshasa on his return flight. In the Congo, having a seat didn't really matter much: most were perfectly happy to squat on the floor of any old plane. Having the Colonel aboard should help police things a little.

Mike had two sayings taped to the CL-44's flight deck. One was a quote from *Platoon*'s Sergeant Barnes: 'There is the way things ought to be and the way things are.' Mike found it peculiarly appropriate for the Congo. The other was in French: 'Je suis entrainé par imbeciles.' *I am surrounded by imbeciles.* It was a classic piece of Snow irony: how it should be interpreted depended upon who was reading it.

It being a Sunday they were late getting airborne, but the flight to Mbuji-Mayi went without a hitch. Upon landing Mike shut down his engines. Mbuji-Mayi Airport had a run-down,

Wild West, junkyard feel about it. It was the kind of place where anything could happen. But Mike needed to rest and test his airplane. The CL-44 had been built in 1962. It was four decades old. By anyone's reckoning that was ancient for an aircraft still in commercial service.

Mike did a walkabout, checking all four engines. One might have been sucking up oil in flight, and the ageing gauges malfunctioning. He compared notes with Renee Illunga, his Congolese flight engineer. Renee had survived two disastrous air-crashes, and Mike valued the guy's opinion. It was Renee's job to monitor the fuel flow, engine temperatures and generators when in flight. And once Mike reached 'V1' – the speed at which take-off could no longer be aborted – he had to pick up the landing gear.

Mike settled into his seat. It was dusk, and the flight back to Kinshasa would be completed in darkness. Beside him sat Roger Barruti, a Congolese pilot who'd been flying for Mike for some time. Renee perched on a seat between the two of them, in easy reach of the throttles. He could swivel his chair around to access a panel of instruments, enabling him to move fuel around the CL-44's tanks – to keep the aircraft in trim, and prevent the wings from warping.

Take-off went smoothly and Mike climbed to a cruise altitude of 10,000 feet. Some pilots liked to have their cockpit lit up like a lighthouse during night flights. Not Snow. He dimmed the lights, so the only illumination came from the instrument panels. If they ran into a thunderstorm – and there were lots of monster storms in the Congo – he'd put the lights back up again, so the flashes of lightning didn't blind them.

Mike had established their cruise altitude when he noticed that the pressure in the CL-44's hold seemed to be dropping.

He handed the controls to his co-pilot, and with Zorro – his 'flying spanner' – to lend a hand, he went aft to investigate. There were twenty or so refugees squatting on the floor – those who Colonel Kibongi had figured warranted safe passage to the nation's capital.

Mike wondered if maybe one of the over-wing exits wasn't fitted snugly, which might explain the pressure leakage. He and Zorro discovered a small problem with one of the seals, but nothing overly significant. The CL-44's pressurization system was fickle at the best of times, so if cabin pressure continued to drop they'd just have to descend to a lower altitude.

Inspection done, he and Zorro went to return to the flight deck. As they did so, Mike felt the aircraft roll and yaw a little, and he presumed they'd hit some turbulence. But as he stepped through the door he heard a blaring wail echoing through the darkened cabin.

Mweeep! Mweeep! Mweeep! Mweeep!

The alarm was emanating from the Annunciator Panel, a bank of lights forming the cockpit's central warning system. Mike's eyes swept across it. It was flashing orange, so not yet the red that would indicate the worst kind of an emergency. Mike could see that the ADLS (the anti-drag limiting system) warning light was on, which meant he had a propeller pushing an engine, not the other way around.

It looked as if they'd lost one engine. No major dramas on a four-engine aircraft. Mike reached over and flipped the cabin lights on. In the glare, he could see his co-pilot, Roger, glancing over his shoulder, eyes wide with fear. In his hands he grasped the stick, but it was pushed fully to the right, which was no way to fly an aircraft nice and steady at 10,000 feet.

Most problems that you experienced as a pilot were predictable. You knew instantly what was wrong. But as Mike sensed the fear pulsing back and forth through the cabin, he couldn't imagine what had happened. He could only think that Roger's artificial horizon had failed, so that it showed the CL-44 in a sharp bank to the left, which Roger was desperately trying to correct.

His eyes flashed to his own artificial horizon, then to the standby device: unbelievably, all three indicated that the aircraft had gone into a 60-degree bank to the left. *What the hell was going on?* If the artificial horizons were correct, that kind of yaw would have put them into a steep, spiralling, corkscrew dive.

Mike had learned a vital lesson during selection into the SAS – to harness your fear and make it work for you. You had to channel the adrenalin, transforming it into energy and focus. He'd made the fear work for him as a soldier, and he'd learned to do the same in Africa, when flying horrendously challenging missions.

He pushed past Colonel Kibongi, who was standing at the rear of the cockpit, and slid into his seat. He checked the exhaust gas temperatures. Engine number one – the outer of the two on the port wing – was showing zero heat, so that was clearly the one that had failed. He glanced out of his side-window, expecting to see nothing particularly concerning. It wasn't the first time they'd had an engine fail.

Instead, he spotted a long tube of blue flame – like that emitted by a Bunsen burner – coming out of the engine's breather unit, a piece of equipment designed to keep the engine cool. Mike now knew that number one engine had a fire, one serious enough to have burned through the central core.

'Where's the emergency checklist?' Mike demanded.

Roger rooted around at his side for a few seconds, before saying: 'Ah, Captain, I cannot find it.'

'Well, get it fucking found.'

It was the co-pilot's job to keep the checklists handy, in case of *emergencies*. Mike ran whatever bits he could remember through his head. First, he needed to put number one engine's propellers into 'feather' mode, aligning the blades directly into the airflow so they offered least resistance, the drag being the only thing he could imagine had sent them into this clockwise spiral towards earth.

In the forty-odd seconds since he'd stepped through the door, he guessed they'd lost a thousand feet of altitude or more. Right now the priority had to be to right his aircraft, which meant dealing with that burning engine.

Propellers feathered, he reached forward to activate number one engine's fire bottle. He was just about to break the seal, when Renee spoke up from his position seated between Mike and the co-pilot.

'Captain, the flaps are fully down.'

Mike felt his heart skip a beat. If the flaps were fully down and one engine was kaput, they would be losing altitude at a far greater rate than he had imagined. It was Renee's job to handle the flaps while in flight.

Mike glanced at him. 'Well, pull them the fuck back up!'

Renee grimaced. 'Erm, they won't come up, Captain. I've tried.'

Mike ran his eyes across the flaps indicator. It confirmed what Renee had said. *Jesus.* He grabbed the flaps lever and yanked for all he was worth, but the indicator needle barely moved. The flaps were fully down and jammed.

What the fuck was going on? It was like some ghost had taken over his aircraft.

In fact, it was worse than that. The flaps were fully down *asymmetrically* – more on one side than the other. The ramifications of this flashed through Mike's head in microseconds: *not good*. He reached out and triggered the number one fire bottle. He glanced out the side-window, but it seemed to have had little effect: if anything, the fire was more evil-looking than ever.

As he went to trigger the number two fire bottle, Colonel Kibongi piped up from the rear. 'Mike, the circuit-breakers have popped.'

The circuit breakers are like the trip switches in a house. They trigger if an electrical system malfunctions. Strictly speaking they were Renee's responsibility, but Mike's flight engineer seemed to have gone gaga with fear.

'Which ones?' Mike barked.

'Flaps and spoilers.'

Maybe that was why the flaps wouldn't respond. 'Reset them for me, pronto.'

Colonel Kibongi ran his hand down the rank of circuit breakers, which covered an area towards the cockpit's rear as big as a bookcase. He flicked four back into position. Mike tried the flaps again. Zero response. *Shit and damnation.*

He triggered fire bottle number two. What the hell else was he supposed to do? It had no visible effect. This was desperate, last-chance-saloon kind of stuff. He had to get those flaps up again, or they were doomed.

A thought struck Mike: maybe with Zorro's help he could go aft, climb into the belly of the CL-44 via the small trapdoor set between the wings, disconnect the flap-motors and wind them up by hand. He knew it was possible. He'd seen it done before, but only with the aircraft on the ground.

Still, what option did he have right now?

Mike indicated to his co-pilot to take the controls. 'Roger, your aircraft.'

Roger rolled his eyes. 'Ah, no, Captain, I am lost. At sixty degrees bank, I am lost.'

Roger was in meltdown, and in truth Mike couldn't blame him. What commercial pilot was accustomed to flying an aircraft at that far off the level and with his flaps gone haywire, an engine gushing flame and the devil himself seemingly at the controls? He could trust himself and Zorro to do the heavy lifting, but that would leave no one to fly the plane.

Mike turned back to the controls. He tried putting full power on number two engine, while placing numbers three and four into idle in an effort to counteract the sixty-degree yaw. It had almost no noticeable effect. Mike had absolutely no idea what was going on any more. They were all out of options.

He glanced at his co-pilot. 'Roger, put a Mayday call through to Mbuji-Mayi control.'

'Yes, Captain.'

Roger tried to raise the Mbuji-Mayi flight tower in English. 'Mbuji-Mayi, Mbuji-Mayi, Tango Sierra. Tango Sierra calling Mbuji-Mayi. Mayday, mayday. Repeat, mayday.'

'Say again, Tango Sierra. Confirm you are returning to Mbuji-Mayi.'

'Speak to the fuckers in French,' Mike growled. They were clearly having problems understanding. 'Explain we got a big engine fire and may need to crash-land.'

Roger did as asked. The response from Mbuji-Mayi control was priceless: 'Tango Sierra, Mbuji-Mayi – *bon courage*.'

They might as well have said: say your prayers.

Mike slowed the CL-44 to 97 knots – as close as they could get to a stall without the plane dropping out of the sky. The stick started to shake and judder, warning him of the dangerously slow airspeed. He was trying keep them airborne for as long as possible, but in a sense it was only delaying the inevitable. Banked over, on fire, and with little control over his aircraft, they were spiralling down to an inevitable doom.

'Captain, should we return to Mbuji-Mayi to land?' Roger ventured.

Mike snorted. 'Roger, we've been flying around in circles for fifteen minutes. I can't even steer the thing. We'll have to put down here somewhere soon.'

Mike glanced at his altimeter: they'd lost 9,000 feet already. *Jesus.* One thousand to go, that's if they were lucky. It was a gnarly old jungle down there, with lots of bluffs and pinnacles and other nasty, rock-hard obstructions.

Mike flicked on his landing lights. Four intense beams speared into the darkness. Some six hundred feet below he could make out thick jungle rushing past. Being able to see the ground just accentuated how hopelessly out of kilter the CL-44 was.

'Right, if you haven't realized, we're all about to die,' Mike announced. 'It's going to be a big cartwheel and explosions, and we're all going to get chopped to shit. So if you have a god, better start praying.'

Silence. Not a word of response from anyone.

As he gazed out over the on-rushing forest, all of a sudden Mike spotted what looked like a clearing in the dense carpet of vegetation. For no apparent reason there were these occasional patches of grassland dotted throughout the Congolese jungle. Pray God it was one of those.

His airspeed was too slow to enable any kind of a safe landing. He piled on the power, accelerating to 160 knots in an effort to reach that patch of open ground. As he did so, the aircraft miraculously began to right herself. He could only imagine that the increased air-pressure had somehow forced the flaps back into line.

For an instant he wondered if he could abort the crash landing and make for Kinshasa, but he was too low and in any case they were on fire. If they lost a wing at altitude, they were going to be toast – obviously. That patch of clear ground was bang up ahead; he decided they'd take their chances.

Their airspeed hit 210 knots. He was flying by sheer instinct now. They swept over the ragged fringe of the jungle straight and level, and he brought the aircraft down without even bothering to lower the landing gear. There was a horrendous screeching and tearing of metal from the CL-44's belly, the aircraft bounced once, crashed down again and Mike saw the propellers on both wings sheer off, as the gearboxes were torn from the engine housings.

Moments later the aircraft slewed to a juddering halt on a spur of high ground, surrounded by eight feet of elephant grass on all sides. They'd come to a stop just thirty yards short of where the terrain gave way to a sheer drop. If Mike had put down the landing gear they'd very likely have plummeted into the open space, with catastrophic consequences.

Mike's greatest worry now was the fire.

Alarms blared through the cockpit.

As they'd hit the ground Mike had felt his back collapse with the impact, but right now adrenalin was blanking out the pain. At any second they were going to get incinerated, as hungry flames flashed through the stationary aircraft.

'Everyone, out!' he roared. 'Roger, open the DV window! Everyone out!'

The direct vision (DV) window lay to one side of the cockpit and it doubled as an escape hatch. Roger booted it open, then went to dive through, but he'd forgotten to undo his seatbelt. Renee, Leon, Zorro, Kema and Colonel Kibongi weren't so constrained: all Mike saw of them were the soles of their feet as they dived into the darkness.

Mike turned to his mechanic. 'Honoré, go get the passengers out.'

Honoré hurried aft. Mike shouted down into the darkness outside. 'Zorro and Kema, look for the fire!'

'No fire, Captain!' the voices echoed back to him. 'No fire!'

Had the fire extinguished itself? Mike couldn't believe it. It was probably just reorienting itself now that the CL-44 was stationary, before flashing through the rest of the plane.

Mike heard the rear cargo door opening and the refugees piling off the aircraft. Then he heard a woman start to scream.

'Bebé! Bebé! Bebé!'

Shit, it sounded as if someone was still left in the hold, and a kid as well.

Honoré poked his head through the door. 'Captain, there's a baby still in the aircraft. I can't find it.'

Mike levered himself up from his seat. Horrific pain shot through his lower back. Gritting his teeth he made for the hold. He grabbed a torch. Where the hell was the missing kid? He couldn't see it anywhere. He paused at the bulkhead that separated the hold from the cockpit, only to hear a tiny, muted cry. He glanced down. A heavy toolbox had broken free from the rear of the plane and slammed down to the front, coming to rest against the bulkhead.

It was lying at an angle, with one end propped up on some cargo netting. Underneath was wedged the errant child. It looked to be about three days old and was dressed in swaddling clothes. Right at that moment it struck Mike as baby Jesus. He'd seen too much death in the Congo. He'd never forgive himself if the baby died. But no way could he bend down to pick it up. His back was agony.

He shone his torch onto it. 'Honoré, grab the baby!'

Normally a CL-44's cargo door sits high off the ground, with the aircraft raised up on its undercarriage. Not now. They were able to reach out and hand the baby directly to its mother, who was crying tears of gratitude.

It was then that Mike noticed the soldiers. A bunch of mystery gunmen had emerged from the bush, hailing from God only knows where. After a few moments thick with tension – were they going to rob the air-crash victims? – it became clear that they were government troops.

Colonel Kibongi grabbed a Motorola Radio off the most senior soldier, and put a call through to the nearest military base, at Kananga town. The fire in number one engine seemed to have completely burned itself out. It was pitch dark, there was zero moonlight, and Mike had no option but to sit there in agony and await whatever fate might hold in store.

After ten minutes a Toyota pick-up emerged from the shadows. Mike managed to clamber aboard, along with the Colonel and the rest of his aircrew.

They roared off into the night, the pickup's lone headlight piercing the gloom. Mike and his crew stood in the rear, holding onto the roof for all they were worth, as the vehicle tore down a dirt road. It led into a small, provincial town: Kananga. There were no lights or electricity and the place was swathed in thick darkness.

From his vantage point in the rear Mike figured he could see a halo of illumination in the far distance. The pick-up made towards it. As they drew closer, Mike could make out what looked like a large English stately home, somehow parachuted into the midst of the Congolese jungle. Unbelievable, but true.

Every window was brightly lit, and it seemed as if a party was in progress. It was around nine o'clock on a Sunday evening, and for anyone who was anyone in Kananga this was clearly the place to be. The pick-up pulled to a halt outside. A formal dinner was under way, and the place was packed with guests dressed as if they were extras in the new series of *Downton Abbey*, only this time set in the Congo.

This had to be the only place with electricity for several hundred miles around, Mike figured. He asked the Colonel the obvious question: *where are we?* It turned out that Mike had chosen to crash-land not far from the Governor of Kasai-Oriental Province's country seat of residence.

A massive Congolese guy in spotless white shirt and full suit and tails came down the sweeping steps. He doffed his hat, and Colonel Kibongi approached to have words.

He gestured at Mike and his crew. 'These people are from the air-crash.'

The Governor glanced at Mike and his men. 'Who is the

captain?' he asked. He spoke in the timbre of an Old Etonian, with just a hint of gravelly Congolese overtones.

'That's me, sir,' Mike volunteered.

The Governor eyed him for a second. 'You are – very – lucky,' he announced, slowly. 'Very lucky indeed.' He waved a hand towards his grand residence. 'Come inside. All of you. You must be feeling hungry after your ordeal.'

Mike gestured at his attire: shorts, T-shirt, desert boots with no socks, and all a little grubby after the crash-landing. 'We can't, sir. Look how we're dressed.'

'No, no, you will come eat and drink,' the Governor countered. 'I'll not have another word said on the matter.'

Mike hobbled inside. He was the only white person in the entire place. As with nearly all African parties he'd ever been to, if you turned up after 8.00 p.m. the guests would generally have cleaned the place out. There were a few chicken legs and some spicy rice left, but that was about it. Mike, the Colonel and his crew hoovered up whatever they could find and made their gratitude clear to their host.

The Governor gave the driver of the pick-up a one hundred dollar bill and told him to take Mike and his crew to a good hotel. They mounted up and roared back into the darkened streets of Kananga. The driver tried several places, banging on the doors, but no one would open up at that time of night.

Eventually, he headed for the last option in town. What had once been a pigsty had been converted into the local brothel. The ladies of the night were long departed, and Mike and his crew were each offered a former sty to rest their aching bones. No sheets; just bare mattresses.

Mike didn't care. He had an injured back, he was shattered,

and his plane lay in ruins in the bush. The lack of sheets was the least of his worries.

The trouble was there were one too few sties to accommodate the entire party. The Colonel was either a real gentleman or a wily old devil – Mike wasn't quite sure which.

'Look, we're both grown-ups,' he told the madam of the place. 'You've been paid your hundred dollars. We'll just have to share the last bed.'

Two weeks later Mike found himself in hospital in Johannesburg, being treated for the malaria that he'd contracted in the pigsty-cum-brothel, and for a broken back.

He'd barely slept at all that night in Kananga. The pain had kept him awake, plus the mozzies had eaten him alive. The following day he'd gone to inspect his aircraft, but of course it was a total write-off. Locals were already looting whatever they could carry and there had been no point in hanging around.

Mike had five broken vertebrae as a result of the crash-landing. No one knew whether he'd be able to fly again. Zorro had also hurt his back. He was being looked after by the Red Cross in Kinshasa. Leon had knocked his teeth out while diving out of the DV window, but Kema, Honoré and the rest were largely unscathed. Renee Illunga, Mike's flight engineer, would never be seen at Kinshasa Airport again. This had been his third near-cataclysmic air-crash, and he'd told Mike the simple truth: 'Captain, I will never fly again.'

Not that Mike had anything left for any of them to fly in. Flight 9Q-CTS had been his last serviceable aircraft. With its death his dream had died. But it could have been worse. They all could be dead. By rights, they *should* all be dead. Whichever way he looked at it, Mike couldn't understand how any of them had survived. He figured it was high time he took up something a little less insane for a living.

But as fate would have it, life was about to get a whole lot crazier for The Bear.

CHAPTER SIX

KIGALI AIRPORT, RWANDA,
SUMMER 1998

Viktor Bout was a physically imposing individual in the flesh, but some suggested he lacked both charm and charisma, plus a sense of fun. A few of his peers at the Moscow Language School had even accused him of being a swot, more interested in academic success than any globetrotting adventures. His life, it would seem, had proved them wrong.

But as the 1990s drew to a close, Bout was starting to attain the singular reputation that would come to dominate every other impression that the man had ever made. He was becoming renowned as the world's foremost arms dealer, an infamy that he would earn primarily in Africa. Or more specifically, in the Congo.

There were lots of legitimate reasons for Bout to be in Africa, many of which bore no relation to the arms trade. Bout believed that business was a 'flowing river'. You needed a thousand projects in development, to ensure a few made good. In Africa he saw opportunity everywhere.

He flew frozen Tilapia fish from Africa's great lakes to Europe; he flew frozen chickens cross-continent to Nigeria – a surprisingly lucrative trade; he flew gladioli from South Africa to Dubai, earning stupendous profits in the process; he flew peacekeepers into active conflict zones, and aid consignments for global charities into areas of intense unrest.

In 1997 Bout's aircraft had provided a lifeline for refugees who were flooding into the benighted city of Kisangani. The Congo's third largest, it lies in the heart of the country's jungle interior, on the banks of the sluggish and steamy Congo River. With its ancient railway buckled and rusted, its roads cratered and unusable, and its streets broken and war-torn, Kisangani's multitude of refugees needed an air-bridge if they were to be saved.

The United Nations World Food Programme had been tasked to intervene, but it possessed no fleet of airfreighters able to do so. Once it had checked that Kisangani's airport was still usable, and that its relief supplies wouldn't be looted, the UN had turned to the only act in town – Viktor Bout. Bout's Ilyushins and Antonovs had started jetting in pallets of food aid and medical supplies, plus plastic sheeting for constructing makeshift shelters.

Each plane wore the unmistakable logo of the United Nations World Food Programme – a stylized hand clutching ears of corn – which should have ensured their safe passage. But upon arrival at Kisangani Airport some of those aircraft had opted to dispense with such safeguards. Instead, they had undergone a rapid and somewhat mystifying transformation.

Once the shipment of aid had been unloaded, steps were rolled up to the aircraft's rear. A member of the flight crew had climbed up, unpeeled the United Nations logo, whereupon the ground staff began loading up crates of weaponry. The transformation took no more than an hour, after which the massive aircraft grumbled along the rutted, cratered runway and took to the skies.

The Congo was riven with conflict, and arms were in hot demand by all sides. By flying in with aid, and flying out weaponry, Bout had deftly adhered to his golden rule: *never fly empty*. Each flight had carried a moneymaking cargo, and each had built the profitability of Bout's airfreight empire. In the late 1990s, his operations were of no great interest to the world powers, and as long as he continued to serve 'obscure' conflicts it looked set to remain that way.

But in 1998 Bout became involved in arming and garrisoning his first major war. A year earlier Joe Reilly – Mike Snow's long-time co-pilot – had started flying for Bout. Recently, Bout had moved his headquarters from Sharjah to South Africa. Captivated by the continent, he'd set up office in the business district of Johannesburg, with his airfreight companies operating out of Pietersburg Airport (now renamed Polokwane International).

But as a result of fierce rivalries with other airfreight operators – and amid suggestions of dark dealings at the highest levels – Bout was driven out of South Africa. His family had been threatened, his home robbed and his offices ransacked. He moved to the Central African Republic, a country lying to the north of the Congo, and Joe Reilly went with him to help set up a new base of operations.

Bout had forged close ties with the nation's President, and Joe Reilly was contracted to fly him around the country on various official visits. In the summer of 1998 the centre of focus for Bout's airfreight operations shifted eastwards – to Rwanda. In the Rwandan capital, Kigali, Bout hired the top two floors of the InterContinental Hotel, where he lodged around one hundred of his aircrew in preparation for the massive airlift that was coming.

Bout's fleet of battle-worn Russian aircraft filed into Kigali

Airport. Ranged across the apron were LET 410s – a Czech light transport aircraft – Antonov 12s, Antonov 28s, plus hulking great Ilyushin IL-76s. Joe Reilly was charged with piloting one of Bout's Yakolev-40s, a three-engine passenger jet dating from the days of the Soviet Union. His role was to ferry high-ranking members of the Rwandan and allied militaries into the neighbouring Congo.

That summer the Second Congo War, also known as the 'Great War of Africa', had broken out. By the time it would run its course – six long years of chaotic strife – it would claim over five million lives, making it the bloodiest conflict since the Second World War.

As with any major war, that in the Congo required men and arms to fight, plus commanders to send them into battle. In his YAK-40, Joe Reilly began shuttling high-ranking military figures between Rwanda, the Congo and Uganda, for this was a war that would be fought between many different nations on the Congo's mineral-rich battlefields.

The small groups of high-ranking men that he flew wore uniforms and carried sidearms. There was little effort made to hide who they were or what they were about, for the world wasn't watching. Shuttling around groups of top brass in an executive jet was pretty standard stuff in Africa, but Bout's fleet of lumbering transport aircraft was there to perform a very different role.

Over the days and weeks Bout's ground engineers swarmed around Kigali Airport, keeping his air-armada operational. More often than not Bout himself was there, overseeing things, his personal plane – a Grumman Gulfstream G1, a US-made business aircraft – parked at the airport.

From a warehouse lying to one side of the runway, consignments of weaponry were shifted across the asphalt by hand, and carried up the rear ramps of the waiting Antonovs and Ilyushins. The arms included AK-47s, crates of ammunition, RPG-7s (rocket-propelled grenades), and light military vehicles.

A snake of men in uniform ran from warehouse to aircraft and back again, loading weaponry into the cavernous holds, while Bout's ground crew and pilots supervised. Vehicles would be brought out from a muster area at the rear of the warehouse and driven up the ramps onto the waiting aircraft. They were mostly Toyota-type 4x4 pick-ups, with heavy machineguns mounted on the rear, but there were also light armoured vehicles.

At times Bout stood beside those open ramps, chatting away with his operations manager, Dmitry Popov, and overseeing the loading. Popov was based in an office on the outskirts of the airport, but he was rarely absent from the runways during daylight hours. At other times Bout liaised with the Rwandan military commanders, supervising the off-loading of weapons crates and inspecting the gleaming new cargoes.

On occasion he would fly away from Kigali Airport in his Gulfstream, keeping a check on what was truly a transcontinental operation. As with his earlier Afghan dealings, Bout had linked up with Peter Mirchev, his Bulgarian arms supplier, for the present airlift. Mirchev had contracted with the Rwandan government to supply the weaponry, with Bout flying shipments in from his Bulgarian arms factories.

Bout's aircraft were heading out of Kigali to two destinations in the eastern Congo, from where the Second Congo War was being orchestrated. One was Kisangani. The other was Goma, a city of one million souls on the shores of the breathtaking Lake Kivu, which itself lies among the foothills of the dramatic Nyiragongo

Volcano, whose crater throws up plumes of steam and smoke from a burning lake of lava.

In the summer of 1998 Goma became the headquarters of a rebel movement, which was backed by the Rwandan and Ugandan governments. The rebels and their powerful supporters would pit themselves against the government of President Laurent Kabila, who had himself forced the Congo's long-time dictator, the fabulously wealthy and maniacal Mobutu Sese Seko, into exile.

Bout's Antonovs and Ilyushins began shuttling into Goma Airport, disgorging not only weaponry, but also planeloads of Rwandan troops. As the distance between there and Kigali was less than a hundred miles, Bout's aircraft could make repeated daily runs.

Three abreast and hoisting their assault rifles, the soldiers headed down the open ramps to link up with the rebel forces, intent on advancing on the nation's capital, Kinshasa. Bout's Congo airlift went on for weeks on end, and few other airfreight operators were involved. In short, he had cornered the market in the Second Congo War.

Little effort was made to hide the nature of the operation, largely because there was nothing about it that was strictly illegal. While the United Nations had placed arms embargoes on many African conflicts, flying in weapons shipments wasn't actually punishable by law. There was no legislation under which arms traffickers could be prosecuted and the rules governing the international trade were markedly ineffectual.

Many argued that the laws were kept deliberately lax so that those countries that profit from the arms trade – the United States and Britain chief among them – could continue to do business unimpeded. Whatever the truth of the matter, it meant that

Viktor Bout was free to mount his airlift into the Congo almost entirely without interference.

Of course, that didn't mean that his activities had escaped the notice of the world powers. Ironically, it was the same agency that had contracted Bout to fly life-saving aid into the Congo who would finger him first as an international sanctions-buster who could seemingly deliver anything, anywhere.

Even as it had contracted Bout to carry its aid, so the UN had sent its people to Angola, to investigate how bulk supplies of weaponry were reaching UNITA rebels. This is what they had discovered: between July 1997 and October 1998 Bout's aircraft had flown thirty-seven flights from Burgas, in Bulgaria, to Lomé, in the West African country of Togo. But Togo was not the end destination for those flights: in truth, they were ferrying the arms south, to UNITA.

The cargo had included 20,000 mortar rounds, 6,300 anti-tank rockets, rocket launchers, AK-47 assault rifles, plus 1.5 million rounds of ammunition. By UN estimates it amounted to $14 million worth of weapons sales. Mirchev had brokered the deals, and Bout's aircraft had delivered all flights bar one. The UN panel of experts discovered that the End User Certificates (EUCs) – basically, the arms export-import licences – had been forged, to hide who was the real customer.

In December 1999 the UN published its report, making all of this crystal clear. But exposing sanctions-busting was one thing; stopping it was quite another. The law simply did not allow for the prosecution of transnational operations such as these. Incredibly, violating UN arms embargoes was a crime for which there was no clear penalty, let alone any enforcement mechanisms.

Bulgarian arms dealer Peter Mirchev argued that he and Bout

were only doing good business. It was his role to load the arms into the aircraft: after that, it wasn't his responsibility where they were headed. Bout argued it was his role to transport those cargoes to their end-destination, not to inspect them or to know what he was carrying. In this sense, their operations had the all-important aspect of 'plausible deniability'.

Within the UN, and other agencies that watch the global arms trade, there was a sense of deep frustration. Bout and his peers seemed able to get away with what they were doing scot-free, and in the Second Congo War the results spoke for themselves.

By 2000, the two sides of the conflict had fought themselves to a bloody standstill. Positions consolidated along a front line that changed little over the course of the war – a war that would earn untold infamy for the terrible atrocities and massacres perpetrated over its six-year history. Millions would end up shot, bombed, blasted or starved to death, or ravaged by disease.

The United Nations accused all sides – including those countries who backed the various factions, and senior military and political figures – of looting the Congo's mineral wealth under the guise of the fighting, including its diamonds and gold. Doubtless, a small group of powerful individuals had grown rich from the grievous suffering of millions.

And those who had armed the conflict were arguably at the front of the queue.

CHAPTER SEVEN

DORSET, ENGLAND, FEBRUARY 2006

As far as Mike Snow was concerned, buying aircraft in Britain had to be far safer than flying them in the African bush. So when the Congo's President announced that he was looking for an HS125 executive jet, and someone to go and purchase it for him, Mike jumped at the chance.

After the air crash that had reduced 9Q-CTS to a battered hulk rotting in the Congo jungle, Mike was more convinced than ever that he'd used up most of his nine lives. If he pushed it, he'd end up dead, of that he felt certain . . . which meant that his days flying museum relics around African war zones were numbered.

He also remained haunted by the brother and sister from the N'Djilli airport explosions. Several years had passed, but still he couldn't get them out of his thoughts. He knew what he needed. He needed a change of scenery and very probably a change of career.

It was February 2006 when the aviation advisor to Joseph Kabila – the Congo's previous President, his father Laurent Kabila, had been assassinated by one of his own bodyguards – contacted Mike with the request to find the HS125. Snow was asked because he had a reputation that he could be trusted. In other words, he wasn't likely to go running off with the President's money.

Mike had called a friend of his, Pierre Villard, a French aircraft broker based in the UK, explaining that he was after an HS125.

'*Mon dieu!*' the Frenchman exclaimed. 'Not so far from here we have one!'

Pierre Villard spoke like an English gent, but with strong Parisian overtones. More to the point the HS125 that he knew of was an absolute peach, by all accounts.

The Hawker Siddeley HS125 was a smart-looking British executive jet, manufactured through to the seventies. Though now somewhat obsolete, it was sufficient for the President's purposes, which was to jet here and there across the 1,000-mile span of the Congo. The aircraft could carry eight passengers in sumptuous comfort, and it was blessed with undeniably classic lines.

It wasn't exactly the aircraft that Mike would have advised Joseph Kabila to buy. It was greedy on fuel and noisy. But if President Kabila wanted an HS125, he was sure to need a pilot, and who better than Snow? It would mean wearing a proper pilot's uniform for the first time in his life, but at least he would be flying a relatively modern aircraft, which vastly reduced the risk of dying.

Mike recruited Joe Reilly to be his co-pilot on the HS125's long flight back to Africa, which they'd complete in a number of 500-mile relays. Joe was the ideal choice: he was honest, dependable, liked a bit of adventure, and didn't start crying for his mother when things went a little out of kilter.

Mike flew in to Gatwick and linked up with Reilly, and from there they drove to Pierre Villard's rural home. The Frenchman had to be in his seventies, and there was something of the louche old soak about him. Small, with longish, foppy hair just turning grey, he dressed like a dandy and still fancied himself with the ladies.

Pierre, like Mike, had done his time as a bush pilot in Africa, only he had flown crop-dusters. It was a bond from which had developed a friendship, despite their obvious differences. In contrast to Snow, Pierre affected a cultured air and was all personable creamy charm, yet even so the two seemed to rub along just fine.

The Frenchman lived alone in a typical Dorset thatched cottage, his former wife having left him after he'd been caught having one too many affairs. *C'est la vie*, he would remark, ruefully. He was too old to fly commercially, so he'd taken to dealing in aircraft instead, arranging deals for second-hand airfreighters and spare parts all over the world.

Mike, Joe and Pierre headed off to inspect the HS125. Its owner took them to a former RAF base, now largely unused. Inside a massive hangar sat the HS125. Mike could tell immediately that it had been scrupulously cared for. It looked clean, well maintained and pretty much ready to go. Shortly after purchasing the HS125, the owner had suffered a sudden heart attack. It was his pride and joy, but he couldn't get clearance to fly it any more. He told Mike he wanted $240,000 for it, which by anyone's reckoning was a snip.

Mike and Joe levered up the aircraft to inspect the landing gear – about the only part of the HS125 that might have suffered during four years' inactivity – using special jacks that slot beneath the wings. They gave it a lube using an old-fashioned grease gun, and cycled the undercarriage up and down via a hydraulic pump. It seemed to work perfectly.

Mike figured it was President Kabila's money, it was a very fair price, so why haggle? They shook on the deal and drove back to Pierre's house to celebrate. That evening, they swapped stories over several bottles of Pierre's wine, catching up on old times. At first, it was one of those classic evenings when each tried to outdo the other by telling the biggest lie from Africa – all based upon a core of hard truth, of course.

But then Pierre made a comment that grabbed Mike's attention. 'You know, I'm working with some people based out of Houston. You should see what kit they have.'

Houston, Texas, Mike mused. Pierre's 'some people' had to be a euphemism for American spooks, most likely the CIA.

'How d'you know 'em?' he queried.

'I sold them a consignment of LET 410s,' Pierre explained, referring to the Czech light transport aircraft that Bout also used. 'Nowadays I mainly sell them the spare parts, to keep them running.'

'So what kind of people are they?' Mike probed.

Pierre Villard had a habit of letting out a high-pitched giggle and licking his lips, whenever he got excited or nervous. He did so just now. 'Well, put it this way: they're interested in Charles Taylor, for war crimes in Liberia. But no one seems to know where to find him.'

Mike snorted. 'I can bloody get him.'

Charles Taylor had been the President of the West African country of Liberia from 1997 to 2003. During his time as the nation's leader he was accused of carrying out horrific war crimes. Facing massive internal opposition and international pressure, he'd finally resigned the presidency in August 2003 and pretty much disappeared. He was now a wanted man.

Pierre challenged Mike to come good on his boast. By way

of answer, he placed a call to a contact of his in South African intelligence. 'Fred, any idea where Charles fucking Taylor is? I've got a guy here needs to know.'

'Hang on, give me thirty minutes,' Fred answered. 'I'll call you back.'

Twenty minutes later Mike's mobile rang. It was Fred. 'Taylor's in a small village situated on Nigeria's border with Cameroon, in a villa called Casablanca. It's a huge place, enclosed with high walls and bodyguards. You can't miss it.'

Fred gave Mike the coordinates, after which Mike logged onto Google Earth. After a few minutes searching he found the place, and zoomed in on the only location that could possibly match Fred's description. The resolution was sharp enough to see the high wall and fence surrounding the villa, and to count the guards.

Mike jabbed a stubby finger at the image. 'There you go. That's where Taylor is. So who wants him?'

Pierre licked his dry lips. 'Like I said, my Houston people might. I'll need to double check.' He took a sip of his wine. 'They're also looking for BMPs. Two, to start. For delivery to some really nasty people in South America. To – tee-hee-hee – stitch them up.'

The BMP – short for *Boyevaya Mashina Pekhoty* – is a Soviet-era thirteen-tonne amphibious tracked infantry vehicle. Mike called Fred in South Africa, and asked if he was able to source some.

'Not a problem,' Fred replied. 'They're $225,000 apiece, plus $35,000 extra if whoever wants them needs training.'

Mike killed the call. Pierre looked suitably impressed. 'My Houston people may need to put some transponders into the

BMPs,' he ventured. 'The people they're shipping them to are rather – tee-hee-hee – evil, so they need to track them. D'you think you can manage that?'

Mike called Fred for a third time. 'Can the delivery aircraft make a diversionary stop over somewhere like Malta, while we fit transponders into the BMPs?'

'Not a problem. We'll act as if we have a technical difficulty, so we have to land. Then we stay grounded for four days – getting it sorted. Gives your guys time to get on-board and do their stuff.'

A transponder is a device that emits a radio frequency that can be detected by a receiver-transmitter. It's a fancy name for a tracking device. If the transponder has the power to transmit to a satellite, it can be detected from outer space and tracked globally: very useful when trying to trace the movements of the bad guys.

It was odd, but after Mike had proved that he could find Taylor, and now source and outfit a pair of BMPs, Pierre seemed to lose interest in both ventures. Mike sensed that he was being tested, and that Pierre and his Houston people were after something else. Finally, Pierre worked his way around to what was really on his mind.

'You know, my Houston people are really interested in Viktor.' Viktor Bout had cropped up earlier in the conversation. 'He's on the wanted list, so they're interested in him.'

'Interested, like how?' Mike asked.

'Interested in nailing him.'

Mike's eyes narrowed. 'Will your Houston people pay?'

Pierre confirmed that they would. He didn't know how much exactly, but if they could snare Bout it would doubtless herald a significant payday.

'The thing is I met Viktor in Angola,' Pierre continued, 'and he seemed like such a nice chap. Just one of the boys, really. He's never done anything wrong in my eyes, so why would we go after him?'

Mike fixed him with a look. 'If he's wanted by your Houston people, maybe he's not so bloody nice, is he?'

'Maybe.' Pierre giggled. 'Apparently he's done some really bad stuff. Sold weapons to the Taliban, or at least that's what they say.'

'There you go.'

'So, d'you think you could get him?'

Mike's gaze hardened: 'I can fucking get him,' he announced, in his bruising tones. 'For sure I can get him.'

Whoever Pierre's Houston people might be, this had the flavour of a seriously adrenalin-fuelled adventure. But as he'd done before, Pierre changed the subject. He reverted back to the HS125 deal and what a steal it was for the money.

'How much do you need, as commission on the deal?' Mike asked him.

'Don't worry about me,' Pierre replied. 'I've not done very much. Just made a few calls.'

'You sure?' Mike pressed.

'No, no, I've not done anything much.'

'Okay, great, 'cause I fucking need every penny I can get right now.'

Mike was being his usual blunt and honest self. Having lost both his CL-44s, he was badly in need of an injection of funds. Shortly afterwards – feeling the after-effects of the long flight from South Africa, and never a big drinker – he made his apologies, leaving Joe and Pierre chatting over a fresh bottle.

As he made his way up the staircase in the creaky old house, Mike felt convinced that Bout was the real focus of interest for

Pierre's Houston people. It had been the lick-factor that had been the giveaway. While Viktor Bout was the topic of discussion, Pierre's tongue had been darting out and moistening his lips every few seconds. Well, if they really wanted Bout, Mike and his network could find him.

Mike had first run into the Russian businessman in South Africa, in the mid-1990s. They'd met through a mutual acquaintance called Andrew Smulian, a fellow Brit. Smulian was ten years older than Mike, and he'd been something of a mentor when Mike had turned up in South Africa wanting to make it as a pilot. Mike had started flying for Inter Ocean Airways, an airfreight business that covered much of South Africa. He'd been loading up a Douglas DC4 – another aircraft from the Second World War era – with a consignment of food aid, when he'd spotted Smulian inspecting a nearby cargo plane.

He was in the company of an unmistakable figure – Viktor Bout. Mike had wandered over to say hello. He'd just turned fifty, and Viktor Bout had to be two decades his junior. The Russian was bound to have heard of Mike Snow – a maverick pilot out there on a limb flying ancient aircraft into war zones. As for Mike, he was more than a little curious to meet the man behind the legend.

Bout was tall and somehow very Russian-looking, with a Cossack-style sweeping moustache and slightly hooded eyes. He was dressed in a slick business suit, but to Mike's eye it didn't sit right upon his shoulders. In fact, Bout reminded him of a lot of South Africans that he knew: rugged, outdoors types who didn't look comfortable in formal business attire. He sensed that Bout was both a man's man and something of a deep thinker – he'd learn more about that later.

Once they'd made their introductions Bout gestured at the nearby aircraft. 'Antonov 8. Russian plane. Russian aircraft very good. Western aircraft too expensive. Russian aircraft very strong. For farmers to fly. Not homosexuals.'

Mike nodded noncommittally. 'If you say so.'

'With this we fly every day to Angola. Every day $175,000 clean profit, each flight. Clean, clean. We not owe anything to anybody.'

Mike nodded again. He sensed that Bout wasn't done.

'Yes, you know, Mike, this,' he patted the Antonov, 'was first turboprop in whole world.'

Mike did a double take. 'An Antonov? Where the fuck d'you hear that?'

'Yes, Russia built world's first turboprop,' Bout insisted. 'First turboprop in world.'

Mike guffawed. 'Fuck off. You want me to believe the Russians had horses and carts in the 1930s and by 1950 they invented the first turboprop? What horseshit.'

Bout seemed somewhat taken aback. 'What is world's first turboprop, then, Mike?'

'It was British. Probably the Rolls-Royce Dart engine, and most likely the Vickers Viscount.'

Mike wasn't entirely certain which model it was, but he was sure the Brits had been first. It was clear that Bout wasn't used to being talked back to or challenged. Mike figured he came from the kind of culture where people tended to doff their hats to the big boss.

That evening Smulian called Mike. 'Hey – Viktor was impressed by you. You stood up to him. He likes that in a man. Said you weren't afraid of him. "Mike is very strong man," he said. "Very aggressive. He did not back down."'

'What did he expect? Russia built the world's first turboprop! Get real.'

Smulian laughed. 'By fuck, though, he's got this woman with him.'

'Yeah, well, he's Russian. What d'you expect.'

'No, no, not that kind of woman. This one's eighty years old and she looks like she's just jumped off her broomstick. If she looks at you and says "*Nyet*", that's it: Viktor won't do business with you.'

It turned out that the old lady was Bout's seer. He used her as a sounding board for all his business deals. There was a spiritual side to the Russian, but not necessarily in an orthodox way. As time went on Mike would begin to view Bout's beliefs as something similar to his own. At age seven he had decided to take all the 'walking on water' stuff with a large pinch of salt. These days he believed in a higher power, but one of his own determining. He was a believer, but not in a traditional way, and he had some sympathy for Viktor with his old lady seer.

After that first meeting Mike and Viktor Bout's paths crossed regularly. They never did any business together, but they led parallel, interwoven lives. They were pursuing the same kind of airfreight deals, and often Smulian acted as the go-between or middleman, feeding each snippets of information about what the other was up to.

The day after his long chat with Pierre Villard, Mike awoke to find the Frenchman gone. He'd left early on business. Typically, he had no food in the house. He was one of those strange individuals who seemed able to survive without eating for days on end. Mike and Joe would have to drive out for breakfast. Before leaving, Mike noticed that the Frenchman had left a note on the kitchen table.

'Re the HS125: no way can I accept setting this deal up and not getting paid. I need a minimum of five thousand dollars from this deal.'

In his cups, Pierre had clearly been overly generous. There was a second surprise in store for Mike. The previous evening Joe and Pierre had stayed up drinking for some time. Finally, the Frenchman had confessed that he'd been secretly recording all that he and Mike had discussed. Recording it for whom, Mike wondered? His 'Houston people', no doubt.

Even if what Joe claimed was true, there was nothing Mike could do about it. And anyway, last night's chat had been just that: tall stories and beer talk. Did Villard really even have these 'Houston friends'? Mike doubted it, or at least to the level that he had implied. Either way, Mike's priority had to be pushing through the deal on the HS125.

Predictably, it took a while to get the money out of President Kabila. By that time Joe was no longer available to fly the aircraft. Instead, Mike found an American who seemed willing to join him on the long flight to the Congo. That man's name was John Costello; he was an Elvis impersonator in his spare time, and his southern Texas drawl was so pronounced it sounded as if he was drunk the whole time.

It was midday when the pair taxied out for take-off and took to the skies. As the HS125 turned south and began to climb, Mike put a call through to Essex Control. They were taking off from a private strip, so they needed to be vectored onto a flight path leaving them safe from collision with any commercial airliners. Costello was actually the pilot for this flight, for he had the licence to fly jet aircraft, and Mike was acting as his radio operator.

'Can't find your flight plan and too busy to help,' Essex Control responded.

'That's not my problem,' Mike retorted. 'I filed it with you two hours ago.'

'Well, try London,' the not-so-helpful air traffic controller suggested.

Mike tried London and got the same response.

He and Costello talked though their options. A jet airliner is horribly inefficient at slow speeds and low altitudes. It consumes more fuel taxiing on the runway that travelling at Mach .8 at 44,000 feet. But the HS125 needed clearance to reach that kind of altitude. Mike needed Air Traffic Control to say something like: fly on X bearing to Y height, then vector onto flight-path Z.

In the absence of such assistance, their only option was to proceed on Visual Flight Rules (VFR) only. Most light aircraft fly on VFR. Working on VFR you don't liaise with Air Traffic Control. Instead, you keep the ground in sight and check all around you for other aircraft. It would be highly unusual to proceed on VFR in a jet aircraft, but what other option did they have?

Mike and Costello decided to push across the Channel on VFR and to land at Ostend Airport, from where they'd chart an onwards course to the Congo. Unfortunately, half way across the Channel the aircraft's radio died. Mike could still hear Air Traffic Control, but they clearly couldn't hear him. The problem was they were about to cross from one Flight Information Region (FIR) to another – the official boundary between one nation's airspace and another.

On crossing from the UK's FIR to Belgium's they needed to

report in. 'Area Control, this is G7-KLH at 2,000 feet ...' But with a kaput radio, that wasn't about to happen. In fact, they'd need to fly into Ostend silent running all the way. That might be acceptable at UNITA's Charlie Two airstrip. It wasn't likely to go down so well at Belgium's Ostend International.

Costello wanted to turn back. Mike made the salient point that they couldn't speak to UK Air Traffic Control either. In short, they were damned if they did and damned if they didn't.

Mike started laughing maniacally. 'We're all gonna die! We're all gonna die!' It was his favourite catch phrase.

Costello clearly thought him crazy.

Maybe Costello was right.

They pressed on. Shortly, Ostend Air Traffic Control came on the air, asking them to check in. Mike couldn't reply. This was six years after 9/11, and it didn't take the brains of an archbishop to work out what a low-flying silent-running jet aircraft might be up to.

'Unidentified aircraft, execute a 360-degree turn and return the way you have come,' Ostend Air Traffic Control ordered.

Mike couldn't respond. Instead, Costello pushed their airspeed to the max and with nerves utterly shredded they somehow made the asphalt at Ostend without being shot down. As they taxied across to the hard standing, the terse voice came up over the radio again.

'Flight G7-KLH, call EuroControl. EuroControl need to speak to you urgently.'

Air Traffic Control had clearly taken a note of the HS125's tail number, and reported the illicit landing to EuroControl, the headquarters of European Air Traffic Control. He and Costello looked to be in a whole world of trouble. But they taxied over to the long-term parking ramp, bluffed their way through customs in their smart pilot uniforms, and split up – Costello heading back to Texas and Mike on to Africa.

The HS125 could remain on the long-term ramp, as long as President Kabila paid the parking fees. In the meantime, they'd need to get it re-registered as a Congolese aircraft. That way it would acquire a new tail number – NQ-CTI, or similar – and would no longer raise a red flag as being the plane that had made the clandestine crossing. Mike headed south by the first available flight. He'd return for the HS125 once it had acquired a new – and safer – identity.

But little did he know that as he settled into his long flight to Africa, he was heading into the coming storm.

CHAPTER EIGHT

LONDON, ENGLAND, JULY 1999

By the summer of 1999, Viktor Bout's position looked unassailable. He was running a global airfreight business boasting some sixty aircraft and employing 300 people. His operations out of Sharjah ranked second only to the German national carrier Lufthansa in terms of volume of cargo. He was still doing business with the Taliban, he'd established an African passenger airline, he was leasing aircraft to Libya's Muammar Gaddafi, and was shipping weapons into war zones.

He remained resolutely apolitical. He never took sides. Indeed, he was happy to do business with anyone, as long as there was money to be made. He relied on the adage that you 'never shoot the postman', plus he had become adept at registering his aircraft with those nations with lax to non-existent regulatory regimes. And nobody was doing much, if anything, to stop him.

Then, in late July 1999 something changed. The politician and prominent anti-apartheid campaigner Peter Hain took up his post as Africa Minister at the Foreign Office. Hain had spent his early years in South Africa, only leaving when his staunchly anti-apartheid parents were forced out of the country, after which he had remained closely involved in African affairs.

In his new Whitehall office he began to receive daily intelligence briefings from Britain's Secret Intelligence Service (MI6), and related agencies, including GCHQ with their wealth of signals intercepts. He was shocked at the reports chronicling private airfreight companies flying weaponry into African war zones – most notably the Congo and Angola – and flying out again with parcels of diamonds.

The more Hain studied the intelligence reports, the more he realized that missiles, landmines, crates of ammunition, small arms and heavy weaponry were being flown into isolated, dusty airstrips with impunity. Clearly, this traffic in death was fuelling conflicts and destroying communities.

Typically, shipments of weapons would be collected in the former Soviet states of Moldova, Ukraine or Bulgaria, and 'officially' flown into Rwanda or Togo. But somewhere en route the aircraft would 'disappear' for several hours, during which time it would make its delivery to the real intended recipients.

Even with British – and allied – intelligence agencies keeping watch, it was easy enough to make an aircraft disappear: a low-level flight executed at night was impossible to track. As the reports landed daily on his desk, Hain realized that while the British agencies were extremely adept at gathering intelligence, there appeared to be few measures in place to do anything about it. Dismayed, he called a meeting of his diplomatic and intelligence chiefs.

'Gentlemen, let me get this straight,' he began. 'We know what these aircraft are carrying. In most cases we know who owns them. We know where they're really heading. But we're doing nothing to stop them?'

Blank faces.

'Erm, Minister, if we did something about them we'd risk compromising our sources,' someone volunteered. 'Remember, in many cases they are risking their lives for us.'

Hain fixed the speaker with a gimlet eye. 'Then why don't we just shoot one or two of these planes out of the sky? Surely that would send the right kind of a message?'

Silence. For several seconds. Then another speaker ventured to raise an objection.

'Um sir, I think that might be a little, um . . . illegal. I mean, for a British Minister of State to order the shooting down of a foreign aircraft over a third country . . . It somewhat smacks of a terrorist act, don't you think? Isn't that the kind of thing we're . . . um . . . trying to stop?'

For a moment you could have heard a pin drop, before the meeting dissolved into laughter. Hain had to admit it – there was something slightly absurd in his suggestion. But beneath the deliberate provocation there was also a deadly serious element to all of this: what was the point in gathering intelligence for endless reports, if at the end of it all there was never any action?

'So you're telling me we can't do anything,' Hain challenged, once the merriment had died down. 'Some of these weapons are being supplied to RUF terrorists in Sierra Leone and then being used against our British troops. But we can't do anything? Here we are, informed up to our eyebrows, but doing bugger all about it while our soldiers are attacked, and death and destruction goes unchecked. How does that add up?'

Hain's blow had most certainly struck home. Since 1997 small bodies of British troops had been stationed in the West African nation of Sierra Leone, to deter the rebel forces in that nation's civil war. Far larger numbers of United Nations peacekeepers had also been deployed in an effort to keep the rebels – the Revolutionary United Front (RUF) – at bay.

Incapable of expressing a coherent political ideology, the RUF's sole aim seemed to be to spread terror as a means of gaining power and control. Their gruesome signature was to amputate the hands of men, women and children, simply to spread fear. They would offer the victim to have their hands cut off 'long-sleeve' or 'short-sleeve' style - meaning above or below the elbows.

Recently, the RUF had vowed to 'do a Somalia' on British troops in Sierra Leone, a reference to the US military's 1993 defeat in the Somali capital, Mogadishu, immortalized in the movie *Black Hawk Down*. Having launched their horrific operations 'Kill All Your Family' and 'No Living Thing', the RUF had decided their next priority was to drive British forces out of their country.

Hain had seen numerous intelligence reports about Viktor Bout running weapons shipments into West Africa, to arm the RUF. Time and again his name came up in the files. If those weapons were being turned against British soldiers and UN peacekeepers, then Bout and his peers constituted a direct threat to British servicemen, not to mention those of Britain's allies.

Hain reflected on what action was open to him, barring ordering one of Bout's Ilyushins to be blasted out of the heavens. He decided there really was only one: he would name and shame the chief offenders in Parliament, where such utterances are protected by 'parliamentary privilege' – an MP speaking in the House cannot be sued for libel.

The initial reaction of the Whitehall mandarins to Hain's proposal was somewhat less than enthusiastic: intelligence had never been used in this way. Hain argued there was always a first time. He spoke to the then head of MI6, Richard Dearlove.

Dearlove actually supported the proposal, as did many of his senior officers.

On 18 January 2000 Hain rose from his seat in Parliament to present his speech. 'It is vital that private individuals and companies engaged in breaking the law by deliberately breaching UN sanctions . . . are stopped . . .'

Hain nailed Viktor Bout as one of the chief sanctions-busters, and he had made sure to alert the world's media to what he would be saying. The story was reported widely, provoking furious reactions from some of those that he had named and shamed. But from Bout there was only silence. The Russian would continue to operate business as usual, no comment.

Perhaps unwittingly, Bout made one fatal error at this juncture: if anything, he strengthened and reinvigorated his dealings with Liberia and Sierra Leone, and, by extension, the RUF rebels. This would put him on a direct collision course with the British government, plus those administrations most closely tied to Britain – first and foremost, the Americans.

In Washington, the same kind of intelligence that had raised Hain's hackles was causing real concern. The summer that Hain took up office, the US National Security Council (NSC) authorized the electronic surveillance of government and rebel leaders in the Congo, Liberia and Sierra Leone. This was in direct response to the upsurge in violence and the scale of arms reaching those countries.

US electronic surveillance aircraft began quartering the skies, picking up calls to rebel groups about arms shipments. Daily, the NSC's analysts cross-referenced those intercepts with the kind of intelligence British sources collated on the ground. Over time, one name jumped out at them: Viktor Bout.

The context of the intercepts was always the same: arms shipments, aircraft routing or diamond deals. Gayle Smith, a top Africanist at the NSC, fired off an email to her fellow analysts about Bout: 'Who is this guy? Pay close attention. He's all over the place.'

By the summer of 2000 the NSC had put most of the pieces together. They figured they had stumbled upon the most extensive, yet secretive, weapons transport and brokering business in the world. By that time Hain had named and shamed Bout in the British Parliament, which added grist to their mill.

Gayle Smith and her colleague, Russia expert and lawyer Lee Wolosky, took their files to Richard C Clarke, then chief of counterterrorism at the NSC. In part, Clarke saw his role as combating the global upsurge of 'drugs and thugs' – the nexus of crime, terrorism and drugs traffickers – and time and again Bout kept cropping up at the heart of that nexus.

Wolosky had spearheaded the NSC's efforts to nail Bout. 'Serving under President Clinton ... we noticed that Viktor Bout was fuelling almost every African conflict the President was trying to resolve. White House officials accordingly sought to build a US response to put him out of business, as he was interfering with the President's efforts to promote peace in West Africa in particular ... Bout was fuelling those conflicts on multiple sides.'

Having reviewed the Bout files, Clarke declared: 'Get me a warrant.'

Saying that was one thing; getting a warrant for Viktor Bout's arrest was quite another. His crimes – that's if they were crimes that could be prosecuted in a court of law – had been committed outside of the USA, which meant that the NSC had little jurisdiction. The NSC shared their files with the CIA, State Department and others. The evidence spoke for itself, but no one could determine the means to nail Bout.

Yet in Britain, the confrontation with Bout was about to be catapulted to a whole new level.

CHAPTER NINE

COPENHAGEN, DENMARK, SEPTEMBER 2007

Mike Snow had barely given a thought to his conversation with Pierre Villard, until the French aircraft dealer got in touch again. His 'Houston people' wanted to meet. They'd invited Mike to Copenhagen, one of their key European centres of operations.

Mike considered their invitation. It was taking a while to spring the HS125 from Ostend Airport, and if nothing else he was intrigued to see if Villard's people really were as Hollywood as the Frenchman liked to make out.

In late September 2007 the two men rendezvoused at the Ryanair check-in desk at Stansted Airport. Mike was feeling a little fractious, especially as he didn't know exactly who he would be meeting. He figured it had to be the CIA, but Pierre hadn't let on, and Mike was playing it too cool to ask. On the flight to Copenhagen he happened to sit next to a woman from the Faroe Islands, an archipelago lying halfway between Norway and Iceland.

He turned to the hapless Faroe Islander. 'So, I bet you think it's fine to slaughter hundreds of pilot whales every summer? That's what you Faroe Islanders do, isn't it?'

Mike was referring to a tradition on the Faroes that every year they'd hunt and kill several hundred pilot whales.

'No, no, really it's okay,' the lady remonstrated. 'You see, we eat them.'

'Well, you shouldn't eat them. What did pilot whales ever do to you? Do they bloody eat you? No, they don't.'

It wasn't until they were in a taxi en route to their hotel that Mike finally got off the issue of the pilot whales, and Pierre felt able to broach the subject of who exactly his Houston people might be.

'So, I guess you figured it was the CIA?'

'I hadn't really thought about it much.'

'Well, it's actually the DEA. You've heard of them, I take it?'

'Drugs Enforcement Administration. I know the name.'

'Good. We're to check into our rooms, and they'll come and find us.'

As far as Mike was concerned it didn't make a great deal of difference what acronym Villard's people went by, but he did wonder what interest the DEA might have in Viktor Bout. A few years back he'd heard tell that Bout was flying drugs, so maybe some bad old birds had come home to roost.

The taxi pulled up at the Radisson Blu Royal Hotel, a slab-sided high-rise looking out over Copenhagen's port area on one side and the Tivoli Gardens – an iconic pleasure park – on the other. As Mike and Pierre strolled into the lobby, a voice rang out in greeting. 'Hey, buddy! Good to see you. How you doing?'

Pierre proceeded to introduce Mike to DEA Agents William Brown and Robert Zachariasiewicz – known to all as 'Wim' and 'Zach'. They struck Mike as looking like your typical American businessmen – crew-cut hair, smart but casual dress, shiny foreheads and beaming smiles. Wim sported a neat but greying beard, and he seemed the quieter of the two. It was Zach who had called out the greeting.

Mike and Pierre took a moment to dump their bags in their rooms, before returning to reception. By now Agents Wim and Zach had been joined by a third figure, who was based in the US Embassy in Copenhagen. Oddly, they started quizzing Mike there and then about the matter at hand.

'So, Mike, how well d'you know Viktor Bout?'

'I'm a pilot. He's a pilot. Or at least he runs an airline business. We're in the same line of work.'

Agent Zach handed Mike something. 'Have you seen this?'

Mike glanced at it. It was a book by American reporters Douglas Farah and Stephen Braun. Though he'd not read it cover to cover, he knew it dealt with Viktor Bout's life and career, hence its tagline: 'Money, guns, planes and the man who makes war possible.'

He eyed the agents dubiously. 'You're going after Viktor 'cause he's had a book written about him?'

'No, no, no. We don't want to get him on what he's done in the past. We want to catch him in the act. Like, d'you think he would swap a load of arms for drugs?'

Mike shook his head. 'Viktor wouldn't do that kind of shit.' He paused. 'But listen, I don't like the idea of standing here in a hotel foyer. I have a big voice and I tend to talk loud.'

The guy from the Embassy chuckled. 'Yeah, I'd like to hear you when you've got a few beers inside you!'

Mike scowled. 'Fuck you! I don't drink much, so that ain't never going to fucking happen.'

The agents suggested they head to one of their rooms. Once there, Mike surveyed the DEA guys a little more closely. Zach was all effusive bonhomie, but Mike sensed it was a little forced.

Below the hail-fellow-well-met act, he detected a smart and ruthless operator. Wim struck him as being quiet, cynical, but efficient, and basically an honest and decent kind of guy.

Time to cut to the chase. 'Right, tell me: what's Viktor done to deserve any of this?'

'We can't tell you exactly. But we can assure you that he is one very bad guy.'

Almost every American agency had been after Bout for years, the agents explained, but with very little success, which was why it had been handed over to the DEA. Wim and Zach actually worked for a specialist unit within the DEA – the Counter Narco-terrorism Operations Centre, part of its Special Operations Division (the SOD) located in Chantilly, in northern Virginia.

'Narco-terrorism' was where the worlds of drugs and terrorism collided, or rather colluded. It was where terrorists and drugs traffickers made common cause to wreak global havoc and make billions. Their role was to coordinate narco-terrorism investigations outside the US: in other words, to combat transnational drugs cartels, high-profile international criminals, global weapons traffickers and terrorist groups operating across borders.

Both DEA agents had long track records. Wim had served in the SOD for four years, prior to which he'd worked for approaching a decade in the DEA's Miami and Tampa field divisions. Before that he'd served for six years in the Marine Corps reserves. Phenomenally bright, he'd graduated from college with a degree in political science. Zach was a former Navy man and had a similarly impressive résumé.

One of Wim and Zach's key tasks within the Special Operations

Division was managing confidential sources – those who worked on the DEA's behalf undercover, penetrating deep within the kind of criminality the agency was targeting.

Mike didn't know it yet, but Pierre Villard was a longtime DEA source, and Wim and Zach had come here to assess whether they could recruit Mike Snow. Most DEA agents received expert training before they took on such a role. There would be none of that with Mike: his experiences in the real world would have to suffice.

Viktor Bout had first come to the DEA's attention in the summer of that year. The Agency's then Assistant Administrator and Chief of Operations, Mike Braun, had been approached by Juan Zarate, President George W Bush's Deputy Counter-Terrorism Advisor at the National Security Council (NSC). The NSC argued that Bout had become the world's most notorious arms dealer, due to his ability to ferry weapons into civil-war zones. They believed he was a serious threat, due to his ability to arm terrorist groups targeting the US or its citizens.

Braun had studied the files. He read reports suggesting that Bout had built a six billion dollar global empire. By shipping tens of thousands of AK-47 assault rifles into the hands of rebels, Bout had 'transformed young, adolescent warriors into mindless, maniacally-driven killing-machines that operated with assembly-line efficiency,' Braun concluded.

But it went further. 'Bout had the ability to acquire the most sophisticated weapons systems that the former Soviet Bloc could offer,' Braun observed. 'He could not have acquired the weapons systems he did without the complicity of the highest ranks of government and military in Russia.' Bout, Braun concluded, was 'one of the most dangerous men on the face of the earth.'

The White House had thrown out a challenge: could the DEA get Bout where other agencies had failed? The Agency certainly had the track record. Recently, they'd orchestrated a string of global arrests, most notably that of Monzer Al Kazar, a global drug trafficker in his own right and then the world's second biggest arms dealer and supplier to terrorists worldwide. Kazar – who'd evaded capture for three decades – was suspected of providing the weapons used by the Palestinian Liberation Front terrorists, to hijack the MS Achille Lauro cruise ship, resulting in the murder of an American, Leon Klinghoffer. After the DEA had nailed him, he was convicted and sentenced to 30 years without parole.

Zarate cited other high profile DEA successes, including the capture of Haji Bashir Noorzai and Haji Bagcho, founders of the Taliban and some of the world's foremost heroin traffickers. Noorzai had been sentenced to thirty years and Bagcho to life, both without parole. In short, if the DEA could get Noorzai, Bagcho and Monzer Al Kazar, why not Viktor Bout? The stakes were extremely high. The illicit arms trade was second only to the drugs trade in terms of profits earned worldwide. Often, the two criminal enterprises ran side-by-side. Braun decided the DEA would give it their best shot.

Right now Agents Brown and Zachariasiewicz were that best shot, and they'd learned enough about Mike Snow to know he offered them a potential breakthrough. Now, in this Copenhagen hotel room, it was all about feeling their way towards some form of common ground, from where they could build a degree of trust.

But they also knew of Mike's reputation as someone who didn't suffer fools gladly. Typically, The Bear was living up to expectations.

'If you're so keen on getting Bout, how come he's flying for you guys?' he barked out a challenge.

The agents seemed nonplussed. 'He's flying for us?'

'What d'you mean?'

'Fact. His aircraft are flying for the US military in Iraq and Afghanistan. If you don't believe me go ask Condi Rice. The flights were originating in France, and the French wanted to stop them. Condi Rice told the French to leave well alone. Surely you blokes know that?'

Condoleezza 'Condi' Rice was then President George W Bush's Secretary of State, and his former National Security Advisor. Bout's airlines were flying military supplies into US bases in Iraq and Afghanistan, and had clearance from the highest levels, or so Mike had heard. The two DEA agents said they knew nothing about that.

Mike considered this for a second. 'Well, maybe we could get him by me saying I had a shipment of arms to organize, but that it fell through. So we ask Bout to take over.'

'Nah,' Wim piped up. 'That won't work.'

Zach leaned forward. 'Let's not sweat the detail. Thing is, can you make contact with Bout? Can you get to him?'

Mike eyeballed him. 'Sure I can bloody get to him. I can do it right now if you want.'

The DEA agents said they'd like that.

Mike composed a text message to Andrew Smulian, his one-time mentor in the African airfreight business. He knew that his old pal was still pursuing various commercial ventures with the Russian businessman.

'I'm with some people who want to get their hands on an Antonov-12,' he wrote. 'D'you think Viktor can help?'

Smulian replied that he'd check. A few minutes later he messaged again. 'I've spoken to Viktor. He can help. He can get you one.'

Mike told him he'd get back with more details.

He flashed the messages at Wim and Zach. 'You may be used to dealing with bullshitters and criminals, but I don't say I can do something if I can't.'

Mike detailed Smulian's relationship to Bout, and why he would be crucial to any efforts to nail him. Smulian was in his late sixties. Ten years back he'd served as Bout's deputy in South Africa. With his shock of white hair above a greying moustache and hooded blue eyes, there was something distinctly grandfatherly about him. Bout had actually nicknamed him 'Babu' – 'grandpa' in Swahili, a language spoken widely across that part of Africa.

Born in England, Smulian had moved to South Africa aged eight. For three decades he'd run airfreight company Inter Ocean Airways, carrying all kinds of cargoes, including occasional shipments of arms for various African governments. For a short while Mike had actually worked as one of his pilots.

Smulian had also served for six years in the South African military, and he'd continued to work for South African military intelligence, as a source. A commercial pilot flying across southern Africa, he'd carried out covert photo-reconnaissance missions. It was Smulian's intelligence work that had earned him the nickname among Mike and his circle of '00-Negative', an obvious pun on James Bond.

It was 1997 when Smulian had agreed to work as Bout's manager in South Africa, setting up a base of operations at Pietersburg Airport, a former military airbase. Towards the end of that year Bout had taken him to Dubai, to visit the DEFEX arms fair, one of the world's largest. While there, Bout had introduced Smulian to Mikhail Kalashnikov, the inventor of the AK-47, as well as Peter Mirchev, his Bulgarian arms broker friend.

Following the Dubai exhibition, Smulian had been in contact with Mirchev, to discuss potential deals. When Bout was forced out of South Africa, he and Smulian had stayed in touch and continued to pursue various business ventures. In 1999, Smulian had been forced to close Inter Ocean Airways, setting him on the road to penury.

Recently, he'd moved to Dar-Es-Salaam, the capital of the East African nation of Tanzania. He was looking to establish a uranium-extraction business there, potential ocean-side casinos, and brokering arms sales to African governments – all with Bout's help. But he was surviving with great difficulty. He was working part time in a local syringe factory, in a hand-to-mouth existence.

Wim and Zach advised Mike to keep Smulian sweet, while they tried to think of a workable plan, something that Bout might go for. In the meantime, they explained, they'd need to sign him up as a DEA confidential source. Mike asked what exactly that might entail.

They needed to photograph and fingerprint him, plus take a copy of his passport, and place all of that in a safe in their Washington DC headquarters. He'd be given a DEA number, and be required to sign an agreement that defined exactly what was expected of him – namely to work with the agency, and remain truthful and honest throughout the period of their investigation.

Mike figured now was as good a time as any to pop the million-dollar question. 'That's all very well. That I can do, no problem.' A beat. 'But tell me ... what's in it for me?'

The agents spread their hands. 'We can't promise anything.'

'We just can't.'

Mike got to his feet. 'Well, then, I'm going home.'

'No, no, wait,' Zach remonstrated. 'We can't say what you will get, but once it's done, if it's done, you get put in for an award. In the meantime, we cover your expenses and provide you with lunch money.'

The agents clarified that Mike should expect to get paid for his services, but only down the road. 'Nothing can be offered up front. It goes to a board, a jury, who determine what your award payment should be.'

Mike considered this for a moment. 'So, basically, I have to rely on the US justice system, pretty much like Viktor will have to, if we get him.' Mike figured he had little to lose and potentially everything to gain. He agreed to be signed up.

He was cautioned about what he could and couldn't do as a DEA confidential source. He would not be permitted to do any drugs deals without DEA prior consent. The same was true of arms deals, aircraft deals or any other type of potentially illegal transaction, including money laundering. Mike's mind boggled: just what exactly did these guys have in mind?

'This is how I'll work with you,' he declared. 'I will never lie to you and I will never bring the DEA into disrepute. But if you trick me or try to make me do something I don't want to do, or if you hide anything, then I'm done. You need to keep me updated at all times.'

'Of course.'

'Goes without saying.'

'I know the game you're in,' Mike continued. 'Deception plays a big part. I do not want to be deceived. If I reach a place where I don't feel comfortable, I'm done.'

Zach and Wim repeated their assurances.

'We'll need to use Andrew as the route to get to Viktor,' Mike continued. 'He's a very intelligent guy and hugely well read, with a pukka English-South African accent. He can talk on any subject – religion, philosophy, you name it. He's got lovely kids and he's basically a real gent. He's a bit of a likeable rogue, but no more than you or me. He'd make a useless crook and he's certainly no hard man.'

'So where's all this going?'

Mike eyed the agents. 'This is my one condition: Andrew Smulian cannot get done for anything. He's going to be an unwitting participant. He's going to be led up the garden path. That makes him an innocent victim and I don't want him convicted. That's my one condition, and it's non-negotiable.'

From the expressions on the agents' faces, Mike could tell that neither of them liked this very much. But likewise, they could tell that Mike was serious. They promised to have a word with the prosecutor – the legal eagle in New York who would be overseeing the case, should they succeed in getting Bout to the US.

Mike asked them to make that call right away. He could tell from the to-and-fro of the conversation that it wasn't going well. Agent Zach came off the line. Apparently, the prosecutor had refused: they needed to be free to prosecute Smulian alongside Bout.

'Then it's no deal,' Mike told them. 'Like I said, either Andrew is granted immunity, or I'm out.'

A second call was placed to the prosecutor. This time he was persuaded of the need to agree to Snow's terms.

Of course, he didn't have anything in writing to confirm that Smulian had been granted immunity, but if he couldn't trust these law enforcement types, who could he trust? And if they double-crossed him, Mike would call a press conference outside the court and tell the media exactly what had gone down.

With Smulian's immunity sorted, they called that first exploratory meeting to a close. Mike left, reflecting on his initial impressions of the DEA. He knew that without him, the agents stood little chance of netting Viktor Bout. But were they actually capable of ensnaring such a man? Somehow, Mike doubted it. He liked them well enough, but he had a distinct sense that they were like little boys whistling in the dark.

As it happened, that impression was just about to be blown asunder.

The DEA enjoyed full cooperation with the Danish authorities, and they'd secured prior approval for their next operation, which was somewhat sensitive. The agents hadn't come to Copenhagen solely to meet Mike Snow. They were here to execute a major sting, one that they'd been developing for some time.

Pierre Villard was an integral part of that operation, but now that Mike was signed up they figured maybe he could play a role. If nothing else, it would give him valuable insight into the way they operated. Plus as a bona fide bush pilot he could well prove useful with what was coming.

In recent years the South American drugs cartels had stumbled upon a new route to traffic cocaine into Europe, via the back door. They'd started buying old cargo aircraft – ancient Boeing 727s and the like – and flying them across the Atlantic stuffed full of narcotics. They'd touch down on remote airstrips in West Africa, from where the drugs were shipped north via Spain and Italy, onwards into Europe.

The cartels were operating fleets of aircraft making regular shuttle runs, with little danger of detection. Once a plane began its transatlantic voyage it would fall off any surveillance systems, there being little radar coverage over the ocean. They'd arrive undetected in Liberia, Mali, Guinea or Sierra Leone, and with customs and airport officials paid off.

So lucrative was the trade that even Gulfstream executive jets had joined the 3,500-mile transatlantic shuttle runs. The amounts of drugs involved were staggering: hundreds of tonnes of heroin and cocaine. And with cocaine use in Europe on the rise, the amounts of money to be made beggared belief.

One of the main countries involved was Venezuela. Two years previously Venezuela's president, Hugo Chávez, had severed ties with US law enforcement agencies, and the Venezuelan military was known to be up to its elbows in the trade. The so-called Cartel of the Suns – a shadowy network of top army and air force figures – was shuttling flights across the Atlantic, evading American and European security envelopes completely.

The global economic slump meant that there was no shortage of second-hand airfreighters going for a song. Big, four-engine planes could be purchased for as little as quarter of a million dollars. The South American cartels had plans to buy entire airports in West Africa, to extend their reach still further, and they were paying aircrews in suitcases full of dollars.

They had one problem: laundering their money. The cartels had hundreds of millions of euros stashed in southern Europe, which they needed to turn into 'clean', usable funds. Transporting the cash through the various nations of Western Europe wasn't a problem, as long as the traffickers stuck to the border-free Schengen zone. But finding a bank to accept their millions, and transform them into 'squeaky clean' wire transfers, was challenging.

Of course, there were plenty of dirty banks; any number of Panamanian, Venezuelan and Middle Eastern institutions were happy to launder hundreds of thousands of dollars at a time. One Middle Eastern bank could accept $10 million a month, no problem. But there were few such facilities available in Western Europe. That was how the DEA had lured Rómulo Ramirez, one of the Venezuelan cartel's top fixers, to Copenhagen, with the prize of a money-laundering bonanza.

The last thing a man like Ramirez wanted to risk was passing through an international airport with millions in hard cash stuffed in his luggage. The offer of a Danish bank ready and willing to take his dirty money was too good to refuse. He was hungry for such a partnership, and that would prove his undoing.

Ramirez had driven up from Spain with 1.5 million euros in the boot of his vehicle. The DEA – posing as corrupt bankers, and working with a cooperating bank – planned to deposit Ramirez's cash, and to provide him with a wire transfer of 'clean' funds. Only, of course, the funds weren't clean. They were tagged as cartel cash, and by following the money trail the DEA could track their entire financial network.

There was no set percentage that such money-launderers charged: it could be as little as five per cent; it could go as high as fifty per cent. It depended on the amount of cash, the level of risk involved and how desperate the 'client' was to clean their money.

For tonight's sting, the DEA had assembled a thoroughly convincing cast. Pierre Villard was point man, for he had brokered the deal with Ramirez. Louis Stavros, a man of Greek extraction – who in truth lived in California, and was another DEA confidential source – would act as the corrupt banker.

Dressed in a slick business suit and with a thick moustache

stained with cigarette smoke, Stavros could speak a dozen languages. His role was to look and act the part of the quintessentially powerful, internationally connected, but bent financial wizard.

As they gathered in the Radisson's lobby, Stavros chain-smoked Camel cigarettes. Hotel security kept asking him to put them out. He ignored them completely. He'd had a beautiful Argentine hooker shipped in for the sting. Or at least, Stavros claimed she was a hooker. Mike didn't know if she was genuinely a lady of the night, or another DEA source. Either way, she was the perfect foil to Stavros' crooked banker persona.

Prior to Ramirez's arrival, a phalanx of very serious-looking individuals swept through the hotel lobby and took the lift. It being autumn, they were dressed in sober black overcoats that reached to their ankles.

Mike nodded towards the lift doors. 'Who the fuck was that lot?' he asked Pierre.

The Frenchman seemed utterly unperturbed. 'As we are doing a money-laundering operation, they bring in the Chief of Police, the US Embassy person, someone from the Danish Treasury, plus their Security Services. You name it, they're here.'

'But they don't sit in on the deal?'

'Of course not.' Pierre waved a hand around the three of them – four if the 'hooker' was included. 'That's for us to execute. The Three Musketeers.'

Mike chuckled. He was there pretty much as an 'observer', but you never knew what might transpire. 'Life is a stage and we are all actors,' he observed.

Pierre nodded. 'The Bard. "All the world's a stage, and all the men and women merely players." Exactly. We are.'

When Ramirez turned up Mike was amazed at how young

the Venezuelan appeared. He, Pierre and Stavros were old enough to be the guy's father. Between the three of them, they had going on a hundred years' experience in their various fields, and the young Venezuelan seemed to take real comfort in their maturity.

Ramirez hadn't brought the 1.5 million with him to the hotel. The actual transaction would take place at a city institution. Tonight was very much a beauty parade. It was all about making Ramirez feel at home with his 'team'. But most of all it was about building trust and getting Ramirez to spill his guts on tape.

Stavros and Pierre heaped praise on the cartel fixer's intelligence, his wiliness and his drive. Stavros dazzled him with flash-talk about the banking world, and how he would make Ramirez a fortune. He spoke of nominee accounts in Paris, Liechtenstein blind trusts, dodgy London commodity brokers and untraceable Swiss numbered accounts – the whole merry-go-round by which mountains of dirty money could be rendered squeaky clean.

The aim of tonight's charade was to lead the DEA to the Big Money, and to the kingpins running Ramirez's operation; to the very centre of the cartel. As the drink flowed and Stavros held forth and the 'hooker' flashed her smile, Ramirez began to open up. He seemed keen to impress and just as the DEA had suspected, the 1.5 million was only the tip of a very large cash iceberg.

'We have two shipping containers,' Ramirez boasted. 'Two twenty-foot containers sitting in Milan and stuffed full of cash. The drugs money in Spain is so big no one can launder it fast enough. So this, it is just like the start. If all goes to plan, there is much, much more.'

'Bring us as much as you like,' Pierre assured him. 'We're ready and waiting. And perhaps in due course we can help you invest some of your funds. That way money breeds money, which is never a bad thing.'

'I think with this money, once it is clear, I will want to buy an Antonov 12,' Ramirez remarked. 'That way, I can fly from Venezuela or Suriname direct with some serious loads.'

Getting hold of an Antonov 12 wasn't a problem, Pierre told him, but loaded with twenty tonnes of cargo it didn't have enough range for transatlantic runs. A few relatively simple modifications should extend that capacity to what was required, and Mike Snow was the man for those kinds of alterations.

Snow explained how a standard Antonov 12 had a maximum range of 2,000 nautical miles, so well short of what was needed. But that was easily dealt with. All you had to do was fit some internal fuel bladders into the Antonov's hold, and you could extend the aircraft's range almost indefinitely.

'You can find one?' Ramirez asked. 'And we can fit it out as you suggest?'

'They're common as muck, An-12s,' Snow assured him. 'We can probably get you one in Moldova or somewhere where the fuckers will take cash. In fact, I know just the man.'

By the time the evening was done, Ramirez had divulged a great deal of his secrets. He'd even revealed some of the names of those at the top of the cartel. And he'd promised to bring Stavros tens of millions more euros, for the magician banker to transform into clean funds.

One matter still eluded the DEA. They suspected Ramirez and his people of having close links to the FARC, the Revolutionary Armed Forces of Colombia – a guerrilla force and terrorist group that used kidnap, ransom and extortion as its chief tactics. Virulently anti-American, the FARC held control of large swaths of Colombian territory, and they financed much of their activities from drugs.

A large proportion of the cocaine flown from Venezuela to West Africa was believed to originate with the FARC. The DEA suspected Ramirez and his people of being the FARC's frontmen, and Pierre suggested that he could provide Ramirez with weaponry. The aim of such an offer was to see if Ramirez would bite, knowing that the arms would very likely be destined for the FARC.

Ramirez certainly seemed interested. He asked about the kind of weaponry that the Frenchman could get his hands on. Pierre said that he'd need to check with his people. They agreed to schedule a further rendezvous at which the arms dealing side of things could be explored.

The meeting broke up. As Snow retired to his hotel room, he realized he'd discovered a talent that he hadn't quite known he possessed – for acting. Upon reflection, he guessed he shouldn't be so surprised. He'd made it into the SAS, and from there into a pilot's seat, and thence to running his own airline, and now to being a DEA asset. He'd been the author of his own life story. But tonight had still felt somewhat like a wild Hollywood production.

He'd also changed his mind markedly about the DEA, now he understood the way they operated. The clean-cut professionals like Wim and Zach orchestrated things from the background, while the dodgy geezers like Pierre, Stavros – and now Mike – fronted-up to sell the bad guys the lie. It made perfect sense: guys like Stavros and Pierre could walk the walk and talk the talk.

And Mike was beginning to figure maybe he could, too.

There was one further upside to tonight's operation. The DEA was empowered to use the 'earnings' from undercover stings to fund future work. In other words, the 225,000 euros that the DEA would take in 'commission' from the 'money laundering' would go straight into their coffers, to cover operational expenses.

When the big takedown came, the DEA would seize millions more in drugs-money and assets, right the way up the cartel's food chain. Luxury cars, yachts, planes, villas, jewellery – all would be grabbed by the DEA and auctioned off, unless required as assets for future sting operations. The beauty of it was that Ramirez and his compatriots would finance their own downfall.

Mike had to admit it, he was impressed.

The following morning Pierre, Mike and the DEA agents did a short debrief on the Ramirez sting. The Antonov 12 deal was of particular interest. If they could locate such an aircraft, one that Ramirez could pay for in cash, he would believe he'd found yet another method of laundering the cartel's money.

Mike could then spend time kitting it out with auxiliary fuel tanks and state-of-the-art navigational systems, while at the same time inserting the all-important tracking device. The transponder would allow the DEA to monitor the Venezuelan cartel's flights, building up a comprehensive map of their operations, including each and every one of their clandestine airstrips. Being able to track and trace the cartel's fleet of dope planes would be the holy grail of DEA operations.

Mike liked the plan. This was a world he knew intimately and something he could get his teeth into. He abhorred the drugs trade and was warming to the idea of nailing the bad guys. But

Zach and Wim cautioned him not to take his eye off the prize: the main purpose of their meeting was to nail Viktor Bout.

They asked Mike to reach out to Smulian. This time he was to say that he had some 'friends' that he'd just sold an Antonov to. He was to inform Smulian those people were interested in pursuing a multi-million-dollar arms deal, but could only pay in cash. And he was to ask if Viktor Bout could provide the arms and take the funds on offer.

They'd think of a more detailed plan if Bout seemed keen to play ball. They shook hands on the deal, and Mike, Pierre and the two agents went their separate ways.

The DEA's Operation Relentless had just gone live.

CHAPTER TEN

LUNGI LOL, SIERRA LEONE, MAY 2000

In the year that Peter Hain named and shamed Viktor Bout's African weapons deals, the UN issued a report into violations of the arms embargo to Sierra Leone. It found that Bout's companies had been running guns into Liberia, Sierra Leone's western neighbour, for almost a decade, from where the arms had been ferried to the RUF rebels aboard Russian-made Mi-18 helicopters.

The UN report concluded that Bout and his accomplices were 'key to such illicit practices, in close collaboration with the highest authorities in Liberia'. Bout's payments came largely in the form of diamonds, from the mines that the rebels controlled.

The RUF had become a force to be reckoned with. In December 1998 they had seized the nation's capital, Freetown, forcing the Americans, British and allied nations to evacuate their embassies. Though they had been driven out again, the rebels retained control of huge areas of the north of the country, including rich diamond mining regions.

Many of the RUF's shock troops were child soldiers. Invariably, they had been 'recruited' when their villages were overrun and forced to carry out terrible atrocities against their own families.

With the initials 'RUF' carved into their bodies, they were branded for life. Their 'family' had become the RUF, and they could never return to their home communities.

Fuelled by alcohol and drugs, they were sent into other villages to wreak bloody mayhem and carnage. Captured villagers were taken as de facto slaves, to work in the rebels' diamond mines. Conditions were hellish. Under the baleful eye of RUF guards, they were forced to labour six days a week.

Stripped to their underwear and working up to their waists in river water, they shovelled gravel and mud into 'shake-shakes' – rudimentary sieves where the diamonds could be picked out. At the end of each day the diamond slaves were forced at gunpoint to strip, and to hose out their body cavities, to ensure they weren't smuggling out any gems for themselves.

Sometimes the pace of digging became so frenetic that the slaves tunnelled beneath buildings and power lines, which came crashing down on top of them. But life was cheap and nothing was allowed to stand in the way of the rebels' great endeavour, the fruits of which were largely spent on arms.

In funnelling weaponry into Sierra Leone and diamonds out again, Bout had dealt closely with Charles Taylor, Liberia's then president. Bout, known simply as 'Mr Vic' in Liberia, maintained a residence in Liberia's capital, Monrovia, complete with a phalanx of heavily armed Russian bodyguards.

He was approaching the pinnacle of his power in terms of his African ventures, and this was becoming of real concern to the British government. British intelligence chiefs zoomed in on Viktor Bout as one of the key 'players' they would have to contend with, especially if Britain was to intervene militarily, with a view to bringing about an end to Sierra Leone's horrific war.

By early May 2000, the RUF were once again in ascendance. Having routed UN peacekeepers, they advanced towards the nation's capital, Freetown. At the same time they announced a new initiative, Operation Kill British, which pretty much spoke for itself. Britain's response was to launch Operation Palliser, in which a force of the 1st Battalion Parachute Regiment was deployed, tasked to evacuate all British and allied nationals.

Riding in Hercules C130 transport aircraft, the elite soldiers flew into Lungi Airport, which lies just across a coastal inlet from the Sierra Leonean capital. Their commander, Brigadier David Richards – later General Sir David Richards and a life peer – knew that the airport needed to be secured, and that meant the rebels would have to be halted in their tracks.

The rebel commanders were alert to the same thing: seizing Lungi Airport was the key priority of Operation Kill British. If they could shut the airport and entrap the British, American and allied nationals in the nation's capital, they could wreak havoc as they overran the city streets.

In January of that year Richards had led a small team to Sierra Leone, to assess how best to halt the rebel advance. Upon returning to London he'd presented his findings to the government: the Sierra Leoneans were in desperate need of support. That trip had left a real mark on the Brigadier and his team. 'We had been witness to some horrific sights,' he remarked, 'things we all hoped never to see again.'

Four months later he was back in the country, tasked with halting the rebel onslaught. Richards ordered the only force he had available to mount up helicopters, to fly north into the jungle and take the fight to the rebels. Twenty-six men of the Pathfinder Platoon – an elite reconnaissance unit within the

Parachute Regiment – were airlifted into the heart of the jungle, facing two thousand heavily armed rebels high on bloodlust and drugs.

'It was a race against time,' Richards wrote of this moment. 'It was vital that the RUF suffered an early blow to their morale, something that would make them pause and think twice about taking on my limited forces.' He sent the Pathfinders north into the jungle as the bait in a trap, and the twenty-six men airlifted into the bush knew it.

This tiny British force faced battle-hardened rebels who were extremely well armed: they boasted armoured personnel carriers, vehicle-mounted heavy machineguns, grenade-launchers, light machineguns, assault rifles and more. Driven on by heroin, voodoo and the thirst to 'do a Somalia' on the British, they vowed to rout the Pathfinders, or worse still take them alive.

Within the first forty-eight hours, the Pathfinders had lost their commanding officer, whereupon seasoned veteran Pathfinder Sergeant Steve Heaney was forced to lead the battle from the front. The mission mutated into an epic siege, during which the British soldiers were forced to survive off giant African land snails, pounded bark and whatever else they could scavenge or kill, as their supplies ran low.

In an effort to compensate for their lack of firepower, they built a series of ingenious defences in the best traditions of British soldiering. They dug ditches from which to fight. They fashioned claymore mines from empty tins filled with plastic explosives, and packed with 'shipyard confetti' – old nails and gravel. They sowed the ground around their positions with fields of 'punji' sticks – bamboo stakes honed to razor sharpness and set to snare the enemy.

Local villagers joined forces with the tiny British unit, as hundreds of terrorized civilians poured into their position, fleeing from the advancing rebels. Wielding machetes, the locals cut back the dense jungle, so as to open interlocking fields of fire. They fetched water, gathered food and cut sleeping platforms for the Pathfinders, who they had started to view as their heaven-sent saviours.

As they hunkered down in their positions, this handful of British soldiers little knew that the rebel forces they were up against had been armed by an elusive Russian businessman called Viktor Bout. It wasn't their need-to-know, and it would make little difference to the coming battle. Knowing who had supplied the rebels' guns, bullets and bombs wouldn't alter whether they lived or died.

At some point as he flew over the West African bush, Viktor Bout had recorded yet another scene on his video camera. His voice – musing, reflective, a little dreamy even – can be heard giving a commentary from behind the camera, as he shoots images of the thick expanse of jungle.

'All is silent in the big old world. Silence. Silence. And beauty ... It's a bit scary to fly at this height. Something bad might happen. Or maybe it won't. You can fall down at any moment. But beauty always comes at a price ...'

In Sierra Leone at the turn of the millennium would be sewn the seeds of that downfall.

CHAPTER ELEVEN

KINSHASA, THE CONGO, NOVEMBER 2007

Once back in Africa, Mike Snow found himself having second thoughts: did he really want to go after Viktor Bout? Did the Russian deserve it, even? And why were the Americans so dead-set on nailing him? On the other hand, he'd seen at first hand the impact the flood of small arms into Africa had on its peoples.

More and more often, he'd encountered guys in their early thirties who knew nothing but war. In Angola, there were villages with no males between the ages of thirteen and fifty. All had gone off to fight. The few who remained had had an arm or leg blown off. It was too much.

In the Congo he'd flown countless young soldiers back from the frontlines, deathly pale from loss of blood. He used to pause and ask of them: 'Soldier, are you okay?' The guy would look at him with eyes that knew exactly what fate held in store. 'No, Patron, not okay.' Mike would hand his water bottle to the medic, so the dying soldier could take a last drink.

More often than not the medic would drink it himself.

He remembered a particularly horrific bombing campaign. He'd seen aircrews loading up crude DIY bombs – old calor gas cylinders packed with nuts and bolts, plus explosives wired to a fuse. They were to be rolled off the aircraft's open ramps over villages, whereupon they would spin violently as they fell, landing practically anywhere.

All African wars basically boiled down to the same thing, he'd concluded: a battle for power, money and resources. But, mostly, he was aware that it was the vulnerable who were the victims. Just like the young girl who'd been thrown aboard his crew bus by her older brother, the day N'Djilli airport had exploded into a mass of rubble, shrapnel and flame. Just like they had been.

Providing thousands of AK-47s and tonnes of ammo was an indiscriminate way to spread death and terror, especially in such anarchic war zones. It was overly simplistic, of course, but if you stopped the flow of arms you'd go some way to halting the carnage. Maybe you could never stop the supply of weapons, but if you removed the lords of war you could begin to take back some form of control.

Mike glanced around the Buddha statues that decorated his study at home. He'd been acquiring them on his travels, and he figured he'd pulled together a fine collection. He did his best to calm his thoughts. Was the karma good or bad for going after Viktor Bout? On balance, he figured it had to be positive.

Mike sent his handler, DEA Agent Zach, an email. 'I enjoyed you guys company, and look forward to a long and fruitful relationship keeping the world a safer place for us "real" humans.' Mike explained that if the DEA wanted a tracker placed on the aircraft they were lining up for Ramirez, he would need 'info on size and antennae requirements', so he could select the best place to conceal it.

From their side, Agents Brown and Zach had concluded that Mike Snow seemed like a sincere kind of guy. Zach had written a debriefing report on their Copenhagen meeting, which reflected the fact that although they didn't yet fully trust the blunt-spoken Englishman, they reckoned they could work with him.

Following their exchange of emails, Mike reached out to Andrew Smulian. He had sold some 'clients' an Antonov, he explained. They were now looking to do an arms deal, but could only pay cash. It sounded like a job for 'Boris' – his and Smulian's informal code for Viktor Bout. Could Smulian help? If so, Snow's people would pay him expenses, plus commission on the deal.

Smulian replied sounding a note of caution. 'Boris situation not so good . . . Our man has been made persona non-G for the world through the UN . . . All assets cash and kind frozen, total value is around 6 Bn USD, and of course no ability to journey anywhere other than home territories. Listed on US black list . . . All access and communications monitored . . .'

Smulian was warning Mike of the difficulties of dealing with Viktor Bout, who faced a UN travel ban and whose assets were sought by US agencies. Bout was heavily involved in the real estate business, he further explained, and might even be out of the 'grey items' business – code for illicit arms sales – altogether.

Mike forwarded Smulian's emails to Agent Zach. It didn't seem to add up, especially since the DEA agents knew that Bout and Smulian were actively pursuing arms deals in various parts of Africa. Various electronic intercepts had revealed as much. They figured they should push, and see what gives.

The DEA had also decided that tracking the Venezuelan cartel's air force was a prime proposition, and that they needed to pursue the Ramirez aircraft deal. As an added bonus, Mike could use it to bolster his story with Smulian: checking out an

Antonov for clients with suitcases full of cash would lend him added credibility.

'I'm off to Moldova tomorrow to check An-12,' Mike emailed Smulian. He added that the deal with Bout would have to be face-to-face, and a possible visit to 'the big Vodka store' – his and Smulian's makeshift code for Russia – might be on the cards.

Smulian's response was decidedly lukewarm: 'Boris had withdrawn, and been told to withdraw from all activities out of the motherland ... Any business which is deemed to be his would be grabbed by the Feds ...'

If Smulian's words were to be taken at face value, Operation Relentless was looking increasingly untenable. Bout was basically untouchable as long as he remained in his home country. But it was then that everything changed.

On the evening of 2 December Smulian sent an email to primus@pisem.net, one of Viktor Bout's email addresses. In it, he alerted the Russian businessman to a demand from Kenya for 'agricultural stuff' – code for military equipment. He also reported on Snow's purchasing an Antonov 12 from 'Paul's place' – a reference to Paul Popov, an aircraft dealer based in the Eastern European country of Moldova.

'The buyer, who is not from this continent, is wanting more stuff,' Smulian messaged. 'All cash. Can I say we can take the matter further?'

Three hours later Bout replied. 'About "agricultural stuff" all possible. What is needed??? You can proceed ... Regards, VIC.' It seemed that the Russian was on for the arms deal, after all.

The following morning Smulian emailed Snow: 'Spoke to Boris. And anything is possible with farming equipment ... I don't think he can move stuff around, but it may be he can get his hands on items you require.'

Mike's response was designed to lure Smulian further into the web that was being spun for him. 'If Boris can help my friends out, you can do well out of the deal. As I said, their problem is they only have cash.'

As far as Smulian was concerned, the cash element of Snow's proposition was a bonus. Cash was untraceable and largely invisible to any watchers. It could be shipped from A to B without the US authorities being any the wiser.

Mike forwarded Smulian's 'anything possible farming equipment' email to Agent Zach. He met with his DEA bosses, and they decided to draw Smulian to a meeting with the 'clients'. Smulian was key to the operation's success: it was time to reel him in.

'AMS [Andrew Michael Smulian] will go anywhere I ask him to,' Mike advised. 'I feel he would be more impressed by flying him far away . . . he would believe it was a real deal . . . more than "here we go again on another waste of time".' Mike warned that whomever they used as the 'client' would have to be 'a very smart gentleman, plausible and neat . . . to con AMS'.

Mike also asked Agent Zach, pointedly, 'Where is my lunch money?'

Zach replied that they should plan on a Smulian meeting for the Caribbean in January. But Mike had been waiting for his expenses for some time, and for him at least the issue had been festering. By 12 December he decided enough was enough. He sent Agent Zach a seemingly terminal message: 'Better we don't continue as in the end you will fuck me over.'

Zach responded immediately, explaining that money seized off the bad guys would be used to bankroll the present mission, but they'd only just gained control of the funds from the Copenhagen money-laundering sting. It had now been allocated to Operation Relentless, so Mike would be getting his money.

Mike accepted the explanation. He contacted Smulian, proposing a meeting on the Caribbean island of Curaçao, which forms a part of the Kingdom of the Netherlands. Being Dutch territory, Brits could visit without a visa, Mike explained. And as Curaçao lay just forty miles off the coast of Venezuela, which was where the 'clients' hailed from, it made perfect sense as a meeting point.

Smulian agreed to the Curaçao rendezvous, but he pointed out there was no point going to see 'Boris' thereafter, unless the 'principals are serious and have the bucks for the machinery'.

Mike emailed confirmation to Smulian. 'I will book you on KLM to AMS to CUR and meet you there at the airport . . . It's a long way to go, just to talk, but they are a bit nervous because they haven't dealt with me on this type of thing before, only the AN12.'

KLM was the carrier, AMS was Amsterdam, and CUR was Curaçao. AN12 was the Antonov cargo plane.

'They think I am raving mad after I told them I can find anything you want and without strings attached,' he added. 'Anyway, they are paying everything, so we must just laugh, take the money and hope all goes well . . . If a goer and B agrees to the deal and a meet, then we go back to EU and regroup.'

'B' stood for Boris – code for Bout, of course.

On 17 December Smulian sent Bout an email, from what he believed was a secure internet connection. 'After sending, these messages are deleted by the server,' his message began. He informed the Russian that he was flying out to Curaçao on 9 January 2008, business class, on a trip funded by Mike Snow's people.

'It seems they are ready to pass major funding,' Smulian wrote, '. . . if we can convince them we can supply. Possibly this means delivery as well, since I can't imagine how they will get the goods to somewhere in that region.'

Writing of his own rustiness in the arms dealing world, Smulian said: 'I really need info on present available items and maybe ball park prices, so I don't look an idiot in front of these people . . . Naturally, I wont try any contact unless I am sure that it is genuine.'

Bout's reply was short and to the point: 'Okay. Noticed. Awaiting exact list what you need.'

That same day, 17 December, Mike and Agent Zach were busy fleshing out plans. 'We must be prepared with the following,' emailed Mike. 'List of materiel required in proper format with full description and quantities . . . End user certificates. Real or fudged. Money for you guys to pass to AS . . . Money for the first deal????????????????? How are we going to get away with that??????????????????'

They planned to make a payment of five to ten thousand dollars to Andrew Smulian – 'AS' – to demonstrate the 'client's' seriousness. But Mike's email reflected the worries he was experiencing in putting such a complex international sting operation together. Zach did his best to calm his nerves.

He advised The Bear not to overly complicate things. The drugs cartel's cash was in Europe, and the Curaçao meet was purely to sketch out the terms of the deal. He suggested negotiating a sample purchase of AK-47s and Surface-to-Air Missiles

(SAMs). They'd buy those items outright, and 'green light' the main shipment once the clients confirmed they approved of the sample weaponry.

The proposal to purchase the SAMs was critical. Man-portable anti-aircraft missiles are the Holy Grail for terrorists and narco-traffickers, few other weapons systems offering anything like as much bang for your bucks. Being able to shoot down an aircraft – whether military or civilian – has a massive propaganda impact. Such weaponry falling into the wrong hands is one of the greatest fears of Western intelligence agencies, hence their sale being so tightly controlled.

Agent Zach suggested that Mike rendezvous with the DEA team in Miami, en route to Curaçao, so they could get comfortable with their roles. Agent Brown would be there, along with one or two confidential sources – Latin Americans with long experience of working undercover with the DEA.

'Okay chief I will comply and look forward to seeing you,' Mike wrote Zach. 'Let's hope we can get some serious work done and not just flit in and out like a bunch of faggots entering a redneck bar.'

On the 18 December Andrew Smulian sent an email to one of his children, outlining his Curaçao travel plans. 'All going well I should have some Uncle Sams [dollars] at the end of it. Will meet with Snow in Islands 3 days after I leave here. Keep the details for yourselves and I will get sim cards as I go along and try to stay in touch. Love Dad.'

The die was cast.

In the SOD's Virginia office, Wim Brown placed a call to one of his long-standing and most trusted confidential sources, Carlos Sagastume – known to all simply as 'Carlos'. Carlos was fiercely protective over his identity and for very good reasons: he had executed over one hundred cases, working deep undercover and in the most extreme situations imaginable.

Carlos had earned the nickname within this dark and dangerous world of 'El Mexicano'. The original El Mexicano had been José Gonzalo Rodríguez Gacha, the fearsome head of Colombia's Medellín Cartel. One of the world's richest narco-warlords during his day, Gacha had been hunted by Colombian forces and the DEA for decades, before being killed in a bloody battle.

In spite of his nom-de-guerre, Carlos wasn't Mexican by birth. He hailed from the Central American country of Guatemala, and he had a long history of involvement in the drugs trade. Basically, he was a bad boy turned good, and over the years he'd become the DEA's star undercover operative.

'Got something we need your help with,' Wim told Carlos. 'You need to meet us in Miami. We're gonna introduce you to this Brit pilot. He's a little crazy, but he can get you to one of the biggest targets in global trafficking.'

'Got it. When you need me there?'

'Second week in January. But listen, don't be offended if the guy seems a little cuckoo. If he talks crap on you or gets a little rough, don't take it personal, okay?'

'I don't give a shit. This is business.'

El Mexicano was good to meet The Bear.

Carlos wasn't particularly daunted by the prospect of working with this crazy, cuckoo Brit. Forty years old, smart, urbane and with classic Roman good-looks, he'd been around the block and then some. The son of a medical doctor, after college Carlos had joined the Guatemalan military's elite G2 intelligence unit. His role was to gather intel on guerrilla activity, Guatemala having suffered from a long civil war.

But after serving in the G2 for five years, Carlos had discovered that a lot of high-ranking officers were up to their elbows in the drugs trade. He had married his beautiful wife young and they had an infant daughter to care for. He figured if the high-rankers were enjoying their ill-gotten loot, why shouldn't he and his family?

The turning point came when he was offered some stolen cars to sell, and the buyers turned out to be drugs traffickers. They asked him to help provide some 'go-fasts' – top-of-the-range speedboats equipped with massive engines, and capable of outrunning coastguard vessels. Carlos was sucked in deeper, and over time he helped run some 2,800 kilos of cocaine north into neighbouring Mexico, for shipment worldwide.

Carlos also helped move the traffickers' cash. One day he was carrying a suitcase stuffed with $3 million, when he was seized by the Mexican federal police and held for ransom. In the ensuing hell of that kidnapping he almost lost his life, but eventually a pay-off was made to enable his release.

Back in Guatemala, he took stock. He realized how his activities had placed his wife and young family in danger. Basically, drugs had corrupted everyone, up to the highest levels. His kids had no future unless the narco-networks could be challenged. He'd made contact with the US Embassy in Guatemala and offered to start working with the DEA.

Carlos had ended up becoming a confidential source. For a year he'd gone deep undercover, turning over the bad guys within Guatemala. Then, in November 1998 he'd masterminded a takedown that went badly wrong. He was arrested along with the targets. When he alone wasn't charged and imprisoned, the bad guys realized that he had to be working for the 'feds'.

The DEA warned Carlos that they had forty-eight hours to get him out of Guatemala, or he was dead. They spirited him to the US, along with his wife and now two small children. At first they weren't happy. They had a one-bedroom apartment with two daughters below the age of eight. Neither had wanted to leave their country, but they consoled themselves with the fact that at least they were alive.

Since then Carlos had gone on to work on scores of cases for the DEA, leading to countless arrests and the seizure of a fortune in drugs and illicit goods and cash. During that time he'd busted top Latin American cartels, lured narco-kingpins to the US along with their planeloads of cocaine, busted boat-loads of heroin, and brought down police chiefs, generals and ministers of state.

He'd worked for the DEA, ICE, the FBI, and the US Secret Service. He'd pursued corrupt American cops, hunted down Pablo Escobar's successor, taken on Hezbollah, aided in the hunt for Osama Bin Laden, and nailed gangs counterfeiting US dollars. On one occasion he'd infiltrated one of the top banks laundering drugs money, bringing it crashing down. Though he wasn't paid a wage as such, awards were offered for suc-cessful cases and these could be substantial, to compensate for the huge risks involved.

In short, El Mexicano was the quintessential poacher turned gamekeeper, and there was no one better in the undercover world. So effective were his methodologies, that he'd become known as 'the King of Sting'.

DEA agents rarely went undercover, because the risks involved precluded it. Carlos often found himself operating far from the USA, unarmed and with little or no backup. He was a firm believer that a confidential source was only ever as good as the DEA agent handling him. On that level, he'd forged an unbreakable partnership with Wim Brown.

Just a few months back Carlos had played the key role in busting arms dealer Monzer Al Kazar, in Spain. The sting had required Carlos – plus his partner, a fellow Guatemalan confidential source – to pose as terrorist arms buyers, while living as guests in Kazar's heavily guarded villa. All the while Carlos had been wired for sound – video equipment secreted on his person recording Kazar's crimes.

After Kazar's arrest, Carlos and his partner's real identities had been leaked to the media. A few months later Carlos' partner and close friend had been at a cockfight in his home town. Two armed men had entered the venue, sought him out and gunned him down. No one doubted who had ordered the hit. As Carlos knew well, he walked the knife-edge each and every day.

In short, he was good. One of the best. And meeting The Bear didn't faze him.

On 5 January 2008 Mike flew into London's Heathrow Airport, en route to Miami. From there he sent a hurried email, half-written in capitals, to Smulian. 'Hi I have prepaid the hotel inc food etc you just sign. Get the HOPPA bus from the airport its 4 quid. takes 10 MINS. I WILL DO THE SAME . . . MIKE.'

By return email Smulian confirmed that all was good.

Oddly, one of Smulian's biggest concerns seemed to be the political persuasion of Snow's people. 'For trimming purposes . . . are your clients to left or right?' he asked. In Smulian's experience of the armed struggle those who leaned left wore their moustaches turned upwards, whereas those who leaned to the right wore them trimmed down: he was anxious to get his appearance just right.

Mike arrived in Miami on the afternoon of 6 January. He checked into the plush Embassy Suites Hotel, at Miami International Airport, all pink marble flooring, warm stucco and gently spinning ceiling fans. Its teardrop-shaped outdoor pool was fringed with sun-loungers and palm trees, not that Mike figured he'd be spending a great deal of time relaxing.

With the arrival of the DEA guys the Operation Relentless team got down to business. Wim and Zach had brought with them Carlos, plus a fourth person. If anything that man, Ricardo Jardeno, had an even more chequered history than did El Mexicano, but his presence on the team would prove invaluable for what was coming.

Ricardo, a Colombian, would be known as 'El Comandante' for the coming sting. Highly intelligent, he'd spent five years at university before joining the Colombian Army. But after a decade's service he'd drifted into the drugs trade. He'd specialized in using yachts, go-fasts, planes and trucks to distribute narcotics globally – smuggling shipments to the USA, Canada, Australia, Brazil, and – via Africa – into Europe.

Over time Ricardo had also begun to dabble in arms trafficking, or more usually drugs-for-arms deals, shipping the narcotics out via the same means by which he shipped the weapons back in again. In the process he'd amassed a personal fortune of some $10–15 million, though by the time of his capture and prosecution in 2005, he'd blown it all.

Ricardo had been arrested on multiple occasions before – in

Italy, Holland, Mexico and Panama – but either the prosecutors failed to make anything stick, or hefty bribes paid to judges secured his release. But on the sixth occasion he'd come to the direct attention of US authorities: Ricardo stood accused of trafficking drugs and weapons on behalf of the FARC.

Secure in the vast tracts of remote Colombian jungle, the FARC had teams growing coca plants and labs refining drugs, while at the same time they deliberately targeted US citizens for kidnap, ransom and murder. The US government had declared FARC a 'proscribed terrorist organization', which meant that anyone with dirt on the FARC was potentially highly valuable – hence their approach to Ricardo Jardeno.

After two years rotting in a Panamanian gaol, he signed a judicial agreement with the US government agreeing to confess all of his crimes, and to assist the authorities in a forthcoming prosecution of the FARC. He was duly moved to the US with his family, and proceeded to testify in a Washington DC court against the FARC members on trial.

In 2007 he'd signed up with the DEA to serve as a confidential source. In the Curaçao sting he would pose as a senior military commander of the FARC, the group that the DEA had decided would pose as the clients for the Smulian–Bout arms deal.

Carlos had the track record of conducting such high-profile stings: he would lead negotiations, posing as the FARC's banker. Ricardo – El Comandante – was the new kid on the block, but he was ideally placed to furnish the specs of the weaponry that the FARC sought to buy. He'd spent years running such arms packages to the terrorist group himself.

As far as the DEA agents were concerned, this was the A Team:

no one stood a better chance of ensnaring Smulian, and hence Bout. All the agents needed to do was to get El Mexicano, El Comandante and The Bear in the same room, and without The Bear deciding to pick a fight with the Colombian or the Guatemalan, or vice versa.

Wim was handling El Mexicano, and Zach was handling El Comandante and The Bear – so no big deal. There was one significant advantage to using the FARC as cover: the group was known to be seeking precisely the kind of weaponry – Surface-to-Air Missiles – that they would request of Smulian and Bout.

On the morning of 7 January the DEA agents gathered the Operation Relentless team in Agent Zach's hotel room. As they made the introductions, they were painfully aware of how crucial this first meeting was. Right now everything rested upon an outspoken and somewhat crazed Brit pilot. Without Snow it was a non-starter, for it was only through him that they could get to Smulian, and in turn to Viktor Bout.

At first things didn't seem to be going so well. As Wim and Carlos lounged on a bed, channel-surfing TV and snacking, and Zach and Ricardo checked messages on their cellphones, Mike paced the room, like a tiger in a cage.

'This is never going to work,' he announced, eyeing Carlos and Wim. 'Look at these guys!'

'What d'you mean?' Carlos countered. He spoke English with a soft Latin American lilt, and a slight lisp. It sounded somehow refined; educated; cultured almost.

'No one's taking this seriously so it ain't going to bloody work,' Mike growled. 'I may as well go home right now.'

'So what you want us to do?' Carlos asked.

'We're supposed to be setting up an arms deal, yet you're lounging around watching bloody TV!' Mike turned to Ricardo. 'Come on, Colonel, let's get doing something. Let's just do a dummy run.'

'No Colonel in FARC,' Ricardo corrected, in his broken English. He pointed to himself. 'Comandante.'

'Okay, Comandante, so have you got a list of the arms you're after?'

Ricardo glanced at the others, nonplussed. 'Does he think I'm stupid?' he asked Carlos, in their native Spanish. 'No one ever carries a list, in case you get caught.'

'Come on, surely you got a list?' Mike pressed. 'You know, one you guys drew up this morning?'

Ricardo eyed Mike. 'You crazy? The police raid this place – you get captured with the list.'

Mike scratched his head. 'Good point. I hadn't thought of that.'

'Tell him I've done twenty arms deals for real,' Ricardo remarked to Carlos, 'and never once did anyone bring a list. That's too risky. It's too obvious.'

Levering himself up on one elbow, Carlos translated what Ricardo had said. Well dressed, well groomed and wearing just the right amount of gold jewellery, Carlos had a more refined manner than Ricardo's barrel-chested bravado.

'Okay, what arms and what transport we gonna use?' Carlos queried of Mike. 'We gonna use a ship?'

'Who's asking?' Mike fired back.

'Me. Carlos. From the FARC. And I'm asking you, Viktor Bout.'

'Planes. Not by ship. This guy's Russian ... I'm Russian ... And I'm very serious and I've got my own airline business, so definitely by planes.'

144

'Okay, so what sort of arms you offer?'

'What're *you* after?' Mike countered.

'You first. You're the salesman. Convince me.'

'Fucking everything. AK-47s up to main battle tanks. You want it, we got it.'

'He got ammunition?' Ricardo fired a question at Carlos. 'I need ten million AK-47 calibre rounds.'

'You got ammo? El Comandante says he needs ten million AK-47 rounds.'

'Wooo ... Ten million. That could take some time to get sorted. But for sure we got ammo.'

As Carlos and Ricardo fired scores of questions at him, Mike found that he was arguing vehemently about how the deal should be sliced and diced. Even with the air-conditioning the room felt hot and claustrophobic, and he had eyes upon him, scrutinizing him closely. He could feel the sweat pouring off his forehead.

Finally, after twenty minutes of such verbal sparring, Mike called a halt. 'Hold on! You got me there like it's for real.' His heavily lined face crumpled into a smile. 'You got me. And you know what, this is going to fucking work.'

Carlos leaned back on the bed. 'You don't say.'

Mike glanced at him and Wim. 'Well you had me fucking going there for a moment, you two, lazing back on the bed like a couple of faggots. I mean, we got to plan this properly!'

'What you want me to do?' Carlos remonstrated. 'What you want me to do? You can't ever plan for this kind of thing, 'cause it'll change as soon as we hit the ground. You just got to be ready for chaos, move fast and think on your feet.'

Mike reflected on this for a moment. Maybe Carlos was right, but he wasn't about to let him get away with it that easily. 'So why do they call you El Mexicano?' he demanded. 'You Mexican or something?'

Mike knew Carlos was Guatemalan. He also knew that Guatemalans hated being mistaken for Mexicans.

'Is nickname,' Carlos responded, noncommittally. 'And I tell you something,' he continued, softly, 'is not about planning. Is about state of mind. My way is like method actor. If I am supposed to be a big drugs dealer, I can see the bales of cocaine stacked up in my safe at home. I can see it in my mind's eye. I got to believe it's there for real. Same with arms or cash. You got to live the deal and the story one hundred per cent. Total immersion.

'I tell you something else,' he added, 'I don't need to get Viktor Bout to trust me. You know why? Because I only need Andrew Smulian to trust me. That is key. And you know how I make Smulian trust me? I pretend not to trust him. Only a genuine bad guy would not trust you upon first meeting; demand to frisk you, and for you to prove you're not a cop. You have to make the other guy believe he has to earn your trust.'

Mike had to admit it – he was impressed.

That evening they went out to grab dinner and a few beers. Carlos and Mike seemed to hit it off. What Mike didn't realize was that Carlos had been briefed by the DEA to work on him; to knock off the rough edges and shape The Bear into exactly what the DEA needed him to be.

In an earlier email exchange with Mike, Agent Zach had made mention of 'The Bear'. It was actually a coded reference to Viktor Bout – the Russian bear. Mike had mentioned how funny it was, because from his schooldays he'd been called 'The Bear'. That duly became his DEA codename.

That evening over dinner, Carlos refined the name: Mike Snow was 'Papa Oso' – Spanish for 'Daddy Bear'.

The next day the five flew to Curaçao as one team.

CHAPTER TWELVE

LUNGI LOL, SIERRA LEONE, MAY 2000

Nine days into their deployment to the village of Lungi Lol, deep in the Sierra Leone jungle, the twenty-six fatigued and malnourished British soldiers were surviving on little more than adrenalin and prayer.

They settled into their dark hours' routine. Just after midnight Sergeant Heaney began his sentry watch. They knew the rebels were massing in the cover of the jungle. All night long there had been these weird animal-like noises ringing out of the darkness. Reportedly the rebels made such calls to signal to each other as they moved, and to terrify those they were about to attack.

They also had a chant, for use prior to battle:

> What makes the grass grow?
> Blood, blood, blood!
> What makes the grass grow?
> Blood, blood, blood!

As Heaney settled down to watch, he detected the odd, inhuman shriek echoing from the tree-line. Of course, it could just be troops of monkeys moving through the trees, but it sent chills up his spine. They didn't sound like any animal cries he'd ever heard before.

His two-hour stint passed without incident, but he could sense a weird, wired tension in the air. Watch done, he collapsed onto the makeshift bamboo cot that the villagers had made for him. Tonight, as with so many nights before, hundreds of women and children had flooded into Lungi Lol, seeking safety.

Heaney had barely dropped off, when he was shaken roughly awake. 'Steve! Maximize! Maximize!'

That was the codeword signifying the rebels were on the move.

All around figures leapt into action. As Heaney shrugged on his belt kit and grabbed his weapon, he tried to tune his senses into the thick darkness, to better assess the threat. The heavy, eerie silence was broken by a single shot. It had the unmistakable dull thud of a low-velocity round, as if a pistol had been fired.

It had come from Heaney's front and slightly to the left – the track leading into the village.

In the Pathfinders' forward-most position – a sandbagged bunker that the villagers had helped dig – 'H', one of their crack gunners, had spotted a column of rebels creeping down the track leading into the village. He'd watched as they drew closer, keeping them nailed in the sights of his general-purpose machinegun (GPMG).

The rebel commander had raised himself into a crouch, and fired one shot with his pistol, signalling the launch of the onslaught. The next instant the darkness erupted in a sea of fire, as the rebels opened up from the cover of the jungle.

Within seconds, the palm-leaf roof of the shelter above Heaney's sleeping position was ripped apart by a barrage of incoming rounds. He saw their radio shack to the rear disintegrate under a withering blast. Trees to either side juddered under the impact, trunks shredding from the sheer volume of bullets pounding into them. The rate of enemy fire was unbelievable.

A deafening wave of sound washed over the village. Heaney had never known a concentration of fire like this, not even during live fire exercises involving entire battalions of the British Army. It was clear that the rebels didn't suffer from any of the shortage of ammo that afflicted the Pathfinders. Each British soldier had been issued with just 300 rounds per man: paltry, when considering the thousands of enemy bearing down upon them.

Among the AK-47 fire the Pathfinders could make out the heavier crack and thump of larger calibre weapons, as the rebel's heavier machineguns began to kick in. This was sheer murder. Either they got the fire down in return, or the rebels would swamp the village.

They could hear wild shouts echoing out of the darkness, plus more and more of those weird, animal-like cries. The blood lust embodied in those savage, ghostly yells was spine-chilling. The rebels knew that time and firepower were on their side: there were hours until daylight in which to outgun, overrun and annihilate the tiny British force.

In every direction muzzle flashes sparked under the canopy. The Pathfinders' fire rose in volume to meet that of the enemy. The popgun bark of their assault rifles cut the night as they let rip with four six-round bursts. There was the hammering *crack-crack-crack* as H's GPMG unleashed punching bursts of fire.

Trouble was, at this rate they'd soon be out of ammo.

The rebels were using tracer rounds. It was arcing into the heavens beyond the village. Tracer takes a good mile to burn out, and the night sky over Lungi Lol had erupted into a fearsome firework display. The number of weapons hammering fire into the British force was beyond belief. Terrifying.

Heaney knew he had to act. Get a grip on the battle. As Platoon Sergeant his place was forwards with the gunners. He grabbed the 51mm mortar tube and began to crawl ahead, ordering one of the others to follow with the heavy sack of rounds. To his front a long line of muzzle flashes sparked out of the jungle. He counted a good dozen, and each had the fast, rhythmical fire of a belt-fed 7.62mm machinegun.

To either side of the path, trees and thick vegetation were getting torn to shreds. This was incredibly accurate and sustained fire. As he tried to push forward on elbows and knees, there was the fierce whoosh of a projectile hurtling out of the darkness. Only one weapon makes that kind of noise: the rocket-propelled grenade (RPG).

This one came flaming out of the night, tearing past just a few feet to the right. It roared across the village, miraculously missing all the huts, and burying itself in the jungle somewhere on the far side. As he pushed onwards, head down, Heaney tried to keep his assault rifle and the mortar tube out of the mud, while staying low enough to avoid getting hit.

It was hellish.

Up ahead H settled into a rhythm on the GPMG, unleashing aimed ten-round bursts. The rebels had to be taking hits, but it didn't seem to be having the slightest effect on them. Heaney's mind was racing: what if the frontal attack was just a probe? What if they'd sent hundreds more around their flanks, to encircle the village?

A solid stream of rounds was hammering past right above his head. He could feel the pressure waves from the bullets thumping into his shoulder blades. He halted for an instant, to get a sense of his position. He reckoned he'd come forward thirty-five yards, putting him right on their frontline. To his left and right he could see figures hunched in their battle trenches, pouring fire back at the enemy. He just knew for sure they were burning through too much ammo.

He had to get further forward. He needed to be in a position where he could use the mortar, and where his fellow soldiers could see and hear him, so as to take his lead. He needed them to slow the rate of fire, and make one shot equal one kill. If they didn't, they were finished.

As he forced himself to cat-crawl onwards, he sensed the ground give way. He tumbled into a slimy hole. For an instant he feared he'd blundered into one of their own punji pits. They'd sighted those fields of sharpened bamboo stakes just forwards of their front line. But as no spikes pierced his combats or tore at his flesh, he figured the nearest punjis had to be a fraction to his right.

To his left he heard H calling out targets. 'Right of bent tree, 2 o'clock; 150 yards!'

Other voices yelled responses, but they were drowned out by the horrendous rate of incoming fire.

Heaney crawled on. He reached a spot where he was right under the enemy guns. He could hear figures thrashing about in the bush just ahead. He hoped to hell it was the forward-most rebels ensnared in the punji traps.

He rose on one knee, planting the mortar base-plate on the earth, driving it into the ground to provide a solid firing platform. He stole a glance in all directions: he was right in the heart of the battlefield – the no man's land between the two sides. Streams of solid tracer were pouring out from the rebel machineguns, plus scores of AK-47s were spitting flame, as fighters unleashed long bursts.

He heard H yelling out more target instructions: 'Sixty yards! Dead ground exit!'

The rebels were closing in through the dead ground – folds and gullies in the terrain where the British soldiers couldn't see them. That meant they were just dozens of yards away. But the Pathfinders couldn't nail them unless they could see them, and for that they needed Heaney's mortar illume rounds.

The 51mm illume fires to a height of 200 feet. It detonates to leave a flare drifting beneath a parachute, burning with a million candles' worth of power. It was light for the British soldiers to see by, but it was also light to signal that Heaney was there, taking charge of the battle.

'Putting up illume!' he roared. 'Putting up illume! Spot your targets!'

Heaney angled the 20-inch-long barrel at the right elevation, held the mortar by the body, tail fin down, and dropped it into the tube, before hitting the spring-operated firing pin. There was a slight vibration in the barrel, a loud *phzuuut*, and the round fired.

He glanced up, following the trajectory. The round burst, hanging like a tiny sun in the heavens. For an instant the murderous fire from the rebels seemed to stutter and stall. They hadn't been expecting to be pinned under the blinding light.

In one smooth movement he swivelled right, the mortar tube turning with him, took the second round and unleashed it. The minute it was airborne he turned 180 degrees left and put up a third round – this one bursting between their furthest trenches west and the tree-line. With three illumes airborne, the whole of the northern end of Lungi Lol was bathed in fierce, burning light.

'Use the light!' Heaney yelled. 'Deliberate fire! Pick your targets! Pick your targets!'

As the illume rounds drifted to earth, Heaney kept spotting for rebel movement and yelling out fire instructions. But the relief from the light was short-lived. Once the rebels realized that whatever light the British soldiers were firing did nothing to hurt, maim or kill, they redoubled their assault.

Heaney fired another three rounds in quick successions, to light the entire front. He needed to keep a check on his own ammo, or they'd run out of mortars. They only had eighteen rounds, all told. In contrast to the RUF rebels, British forces had been deployed with a woeful lack of ammunition, and the logistical supply chain from Britain to Sierra Leone still hadn't caught up.

All such worries were wiped from Heaney's mind, as he saw figures rear up from the bush. They came surging forward, muzzles sparking fire. Heaney dropped the mortar, swept up his assault rifle, flicked off the safety and let rip, firing short, targeted bursts. He heard the distinctive sound that 5.56mm bullets make as they rip into human flesh. He kept firing until all movement ceased, pumping rounds towards any sign of life or human cries.

He ceased fire, but kept his weapon in the aim, eyes down the sights and sweeping the night. He heard agonized groans and moans from the vegetation all around. The flare round above drifted silently into the trees. The darkness became thicker, as mortar rounds five and six were snuffed out in the jungle.

He dropped onto his belly, so he was laid next to the mortar tube. For the first time since crawling forward he was pretty much out of the enemy's line of fire. He was dripping in sweat, his heart was going like a jackhammer, and he was high as a kite on adrenalin.

Moments later, as if on a command, the rebel's fire petered out. Silence.

The eerie quiet drew out: ten seconds became twenty . . . What the hell were the rebel commanders up to now? They would be as cunning and battle-savvy as any adversary that the Pathfinders had ever faced.

Woe betide anyone who underestimated the rebel's dark intentions, or their sheer punch and firepower.

CHAPTER THIRTEEN

WILLEMSTAD, CURAÇAO, JANUARY 2008

Curaçao is a beautiful, sun-washed Caribbean island – a haven of peace and tranquillity, with a booming cruise liner industry. But with its innumerable inlets it is also a transit point for all kinds of undesirables, running cocaine north by go-fast, aircraft or even submarines – the biggest cartels have them – towards Mexico and on to the USA.

The DEA agents would need to maintain a firewall between themselves and the undercovers – The Bear, El Mexicano and El Comandante – while on the ground here. At the same time, they needed to stick close: El Mexicano would need to deliver recordings direct into their hands immediately after they'd been taped.

Accordingly, they booked the undercover team into the Curaçao Hilton, while they billeted themselves in the neighbouring Marriott. The Hilton was wide open, with an airy lobby that led directly onto a stunning beachside bar and dining area. The open-plan design made it easy enough for the DEA agents to wander in without attracting attention, should they need to get there in a hurry.

Curaçao's capital, Willemstad, consists of neat rows of gaily painted classic Dutch houses, the warm yellows, blues and greens of the quayside façade offset by the giant forms of gleaming white cruise ships lying alongside. Imagine old town Amsterdam parachuted into the midst of the Caribbean.

As the DEA enjoyed a close working relationship with the Curaçao police and security services, Willemstad was a good place for them to mount such a sting, and they'd cleared the present stage of Operation Relentless with the authorities.

The Hilton lay two kilometres east of downtown Willemstad, on a prime slice of beachfront adjacent to the Pirate Bay Curaçao Beach Club. With its two private coves lapped by aquamarine waters, its Y-shaped infinity pool and palm-thatched bars set on crystal white sands, it struck Mike Snow as being the perfect place to bewitch and beguile their target – Andrew Smulian.

They gathered for a heads-up that first afternoon at the Celeste Beach Bar, the beachside dining terrace of the Hilton. There were two new figures, in addition to the DEA team that had coalesced in Miami. One was Pierre Villard, the French aircraft dealer and DEA source. He was here solely to facilitate the Ramirez sting, and would play no role in the Smulian–Bout operation. The other was Louis Milione, the DEA's supervising agent for Operation Relentless, never known by anything other than 'Lou'.

Clean-cut, square-jawed and super-efficient, Lou Milione had worked as an actor before joining the DEA. He'd appeared in the 1980s movie *Risky Business*, a rite-of-passage romantic comedy that catapulted Tom Cruise to stardom. The film explores the themes of coming-of-age, loss-of-innocence and materialism. In many ways it was perfect schooling for the kind of operation Milione was now overseeing.

He was Wim and Zach's immediate boss, which made him

Mike's boss as well . . . at least, in theory. The seven sat around nursing drinks and talking through the coming operations. As Mike studied their team leader, he sensed that Milione wasn't much accustomed to being around a crazy, cuckoo Brit like The Bear.

Lou Milione set out the ground rules up-front. Unless they were meeting with Smulian to cut the deal, Snow was to keep the target away from Carlos and Ricardo. The longer Smulian spent with the two 'FARC' undercovers, the greater the chance that one or other might mess up.

He counselled that the 'FARC' guys – Ricardo in particular – could afford to act a little desperate. The FARC was embroiled ih a fight to the death against the armed forces of the Colombian state and their American advisors. They had piles of drugs money, but they needed new and more sophisticated weaponry if they were to win the bloody war. Their need for such hardware was urgent and compelling.

As the afternoon wore on, Mike sensed a growing unease on the part of the DEA agents. They were worried that Smulian wasn't going to fall for what they intended, or Bout for that matter. And there was no doubt about it – nailing Bout was the number one priority here in Curaçao. Reeling in Ramirez was very much a second-string operation.

Smulian was absolutely pivotal. It was clear from their previous dealings that the Russian trusted him absolutely. Lou Milione was acutely aware that if Smulian didn't buy the sting, then they were going home empty-handed. Conversely, if Smulian was suckered in it was game on.

'Don't stress,' Mike counselled. Then, somewhat enigmatically: 'Remember, thoughts become things.'

'What d'you mean?' Lou asked.

'Everything you have seen or used or touched today, began as a thought. Everything you think of can become concrete, because that's the law of the universe. Thoughts become things.' Mike paused, for emphasis. 'I am a great practitioner of "thoughts become things" . . . If we think that way, we'll get him.'

Mike was being genuine. He was a firm believer in the power of positive thinking, including when it came to ensnaring Viktor Bout. But he sensed that Lou Milione wasn't exactly of a mind with him, and that there was a certain friction between them. That evening, it all came to a head.

Lou had been asking Mike about his family. He'd suggested that if all went well with Operation Relentless then maybe they could get a green card and move to the US. It irritated Mike. He didn't appreciate the way some Americans tended to believe that everyone wanted to live in the States. Lou was acting real friendly, but Mike felt as if he was being talked down to.

'Don't you speak to me like I'm your garden boy,' he growled. 'I'll be out the fucking door. I don't work for you.'

Lou raised one eyebrow. 'Well, right now you kind of do.'

Mike was on his feet in an instant. 'I don't fucking think so! You might think you're clever, but I've got ten times more dog fuck than you. I've shit more dog fuck than you have. You think you can fuck with me? I'll be ten times tougher than you'll ever be.'

It had all gone very quiet.

Lou appeared utterly taken aback.

Mike eyed the people around the table. 'Look, I'm about to move into a phase where I've got to deceive a good friend. You guys lie for a fucking living. After all, that's what you do. Deception is your trade. Not bloody me.'

Mike led a very nonplussed Lou Milione to one side, for a private word. They faced each other beneath the palm trees. 'That . . . that was all a test,' Mike ventured. 'I just needed to test you. If you'd lost it, I would have been out of here. As it is, you're cool.'

Lou pursed his lips. 'Okay . . . Well, I don't understand it. But it's okay with me, I guess.'

They rejoined the table, to a few anxious glances.

'So, for those of you wondering, "dog fuck" is an African aviation term,' Mike announced. 'It's bush-pilot speak for common sense, but it goes a lot deeper than that.'

'What's the phrase again – fuck of the dog?' someone queried.

'Fuck of the dog,' Zach confirmed. 'It's like animal instinct and nous, I guess.'

No matter how many times Mike might try to correct them, that would become the catchphrase of Operation Relentless: 'fuck of the dog'.

Later that evening Carlos steered Mike to the bar, so it was just the two of them. He shook his head and chuckled. 'Fuck of the dog . . . Come on, we gotta get a beer.'

'It's dog fuck, Carlos. Dog fuck. How many times . . .'

Carlos glanced at the agents drinking at the table. 'You know what "DEA" really stands for?'

'Nope.'

'Drunk Every Afternoon.'

They laughed.

Carlos turned to Mike. 'You seem on edge, my friend. You gotta calm down. Relax, Papa Bear. Tomorrow morning we have Ramirez – the dry run. No big deal. Then we do Smulian.'

'Yeah.' Mike paused. 'That with Lou, that dog fuck moment, it was all an act. I had to test him somehow.'

Carlos shrugged. 'No big deal. And you know, tomorrow, only one rule you gotta bear in mind, with both of them, Ramirez and Smulian. Always remember, you just gotta appeal to their greed. A bad person has no principles – just appeal to his greed. *Always.*'

The following morning, Mike joined Carlos in his hotel room. El Mexicano was prepping his recording equipment. It consisted of a small, hand-held leather satchel concealing a recording device, and a lens secreted in a stud at one end.

Mike stared at the contraption, in amazement. 'Where the hell did you get that? It's horseshit.'

Carlos chuckled. 'It work fine for me with Monzer.' By Monzer he meant Monzer Al Kazar, the Syrian arms dealer that he'd busted a few months back, in Spain.

'You used that shit on Kazar?'

'Yeah. I place it on the arm of my chair, when sitting opposite Monzer, and I record everything. All the shit he talk.'

Mike shook his head in disbelief. 'What if Monzer had picked it up and opened it? You'd have been shafted.'

'Yeah, but he didn't. After a while, he treat me like a brother or maybe more like a son. Monzer, he was very protective over me.'

Mike snorted. 'You were just bloody lucky. I'll show you the kind of kit you should be using.'

He logged on to the internet, and walked Carlos through the kind of bugging equipment you could buy commercially – secreted in watches, key-fobs, mobile phones, and even a pair of heavy-framed glasses.

Carlos patted his man bag. 'Don't worry, Papa Oso. This – it go with my image. Today, Carlos is the smooth-talking moneyman for FARC. Tomorrow, who knows?'

They headed for the lobby.

As they did so, Carlos warned Mike that as soon as the meeting with Ramirez was done, he'd have to disappear. He had to hand the recordings direct to Agent Brown, to maintain the 'chain-of-custody'. In a court of law, the recordings would be treated as irrefutable evidence, but only as long as they were sealed by the DEA right after they'd been made.

If not, a clever defence lawyer could argue that in the time that had elapsed between recording and handover, the tapes might have been tampered with. Although extremely unlikely, it was the kind of thing a defence attorney might use to plant a seed of doubt in the mind of the jury.

Ramirez was waiting for them on the hotel terrace, along with Pierre. He greeted Mike almost as an old friend. Mike, of course, was needed for the Antonov 12 purchase. That plane was presently sitting on a remote and discreet airstrip, awaiting conversion into a transatlantic dope-carrier – a procedure that Ramirez expected Mike to oversee.

Villard had briefed Ramirez that Mike was actually a former South African mercenary, with great standing in the arms trade. Carlos was Mike's moneyman, the guy who cut his deals. With El Mexicano's bag sitting on the table, lens pointed at Ramirez and recorder running, they got right down to business.

The Venezuelan explained that he'd spent the last two days flying up and down the Curaçao coastline in a light aircraft, scoping out drugs landing points for the cartel. Now, he was keen to move onto the business of the day – weaponry.

'To start, I need two thousand 9mm pistols,' Ramirez ventured. 'Is to equip the Venezuelan police force. I don't care where you get them, but maybe Russian?'

'If you want Russian kit and it's bona fide, why not get your president to approach Putin direct?' Mike challenged. 'Putin sends five planeloads for your police force. Job sorted. Why the need to use us?'

'I could do that,' Ramirez conceded. He spread his hands. 'But then, no one make any money on the side.'

Mike didn't believe a word. Whoever the real customer was for his pistols, he doubted it was Venezuelan cops.

He turned to Carlos. 'We don't normally do such . . . modest deals. But I guess we can make an exception, if there's more and bigger things coming?'

Carlos gave an easy shrug. 'Maybe we all make a bit of money, this one. But we all wanna make a lot of money, so we need the big deals.'

Mike and Carlos wrapped up the meeting, agreeing to source Ramirez's arms for a price, but with the promise of more and bigger things to come. It was approaching mid-morning, and Smulian would be arriving at Curaçao's International Airport around lunchtime. They needed to get into role and get ready.

As they went to leave, Mike paused, theatrically. 'We're doing a few deals while we're here,' he remarked to Ramirez. 'So, if we see each other in the hotel, we don't let on we know each other, okay?'

Ramirez nodded. 'Got it. No problem.'

As they strolled into the lobby, Carlos congratulated Mike on his performance. 'Like I say, is easy, huh?'

'Yeah, Matt Damon eat your heart out.'

Mike was only partially joking. Pierre Villard was left with Ramirez, for his part in the Curaçao drama was now over. Carlos, meanwhile, hurried out of the Hilton to hand the DEA agents the Ramirez tapes. To Mike, it was like being on a film set. There were several different scenes all going on simultaneously, and he and the rest of the players were ducking from one to the next and the next.

People flitted from scene to scene, getting into role as they made their way along corridors or up flights of stairs. And, as former actor Lou Milione had told them, if you weren't 'on stage' you went to your room to lie low. If Mike ran into Milione as he made his way to the Hilton lift, he'd have to act as if they'd never met, or turn around and walk the other way.

To Mike it felt wild. Crazy. Cool. And he had to admit – he was on some kind of a high right now.

Back in his room, he prepped for Act Two: collecting Smulian from the airport. He'd originally advised him to get the Hoppa shuttle bus, but after the last few days he was beginning to appreciate the value of theatre. Smulian had to be stroked; made to feel the key man. The focus of everyone's attention.

Mike hired a car and drove to the airport. It was 10 January 2008, and Smulian was due in at around 1.50 p.m.

Smulian arrived looking somewhat the worse for wear, not that he was ever the nattiest of dressers. Having fallen upon hard times, his short-sleeved shirt and chinos appeared frayed and worn. Mike noticed there were holes in his deck shoes. He was also looking distinctly harassed. Mike soon discovered why. Smulian had had to overnight in Miami, in transit, and Mike had messed up the booking.

'My God, but it's a long way,' Smulian complained. 'And you know what? You fucked up the Miami hotel. It was all a day out.'

'Shit. Did you have to pay?'

'Yeah, but luckily I had seven hundred dollars cash. Otherwise ...'

Mike held out a hand. 'Give me whatever you got left.' Smulian dug in his pocket and pulled out a crumpled roll of dollars. Mike took it, peeled off seven crisp one hundred bills from the expenses money that the DEA had given him, and handed them to Smulian. 'Take it. And call it quits.'

Back at the Hilton he got Smulian checked in, then took him to his room. There Mike delivered his carefully rehearsed cover story.

'You remember when you called me several years back and told me the boys from Pretoria were not happy with me?' The 'boys from Pretoria' was a coded reference to South African intelligence.

'Yeah, I remember well.'

'Okay, well, I put the word out I was doing flights for Savimbi, so that was why. Remember?'

'I do.'

'Right, well, in truth I'd picked up this guy from Ouagadougou and flown him transatlantic to Suriname and back again. Now, as you'll appreciate, that's a hell of a lot of flying.'

Ouagadougou is the capital of the West African state of Burkina Faso, a known transit point for South American cartels moving drugs into Europe. Suriname is the South American country bordering Brazil, known to be a launch point for such transatlantic dope shipments.

Smulian eyed Mike, curiosity burning in his gaze. 'What d'you think the guy was up to?'

'Put it this way: I got paid very handsomely for it. A very large amount of money. So, I think maybe they were exchanging drugs for diamonds, or maybe weapons as well. As you can appreciate, I didn't probe too much.'

'No, no, you wouldn't.'

'That guy – he's a Latin American. He's the guy we're here to meet. He, or his group, they're the clients.'

'Right. Got it. So are they left or right wing?'

'They're lefties. Commies.'

'Oh, right.' Smulian glanced in the mirror. 'I was worried about my moustache. If they're left, it's supposed to curl up. I thought maybe they were right, so I turned it down.'

'Frankly, Andrew, I don't think they give a shit.'

'Oh, right. Did you notice there are loads of cameras in the hotel foyer? Seems like a bit of an open kind of a place to meet?'

Mike chuckled. 'Don't you fucking worry about that. These guys – they *own* the hotel.'

Mike left Smulian to get some rest. They agreed to rendezvous on the terrace around 6.30 that evening, where they'd be joined by the 'client' for dinner.

At the appointed time Mike headed to the al fresco dining area. He took a seat at a table to the right of the Celeste Beach Bar. It offered a breathtaking view of the sands below, dotted with sun-loungers and rustic-style sunshades roofed with coconut palm. To his front lay a wooden jetty, reaching out into the shimmering waters of the bay, with a couple of luxury yachts moored up.

During Mike's years in the SAS he'd got involved in training the raw recruits. He'd taken a somewhat different approach to selection from the one he had experienced. He'd gathered together the young hopefuls and explained that a good proportion was destined to fail because they had a skeleton or two in the closet. Any with criminal records or other insurmountable problems were encouraged to fess up, and drop out there and then.

With those who remained he'd adopted the following stratagem:

he'd get as many through as he could, quietly supporting them behind the scenes. Over the coming days he'd study the recruits, working out each man's strengths and weaknesses. That way, if one individual liked to lead from the front, but tended to tire relatively quickly, he'd give the guy his head, but replace him later with one of those who tended to get a second wind.

It was a strategy inspired by a book he'd read – Peter Watson's 1978 tome, *War on the Mind*. In it, Watson, a trained psychologist who went on to work for the *Sunday Times*, explored the long love affair between the military and psychology. Based upon a wealth of documents from the Second World War and thereafter, Watson's book revealed the sophisticated exploitation of psychology by the armed forces.

Nowhere was this more apparent than in Special Forces. The book revealed how in 1972, a troop of SAS had left their Hereford base en route to Malaysia, ostensibly for training. In truth, a bunch of army psychologists had flown out ahead of them. The SAS men were guinea pigs: they were scrutinized and subjected to various psychological tests during weeks in the jungle.

The psychologists had concluded that those who performed best over the first forty-eight hours were by no means the best over the long term. Moreover, they realized they could predict who would be the best long-term operators, based solely upon a series of tests they could carry out in wet and chilly Hereford. The tests remained secret, but they were adopted to select those men most suited for emergency deployment overseas.

Mike knew what type Smulian was. He was the enthusiastic early starter, who tended to tire and lose heart as the mission progressed. He would have to massage Smulian through the coming operation. He would need to be supported and encouraged to last the course, and others would need to be ready to lead the way.

Right now, as he relaxed at his beachside table, Mike saw Smulian as a member of his team, albeit an unwitting one. He was to be lured into wrongdoing, but for a greater good. Since he would escape prosecution at the end, maybe Smulian could even start working as a covert DEA source.

In his room, Smulian had just finished showering. He paused at the balcony. Bright blue waters stretched to the far horizon under a sky flecked with the odd wisp of cloud. He grabbed his camera and took a souvenir photo. Whatever might result from the coming meeting, he sensed that he was warming to the island of Curaçao.

He left his room and took the lift down to the lobby, joining Mike on the terrace.

Carlos, meanwhile, was also making his way to the rendez-vous. As he stepped out of his room, he'd already set his recorder running. He headed through the hotel and joined Mike and his companion at their beachside table. The two Brits rose to greet him, whereupon Carlos and Mike executed a showy embrace.

'Hey, amigo!' Mike declared.

'Amigo!' Carlos patted Mike's stomach. 'Ah, my friend, good to see you are getting fat. Fat is good. Is comfortable.'

Mike laughed. He turned and introduced Smulian.

Smulian gestured at the table and its position, set to the far right of the dining terrace. 'Uh, I think here is fine, because nobody's watching us?'

Carlos agreed. 'Is quiet just to talk a little bit. Tomorrow, when my partner's coming, we'll finish . . .' By his partner, he meant El Comandante.

Carlos went to take a seat, with Mike to his left and Smulian across from him enjoying a fine view of the ocean. He was hungry. He eyed the others. 'You guys hungry? Yeah? I'm hungry. Let's eat.'

To the right of their table lay a rocky bluff, thick with vegetation. As they went to order, Carlos could hear something large rooting around in the undergrowth. It turned out there were big iguanas lurking in the bush; they were in the habit of scavenging food out of the Hilton's bins. Smaller lizards scuttled around the beach, the tamer ones even taking titbits from the guests' hands.

The rustling of the lizards made a surreal kind of background beat for what was coming. They finished the main course, and with coffee and desserts ordered, Carlos figured it was time to talk turkey.

'Let's see if we can talk a little bit about business,' he ventured. 'See if you guys can help us.'

Mike feigned surprise. 'You, you want to talk today?'

Carlos shrugged. 'Uh, right now, with the coffee, just talk a little bit . . .'

Smulian fiddled with his napkin. He'd done his best to mug up on the arms trade. He'd got some guidance from Bout, and augmented that with his own research on the internet. He guessed he was ready.

'All you have to do is you have to give me a list of what you want . . .' he began. 'Except if you want information on new stuff.'

Carlos took a sip of water. 'Actually . . . how big is your market? That's what we are interested in.'

Smulian smiled. 'What you ask for, we can supply . . . What are you using? Equipment from the East? . . . If you're using Eastern equipment then that's very easy.' By the 'East' he meant Eastern Europe.

'We use anything we can get.'

'You're on the left?'

'Yes.'

Smulian turned to Mike. 'I asked you, didn't I . . . I said to him: "I want to change my moustache."'

The three men laughed.

'Yeah, normally what happens is that we are in the middle of the jungle . . .' Carlos began again.

'You?' Mike butted in.

Carlos shook his head. 'Not me. The people that I work for . . .' Carlos explained that he was a roving buyer for weaponry and other goods the FARC might need.

'So you work with them, or you're a broker?' Mike queried, slipping further into role. As far as Smulian was concerned, Mike's only connection to the FARC was flying their people around and procuring aircraft for them. In theory, he would know little about their wider operations.

'You can say both . . .' Carlos explained that he brokered arms deals and was the FARC's moneyman.

He knew exactly what he needed to secure on tape, to be able to nail this down in a court of law. But he couldn't push too hard or too quickly. This was all about throwing out a little bait a piece at a time, and having the patience to reel the guy in.

As the FARC operated in the deep jungle, did they have limits on the types of weapons they could utilize, Smulian asked?

'Oh, no, no, no, no, no, no,' Carlos assured him. He was about to elaborate, when the waitress appeared with two gigantic portions of cake. She eyed the three men at the table: *so who are these for?*

'Whoooo!' Smulian exclaimed.

'Oh, the cake? That's for him,' Mike told the waitress. 'That is very big. Thank you. That is bigger than the main course!'

The waitress handed the first slice to Smulian, and the second to Carlos, who had something of a sweet tooth.

Carlos took a forkful, settling deeper into his chair. 'Let's see . . . What happens is that sometimes it's a little hard for us to find the people to supply us . . . If you're telling me that you can get us a lot of things from the East, uh, we're interested.'

Smulian confirmed it was easy to source arms from Eastern Europe.

'We normally use a lot of things from there – China, Russia . . .' Carlos continued. 'And we're interested in a lot of things which is hard to get. I don't know if you can get those things to us?'

Smulian paused. 'Have you got money?'

This was more like it. Carlos could sense they were closing in. *Play to his greed.* 'They got money,' he confirmed.

'The money is where? Is it here? Or in Europe?'

'That's the other thing. We got money in different places, but it's cash.'

Smulian moistened his lips. 'Is it . . . Is it . . . Uh, is the money in places where one can fetch it in an aircraft and move it?'

'I don't know if that's possible . . .' Carlos paused to clear his throat. He needed to play for time, while he worked on a convincing answer. 'We got money in different places.' He cleared his throat again, nodding at the cake. 'Sorry, it's too sweet.'

Mike grabbed a carafe of water and poured some. 'Here. There's water here. Want more?'

'No, no, no. That's fine . . .' Carlos glanced at Smulian. 'The only problem we got is cash.'

'You got a problem with cash?'

Carlos nodded. 'We have cash. Only cash.'

Smulian smiled. 'You've got cash.'

'Cash,' Carlos confirmed. *Play to his greed.* Their problem, he explained, was laundering their cash so they could use it as they pleased.

Smulian's smile broadened. 'That's not a problem. It's a question of, um, collecting it and, um, moving it . . .' Smulian suggested they needed to purchase an aircraft, to move their cash around. He explained that he used to make flights across Africa, with parcels of cash, gold or diamonds secreted in the aircraft's instrument panels. They could do the same with the FARC's cash now.

'How much money can we put in there?' Carlos asked.

'We can move as much as you like,' Smulian replied. 'I moved 375 thousand dollars in gold . . .'

Just as they seemed to be getting to the heart of the matter, Mike signalled the waitress over, asking for a fresh round of coffee. Everyone was settling into role, and he seemed to be playing that of the bon viveur. Carlos knew he needed to roll with the punches. Go with the flow. He couldn't appear too eager or hungry.

'Sorry, what did I miss?' Mike asked, once he was done ordering.

'What I'm telling him is this,' Smulian explained. 'The best way to move the money is to get a suitable aircraft.'

'I'll start fucking looking!' Mike exclaimed.

'Okay, but . . . look, we're just talking,' Smulian told him. 'If the money is in different places and has to be collected, then the best way to do that is to operate an aircraft.'

Carlos leaned across the table, his open-necked shirt flashing just enough gold chain. He lowered his voice a little. 'Let me ask you: can you launder money for us?'

Smulian nodded. 'I can arrange it, if you want . . . Have you got diamonds for me? Rough diamonds?'

'What you said?' Mike butted in, "cause I'm deaf as a post in this ear . . .'

'I asked him if he can launder little bit of money for us,' Carlos repeated.

Smulian asked again if Carlos had any supplies of diamonds.

'No, no.' There was a glint in Carlos' eye now. 'We got a different thing . . . Little bit similar like diamond, but not diamond . . .'

Carlos saw the realization dawning in Smulian's eyes: the money came from drugs. 'Ah, okay, I'm with you,' he confirmed. 'Uh, that's a bit tough for anybody.'

'Yeah,' Carlos agreed. 'You don't wanna go there . . .' Drugs were too hot to handle, but cash wasn't. *Appeal to his greed.* 'Money is no problem. We have the money.'

Mike signalled to the waitress again. It was good to get Smulian's mind off the realization that the money they were discussing came from narcotics. He indicated the crème brûlée that he had just finished eating: 'Me, I want another one of these, my darling.'

'But I asked for coffee,' Carlos protested.

'Yeah, me also,' added Smulian. 'I asked for coffee.'

Mike ordered a second crème brûlée and a fresh round of coffees.

'Hey, first the fish is too small,' Carlos grumbled, once the waitress had left. 'Now, no coffee.'

Mike flashed a sideways look at him: time to get things back on track.

'I know you and I know him,' Mike began, jabbing a fork in Carlos and Smulian's direction, 'and I know the other guy.' By the 'other guy' he was referring to Viktor Bout. But as former SAS, visiting Russia was out of the question, he explained. He eyed Carlos. 'So, you have to agree . . . to pay out commission.'

Mike told Carlos that he had to agree the prices for the weaponry and pay him and Smulian a flat rate of commission, to avoid any problems down the line. 'For instance, we buy it for, uh, ten,' he explained. 'Then we tell you it's twelve. Human nature makes people greedy. So next time it's not twelve, its thirteen. And then you start to get pissed off.'

Mike found himself haggling as if the deal were for real: it was amazing how quickly such scenarios started to feel as if they were actually happening in reality.

'If it's a long-term thing, it's better to have a small thing for a long time,' he explained, 'than to start to be greedy and get fucked out of it. And me, an old guy . . . all I want is that you are honest with us . . .'

'Oh, okay.' Carlos was quiet for a moment. 'You know that if we agree on the commission, you know I promise . . . you going to receive your, your commission.' Carlos was asking Mike and Smulian to trust him.

'Yeah . . .' Mike shook his head, feigning unease. 'I don't know.' He glanced at Smulian. 'Andrew, you've gone quiet.'

Smulian shrugged. 'No, I'm just thinking. I'm just thinking about what position I will require when the game is finished.'

Good question, Mike thought. *If you only knew.*

They'd been talking for ninety minutes now, and after thirty-six hours of travelling Smulian was looking tired. Carlos was determined to use the wrangling over the commission to get to the crux of the matter. He explained they would need to go and meet the arms supplier face-to-face, to agree prices for the weaponry.

Mike asked Smulian if the arms supplier – Bout – would have a problem with that.

'No, no, no. He'll do it if I ask him to do it. He'll do it.'

'So please, I only ask you one thing,' Mike interjected, speaking to Carlos directly. 'If it goes wrong, any of it, you don't fucking blame me . . . I'm just telling you like that, Carlos, eh?'

Carlos laughed. 'Listen, on this type of business . . . I never going to blame you nothing.'

'I believe the guy will treat you properly,' Mike added, referring to Bout. 'But don't come fucking looking for me to cut my fucking throat and pull my tongue out.' Mike was being deliberately provocative. All part of the act.

'No, he's, uh, he's a very good guy,' Smulian tried to smooth things over. 'Uh, top, top dog . . . He can't travel, unfortunately, because of circumstances. But you can go there, no problem . . .'

At that moment a waiter paused by their table. 'You need something else?'

Carlos nodded. 'We asked for two crème brûlées.'

'You sure?'

'We asked for two more crème brûlées.'

'You already asked?'

'Yes,' Mike cut in. 'Go check in the kitchen and see if they are doing it. Please.'

As the waiter went to check on the crème brûlée situation, Carlos slipped in some more details about the buyer of the weaponry, explaining that they were fighting against the Colombian government and 'the gringos'. By the 'gringos' he meant the Americans. He needed to make it clear that the Americans were as much their enemy as were the Colombian troops. He needed Smulian to know – and for it to be captured on tape – that the weapons would be used against Americans.

Just then, a waitress arrived with the two missing desserts.

'Oh, *merci beaucoup, madame*. Yes. Yes,' Mike effused, as one was placed before him. The fact he was using French in a Dutch-speaking territory didn't seem to bother Mike. French was the language of fine dining, after all.

'Yesterday, in Miami, they took my photograph and they fingerprinted me,' Smulian ventured, picking up on Carlos' anti-American sentiments. 'That was the end . . . Fucking bastards. Who the fuck do they think they are?'

Mike paused over his crème brûlée. 'It's their country.'

'But you don't treat people like that,' Smulian protested.

'Well, *they* do.' Mike took a spoonful of the dessert and grimaced. 'I must go show them how to make a fucking proper crème brûlée . . . they never burnt it properly. I'm only eating it because I'm fucking starving.'

Mike knew exactly what he was doing here. Genuine bad guys would sweat the small stuff: the coffee; the sizes of the portions; the quality of the dessert. Somehow, it made their act all the more convincing. It helped hide what was actually in train here, and that all was hanging on the sting.

He glanced at Smulian. 'So how long d'you think it could take to organize?'

Smulian explained that he'd need to sort a visa to go and visit the arms supplier and explain the nature of the deal in person.

'Visa to where?' Carlos asked.

Above: A thing of grace and beauty. Former SAS man turned bush pilot, Mike Snow (left of picture) rescued WWII-era aircraft to fly cargoes into war zones. Grounded after a string of near-disasters, he was recruited to hunt down one of the world's most-wanted men.

Left: The cockpit of a giant Ilyushin air-freighter, built to project Soviet power around the globe, and capable of carrying fifty tonnes into just about anywhere.

Above: Flying for Russian-based airfreight company, Airstan, this Ilyushin was forced down in Afghanistan, its hold packed full of ammo, shells and guns. The Russian crew were held hostage for 378 days, until a daring escape executed via their own aircraft.

Left: The Airstan crew were just one of dozens flying for entrepreneur, reputed billionaire, former Soviet military and suspected Russian intelligence agent, Viktor Bout. Due to his reputation for flying anything anywhere, Bout had become renowned as the world's foremost arms dealer, earning the nickname 'The Merchant of Death'.

Right and below: From assault rifles and RPGs – these in the hands of Sierra Leonean rebels – to fearsome Mi-24 helicopter gunships, Viktor Bout flew sanctions-busting missions to everyone and anyone. But Mi-24 gunships aren't available over the counter; it took connections at the highest levels to finesse such deals.

Left: Bout's arming of rebels put him on a direct collision course with Britain and America, as troops deployed to Sierra Leone to stop the war there: suddenly, NATO and UN soldiers faced rebels boasting terrifying firepower supplied by the Russian.

Right: Task Force Bloodstone. Viktor Bout would take payment in uncut gemstones, gold or other precious minerals. T. F. Bloodstone – named after the trade in 'blood diamonds' – was a top-secret MI6/Special Forces unit tasked to hunt him down.

Above: By 2007, Bout was one of the world's most-wanted men, but every effort to capture him had failed – cue the Drugs Enforcement Agency (DEA), fresh out of a string of sting operations. If Bout couldn't be cornered, could the DEA lure him into a trap?

Above: In Colombia, the notorious FARC rebels – the Armed Revolutionary Forces of Colombia – were known to be seeking sophisticated weaponry to further their war against the state: could Bout somehow be drawn into a deal to sell arms to the FARC?

Above: FARC earned hundreds of millions of dollars from the drugs trade, using 'go-fasts' – hugely-powerful speedboats – Boeing 727 air-freighters and even submarines to run drugs into the USA and Europe. They had money to burn on such an arms deal.

This page: The FARC were 'narco-terrorists': they shipped bales of cocaine and heroin out of Central America and guns back in again. The DEA recruited its team for Operation Relentless - the mission to lure Viktor Bout into such a deal – starting with Mike Snow, who knew Bout from his years flying into war zones. Snow teamed up with DEA confidential sources Carlos and Ricardo – former drugs and arms dealers turned good guys – the plan being to "use a thief to catch a thief." Their first tasking was a multi-million-dollar money laundering hit on a major drugs cartel.

Above and below: The Russian Igla – 'needle' – man-portable heat-seeking surface-to-air missile: the FARC were desperate to acquire such weaponry, to shoot down the US helicopters flying missions to combat their drugs smuggling networks.

Above and below: Viktor Bout and Briton Andrew Smulian, a former pilot and business partner of Bout's, in Moscow's Red Square. They met to agree a multi-million dollar deal to sell tonnes of weaponry to the FARC, including hundreds of Igla anti-aircraft missiles. Those weapons would be air-dropped from Bout's air-freighters at night direct into the FARC's bases deep in the Colombian jungle. [Photos marked 'Government Exhibit' were used as evidence in Bout's US trial].

Below: The Operation Relentless team celebrates the success of the sting. From left of picture, standing: Carlos Sagastume 'The King of Sting', Pierre Villard, Ricardo Jardeno 'El Comandante', Mike Snow 'The Bear'. Faces obscured, as they still serve on undercover operations.

Above: The conference suite in the Sofitel Hotel, Bangkok, to which Bout, and his Russian bodyguard Belozerovsky, were lured by the DEA undercover team, and where the hit went down.

Above: After a two-year extradition battle, Viktor Bout was flown to the USA in the custody of DEA agents William 'Wim' Brown and Robert 'Zach' Zachariasiewicz, who along with supervising agent Lou Milione masterminded the case.

'Russia.'

'To *where*?' Mike asked.

'Russia.'

'I'm not going there,' he snapped.

'No, I know. And it's not a problem . . . my contacts are very, very high.'

Carlos frowned. 'Maybe it's going to be a problem for my friend and me . . . We gotta be very, very careful, because I don't want nobody have problems, and I don't want to have problems.' Travelling to Russia wasn't on the cards from their side.

'You don't have to worry,' Smulian soothed. 'This is a game we've been doing for a long time . . . So, my friend, the reason he can't travel is because there's an INTERPOL Red Card. So he can't go anywhere out of Russia. In Russia he's protected at the very top.'

Carlos nodded. 'Uh-huh . . . So that means he cannot get out from there?'

Smulian confirmed that Bout's ability to travel was extremely limited. 'Belarus he can go . . . Moldova he can go, and Albania and . . . probably Armenia . . . Whatever the case . . . it's not going to be cheap.'

'What makes it easier is . . . it's money that's not, uh, in banks,' Carlos told Smulian. *Appeal to his greed.* They had heaps of cash they needed rid of. Mike added that there were 'fucking big buckets full of money' that needed laundering.

Smulian confirmed that Bout would have no problem cleaning such funds.

The waitress was hovering, keen to clear the plates away. 'Thank you, sir. Finito?'

'I'm finished,' Smulian confirmed.

Mike stole a glance at Carlos: this seemed as good a time as any to call the meeting to a close.

'Yeah, like, so you know, we got the money,' Carlos reiterated, throwing one last chunk of bait.

'Uh-huh.'

'We don't have banks. We've got cash money.'

Smulian smiled. No problem, he assured El Mexicano. They'd get the client's cash cleaned and sorted.

Carlos made his excuses and strolled away from the table, nonchalantly. He exited the hotel via the lobby and turned right towards the Marriott, just a short walk away. They'd danced around the subject a little – especially the identity of the arms supplier, which he still needed to capture on tape – but he figured they'd made a damn fine start.

He needed to get the tapes into the hands of Agent Brown.

CHAPTER FOURTEEN

LUNGI LOL, SIERRA LEONE, MAY 2000

Heaney yelled around the darkened battlefield, asking for any casualties. He figured they had injured, but with all the deafening noise of the firefight no one had been able to use the radios. He wondered for an instant if the rebels were withdrawing. Then he heard it – the faint, distant snort of what sounded like a heavy diesel engine moving on the track up ahead.

Oh shit. Maybe the RUF were bringing up their armour and their heavy guns.

As if to usher them in, the rebels opened up again with seemingly every weapon they'd got. The incoming fire was murderous, yet now it was coming from a different direction and concentrated on a whole new target.

The Pathfinders' position to the far west was taking a massive pounding. It was getting totally smashed, tracer like a solid stream of flame scorching into it. Heaney rose on one knee, grabbing the mortar tube. As he did he saw the Pathfinders in those western trenches opening up on the advancing enemy. But their rate of fire really scared him now: it was too much, too quick. Keep this up and they'd be down to fighting with machetes and their bare hands.

He reached for a round and dropped it down the tube, launching a flare high above the position now under assault.

'Watch and shoot!' he yelled. 'Pick your targets. Watch your fucking ammo!'

Heaney spotted scores of rebel fighters sprinting across the dirt track. They were pouring west, heading across to join the main thrust of the battle. Maybe his instinct earlier had been right. Maybe the rebels had hit them front-on as a feint, to mask a move to outflank their positions. It was a chilling proposition.

The desperate firefight that night at Lungi Lol would continue until just before daybreak. At one point the Pathfinders were poised to pull back from the village, as the rebels threatened to overrun it, but they'd held firm. Come first light, the rebels melted back into the jungle.

For now. The RUF had vowed to take Lungi Lol and execute Operation Kill British: no one doubted that they'd be back.

As the sun rose above the jungle it was as quiet as the grave out there. Even the moaning of the rebel wounded seemed to have stopped. The Pathfinders asked for any wounded villagers to be brought to the square, so they could assess their injuries. The thin-walled village huts would have offered little cover from small arms and machinegun fire, let alone RPGs.

Bryan Budd, who would later go on to win a posthumous Victoria Cross in Afghanistan, was the Pathfinders' medic. A young girl had been hit in the shoulder. She was cradled in her traumatized mother's arms. Budd inspected her wound. Luckily, it was a 'through-and-through' – the round had passed clean through the girl's body. Budd managed to stop the bleeding and get her stabilized. She'd live.

Miraculously, there were precious few other casualties. It

would have been a very different outcome had the RUF overrun the British positions. That didn't bear thinking about, and the Pathfinders vowed to redouble their vigilance. No matter how well armed they might be, no force was taking Lungi Lol while the elite British soldiers still had breath in their bodies.

In the early morning light, they could make out corpses lying on the track leading into the village. The rebels were dressed in a mish-mash of shell-suits and combat fatigues. One cradled an RPG-launcher in his arms, plus there were others armed with AK-47s, and a belt-fed RPK – a Russian light machinegun.

Now the British force commander knew for sure the rebels' intentions – to fight their way through Lungi Lol – he could afford to reinforce the Pathfinders. A Chinook helicopter flew in that morning carrying a platoon from the Parachute Regiment, plus a mortar unit. The newly arrived men filtered into the Pathfinders' trenches, enabling the exhausted fighters to stand down.

But being Pathfinders, they didn't rest for long. Instead, they decided to do the utterly unexpected – going after the rebels in a seek-and-destroy mission. The plan was simple. They would move west through their trench positions, sweep north from there into the jungle, advance a kilometre, and from there strike east to the dirt road, clearing as they went. They'd cross the track, and come back due south, which would bring them into the eastern flank of the village.

Heaney formed up a stick of nine operators. In single file they moved through the waist-high vegetation, each man with his weapon in the aim and scanning his arcs, poised to unleash hell. They pushed ahead stealthily towards the canopy, some 200 metres away.

They came to the edge of a shallow depression, the entrance

into a V-shaped gully. The lead scout went down on one knee and Heaney closed in on his right shoulder. The scout indicated the footprints that crisscrossed the soft, loamy soil. Dozens of rebels had been through here.

In among the crushed foliage were bright red strings of congealed goo: blood trails. As they moved off, Heaney gave the man behind him the signal: two fingers into his eyes with the one hand, then pointing at the gully. *Look in the ditch*. The signal was passed silently down the line, so that everyone got to see the evidence of battle.

They reached the edge of the jungle, and nudged into the musty, claustrophobic interior, the smell of rot and decay heavy in their nostrils. The forest closed around them, silent and foreboding. The lead scout motioned to the ground. The leaves underfoot were thick with pools of congealed blood. This was where the rebels had regrouped, and by the looks of things a lot had been wounded.

By the end of that day, the Pathfinders had cleared the jungle surrounding Lungi Lol and reinforced and consolidated their positions. In doing so, they encountered scores of refugees fleeing from the rebels. Villagers had been rounded up and forced to dig graves, to bury the RUF's dead. The stories of the horrors the rebels had inflicted on the locals were chilling.

In the coming days there were further probes by the RUF forces, but neither the village of Lungi Lol nor Lungi Airport itself fell. A few hundred men – Paras and Pathfinders – had halted the rebels in their tracks. Sergeant Steve Heaney was awarded the Military Cross for his actions at Lungi Lol, and their mission would be one of the most highly decorated in modern British military history.

Just three months later, a last-gasp operation would see the 1st Battalion Parachute Regiment back in action. Rebels had taken hostage eleven men of the Royal Irish Regiment, on peacekeeping operations in the country. The SAS and the Paras were sent in to rescue them. Their daring mission resulted in the freeing of all the British hostages, but it led to injury and loss of life among the rescue force.

It also signified the end of the bloody civil war in Sierra Leone. By the autumn of 2000 the leader of the RUF was in captivity, facing war crimes charges, and the rebels had disbanded. But the decade-long strife had taken a terrible toll in terms of human lives, plus those who were permanently disabled due to the horrific amputations. While the fighting may have been brought to a close, the war would cast a very long shadow.

That winter, Viktor Bout's role in arming the Sierra Leonean rebels was highlighted most powerfully. Africa Minister Peter Hain had played a key part in steering British policy, and on 7 November 2000 he rose to speak for a second time in the British Parliament regarding sanctions busting and the arms trade.

Once again, the press would prove crucial to what Hain intended. He'd thought long and hard about this speech. He knew that the media could prove a hugely powerful tool for good, but there was little scope for nuance or subtlety. He decided he needed a catchy, but accurate tag to encapsulate the threat posed by Viktor Bout.

'Sanctions busters are continuing to perpetuate the conflict in Sierra Leone . . . with the result that countless lives are being lost . . .' he began. 'Viktor Bout is indeed the chief sanctions buster, and is a *merchant of death* who owns air companies that ferry in arms . . . and takes out diamonds which pay for those arms . . . aiding and abetting people who are turning their arms on British soldiers.'

The 'merchant of death': the phrase had come to Hain spontaneously, as he'd read yet another intelligence briefing on Bout's activities. It struck an immediate chord, and the press took up the hue and cry. The very idea of a Russian multimillionaire trafficking arms to vicious rebels, only for them to be turned on British troops, proved a powerful story.

Hain's name-and-shame campaign proved remarkably effective. That phrase – the merchant of death – stuck. But Hain was far from done. He established a top secret Task Force, combining agents from MI6, GCHQ and other agencies, plus Foreign Office officials, to go after Bout globally. The Task Force was codenamed Bloodstone, an apposite choice bearing in mind Bout's line of work and its links to the illicit diamond trade.

Let off their leash, the MI6 officers leading Bloodstone proved particularly enthusiastic. At the same time Hain pressurized the Crown Prince of Abu Dhabi, plus his defence minister, Sheikh Mohamed bin Zayed, to close down Bout's operations in Sharjah. Yet despite such efforts Bout continued to enjoy high-level protection from Moscow, where he remained something of an untouchable.

In February 2002, Task Force Bloodstone drew first blood. A fearsome Mi-24 helicopter gunship – the nearest Russia equivalent to the NATO Apache – was seized in Slovakia, en route to Liberia. By means of a dizzying system of front companies and bogus documentation, Bout's people had already shipped one Mi-24 to Liberia, on-board an Ilyushin, but the second was stopped and impounded.

That same month a British field agent sent an encrypted message from Moldova to London, reporting that Bout had boarded an aircraft routed from there to Athens. Moldova, a former Soviet

Bloc country, was one of Bout's regular stalking grounds, somewhere where he felt protected. Task Force Bloodstone swung into action, preparing to arrest Bout upon his arrival in the Greek capital.

But the encrypted message sent by the British field agent must have been intercepted, for the flight suddenly veered off course, disappearing from radar coverage for a good ninety minutes among mountains. When it did eventually land at Athens, MI6 agents and British special forces – along with their Greek counterparts – stormed the flight, only to discover there was no sign of Viktor Bout.

Someone with the technology to rapidly break MI6's encryption must have sent Bout a warning. Only two countries in the world possessed such a capacity: the Americans and the Russians. Still, it was the closest Bout had ever come to being nailed.

By now, efforts were under way to slap a global travel ban on Bout, and to freeze his assets worldwide. If the elusive Russian businessman couldn't be captured, then at the very least his global dealings could be hamstrung via such measures.

Despite his narrow escape in Athens, the walls were closing in.

CHAPTER FIFTEEN

WILLEMSTAD, CURAÇAO, JANUARY 2008

The morning after their first meeting, Mike, Carlos and Smulian gathered for a fine Hilton breakfast. Smulian seemed refreshed after a good night's sleep. He was keen to talk more about the business of the day, but Carlos demurred. They needed to await the 'Commander's' arrival. Smulian had met the client's moneyman; he now needed to speak to their weapons guy, El Comandante.

The four rendezvoused at the Hilton's beach bar. Mike did the introductions, after which there were a few moments' confusion as to which table to take. Carlos had noticed that someone – quite possibly just a nosey tourist, but you never knew – had become very interested in their gathering.

They moved to a furthermost table, well out of earshot. There they ordered drinks. Carlos leaned back in his chair, gesturing at the sun-drenched beach and the well-stocked bar. 'This is the good life. This is the good life here . . .'

Ricardo – El Comandante – didn't appear too interested in taking things easy. He dived right in, jabbering away in Spanish and waving his hands about expansively. Carlos had to slow the guy down, for he was playing the role of translator.

'So, he said . . . he is very interested to see what you can offer to us. That we need a lot of different things.'

Mike squared his shoulders and eyed Ricardo. 'It's not necessary to beat around the bush . . . All general Russian . . . infantry weapons we can supply.'

Ricardo glanced from Mike to Smulian, as if measuring them up. 'Does he have access to Iglas?' he barked in Spanish. 'Ask him.'

'You can find us . . . Iglas?' Carlos ventured.

Smulian looked nonplussed.

'Iglas,' Carlos repeated. 'Iglas.'

'Eagles?' Mike queried, feigning ignorance.

As well he knew, the Igla – Russian for 'needle' – was a man-portable heat-seeking surface-to-air missile (SAM). By asking for the much-coveted anti-aircraft missiles up front, El Comandante had plunged in at the very deep end. Mike studied Smulian's face for any telltale reaction; any sign of suspicion at the mention of the SAMs.

Ricardo leaned closer to Carlos. 'Tell him it's the new generation of the SAM-7.' Carlos translated, the SAM-7 – also known as the 'Strela' – being the precursor to the Igla.

For a moment Smulian appeared flummoxed. 'Ooof!' he exclaimed.

'Iglas,' Carlos reiterated.

'*Nueva* Strela,' Smulian ventured – the 'new Strela' – trying out a touch of Spanish. He reckoned they *could* supply the Igla, but he'd clearly need to check with his boss. Carlos explained that whatever anti-aircraft hardware they purchased, it had to be 'something simple', because they were guerrilla fighters operating in the bush.

'What I think you guys need is, uh, RPG-29V,' Smulian suggested.

At the mention of the RPG-29V Ricardo leaned forward excit-edly. Everyone in this line of work recognized that acronym: R-P-G. Ricardo knew the 29V – V for Vampir; vampire. The war-head could penetrate the frontal armour of a NATO main battle tank, and it was simple to operate, reliable and robust.

Smulian had actually fired the weapon when serving in the South African military. Previous RPG models were accurate up to 800 feet, but the RPG-29V extended that range to close on 3,000, and that made it a passable anti-aircraft weapons system, he explained, especially against low-flying helicopters. The West didn't have an equivalent, he boasted, and he was happy to supply them.

'Ask him where they are,' Ricardo told Carlos, eagerly. 'I want to see them.'

Carlos translated his question.

They'd be sourced from Russia, Smulian explained. 'I know more or less what you want. I mean, if you're working in the bush and you have foot soldiers, then, well, I know what you want.' But he and Snow would need to charge their commission on whatever price Carlos and Ricardo agreed with the supplier.

'How much?' Ricardo barked.

'How much you want for commission?' Carlos added.

Mike's expression hardened. If the deal was for less than one million dollars, they'd need to take fifteen per cent commission. Between one and two million would be ten per cent; above two, their cut would reduce to five per cent only.

Ricardo shook his head. He looked daggers at Mike: he was being way too greedy. Despite knowing that this was all a sham, at the same time it felt suddenly so very real. Mike found himself arguing over whether Carlos and Ricardo were trying to do him and Smulian out of a fair cut.

It was far too early in the deal to be arguing over money, Ricardo protested. It was Mike's turn to act aggrieved. 'This is bullshit, because first we didn't prove we can do anything . . .'

Ricardo held up his hands in mock surrender. 'Okay, okay, okay, okay . . . Money is not the problem.'

'We don't have problem with the money,' Carlos echoed. 'We don't have problem with the money.'

Time to jack down the confrontation level, Mike figured. 'We know that . . .' He glanced at Carlos. 'I trust you.'

With the items they were now discussing – a dozen Iglas alone would cost well over a million dollars – the commission was going to be considerable, said Ricardo, no matter what Mike and Smulian's cut might be. There would be plenty of money to go around.

Ricardo listed their needs: AK-47 assault rifles, ammunition, fragmentation grenades. He and Smulian picked over the advantages of different calibres of assault rifles. They talked about a training team being provided with the weaponry. But with the shopping list lengthening, Ricardo circled back to the issue of the commission.

'Tell him it's five per cent,' he declared. Non-negotiable. Carlos translated: five per cent was the maximum they were willing to pay.

'Across the board?' Mike challenged.

Across the board, Carlos confirmed. This deal alone would be three million dollars' worth of arms, and there would be plenty more to come.

Mike glanced at Smulian. He could almost see the figures whirring through the guy's brain, as he calculated five per cent split between the two of them. That amounted to $75,000 each, and on a recurring basis, by the sound of things.

If something seems too good to be true, it generally is: but as Carlos had stressed, all you had to do was play to the guy's greed.

In his excitement, Smulian blurted out the million-dollar question, the answer to which should fully ensnare him in the web that was being woven here. Who exactly was the group that Ricardo and Carlos represented?

Ricardo responded with a teaser. 'We are people who buy . . . for a very important group in Colombia . . . Who needs weapons in Colombia? Aside from the army?'

'And who is the group?' Smulian parried. 'It's because the guy in Russia . . . I'm sure, he will ask me'. Smulian's supplier was close to the Russian President, so he had to be very careful.

Carlos picked up a napkin and handed it to Ricardo. 'Write the name down for him there. Write the Fuerzas Armadas Revolucionarias . . .' Ricardo scrawled out the FARC's full name – Fuerzas Armadas Revolucionarias de Colombia – and handed the paper to Smulian.

Smulian glanced over it, his face registering little surprise. 'It's, uh, nyet problemy in Russian.'

'Nyet problemy,' Mike echoed.

'Nyet problemy,' Smulian repeated.

No problem.

'F-A-R-C . . .' Ricardo spelled out, just to be sure to get it on tape. 'Which means Armed Revolutionary Forces of Colombia.'

Smulian nodded. 'Okay, that's what I thought, anyway, so okay.'

Legally speaking, Smulian was now totally stuffed. He'd

seemingly just organised the sale of an arsenal of weaponry – including anti-aircraft missiles and grenade-launchers – to the FARC, a proscribed terrorist organization.

Ricardo ripped up the napkin, reminding the others how you could never be too careful, and then the discussion moved on to next steps. Mike suggested that he and Smulian would fly to Copenhagen, from where Smulian could flit across to Moscow, to meet with Bout and seal the deal.

With Ricardo presently in the hot seat, the discussion lacked some of the order of the previous evening. A hot-blooded, fiery Latino, Ricardo didn't need to play up to the FARC commander act. He pretty much just had to be who he was, to appear entirely convincing.

Ricardo circled back to the weaponry. They had need of Dragunovs, he explained, a semi-automatic Russian sniper rifle that packs a ten-round magazine. Smulian pointed out that the Dragunov had been superseded by a new Russian heavy-calibre sniper system, the Bison, chambering a 12.7mm round, the equivalent of the .50 calibre NATO bore.

'Yeah, .50 . . .' Smulian enthused. 'And I'll show you a photo . . . of it blowing these people apart.'

'*Es muy bueno*,' Ricardo confirmed.

'Yeah. *Muy bueno*,' Smulian echoed. '*Grande*.'

Ricardo proceeded to reel off the long list of weaponry that Smulian had agreed to provide to the FARC. 'The AKs, the new version of the Dragunov, uh, the ammunition, the Iglas, uh, the RPGs – the entire spectrum of the RPGs . . .' But how and where could Smulian and his people deliver them?

Smulian said they'd need a safe coastal area where they could land an Ilyushin airfreighter stuffed full of arms.

Carlos had got exactly what he needed on tape, and he was keen to draw the meeting to a close. You had to walk a fine line between pushing it, and forcing it too far. He and Ricardo would have to see the seller face to face, and that would mean finding a country where both sides were happy to meet.

'You said that you once met someone in a boat, in the middle of a . . . river,' Mike suggested.

Smulian nodded. 'Yeah. Yeah, that's possible . . .'

'What about in the . . . Baltic?' Mike pushed. 'He can come from Russia, we go in the Baltic, and we meet at night in the yacht . . .'

'Look, I have to ask him, and he'll tell me,' Smulian objected: this would be Viktor Bout's call.

Mike shrugged. 'Yeah. Yes, yes. But I'm just, I'm just talking shit . . . Romania's now in the EU. Go from Romania on the Black Sea, and he comes from Moldova, somewhere like that. I don't know. I'm just talking crap, eh?'

'Yeah. I have to ask him,' Smulian repeated. Their exact rendezvous point would be down to Bout.

It couldn't be Russia, Carlos explained, because a Russian stamp in their passports would be the death knell for them as FARC operatives. But, equally, it couldn't be somewhere where the 'gringos' had too heavy a presence.

It was now that Carlos produced a smart new cellphone. He pushed it across the table to Smulian. He explained that for security reasons, the FARC changed their phones every few days. As Smulian was now working on their behalf, he would need to do likewise. This one was pre-paid, so he was free to make international calls.

In truth, this was one of several phones on which the DEA had secured prior legal consent to place a wiretap. Mike had been given one, as had Carlos and Ricardo. Now that Smulian had his, the calls between the principals involved in the FARC arms deal could be legally captured on tape – 'judicially intercepted', in DEA parlance.

This was a crucial moment. If Smulian suspected anything, he'd baulk at taking the phone. Instead, he just seemed happy that he was 'on the team'. That in turn was testimony to the power of the last forty-eight hours of theatre, which been hugely intense and all-consuming.

In fact, Mike had barely noticed when Agents Milione, Brown and Zachariasiewicz had done a 'walk-by' of the meeting, so focused had he been on the negotiations. The DEA agents had done so in case they needed to testify in court about the meeting taking place: its location, who attended and when.

As Smulian admired his gleaming new cellphone, Mike badgered him to give Bout a call. This was a multi-million-dollar deal, and it had every promise of being hugely lucrative. They needed Bout to get on the case with Smulian's Russian visa application, so they could move to the next stage.

'And tell him to fucking move his butt,' Mike cajoled.

Smulian dialled Bout, but he couldn't seem to get any response. He figured it had to be due to the time difference – Curaçao is seven hours behind Moscow. It would be twelve o'clock midnight with Bout right now, which doubtless explained why he wasn't answering.

Unable to raise Bout, Smulian called a mutual friend in Tanzania – a partner in their African business ventures. He explained that he planned to be in Copenhagen in three days, so that was where he wanted to collect his Moscow visa stamp, and

Bout needed to understand that this was 'very urgent'. Call done, Smulian raised another point that had come to mind: did the FARC have communications needs?

'We need communications,' Carlos confirmed. But he cautioned that there were American forces on the ground, intercepting their electronic signals, so sometimes they had to send human couriers carrying messages by hand.

'You know the story about Somalia and the Black Hawk – the Arabs they shoot the Black Hawk?' Smulian queried. 'You know how they got the message the aircraft was coming?'

He was referring to the 1993 battle between American forces and Somali militia, in the Somali capital, Mogadishu, in which two US Black Hawk helicopters were shot down. He explained how the militias had placed 200-litre steel drums around the US airbase, on which they hammered out a beat whenever a helicopter took to the air. The drumbeats signalled the direction of flight, so the choppers could be targeted by RPGs.

The drumbeat system was low-tech, but it was totally invulnerable to American countermeasures. Smulian proposed supplying the FARC with HF radio backpacks, which switched frequencies regularly to foil interception measures. Carlos and Ricardo confirmed those might well suit the FARC's requirements.

In addition to the communications systems, Ricardo realized he'd left one other crucial item off their shopping list of materiel. 'The explosives. Essential.' Smulian confirmed providing plastic explosives wouldn't be a problem.

He asked if there were any medical supplies that the FARC might require. Right now he had in mind a side-deal for himself and his Tanzanian business partner. The syringe factory he worked at could provide general medical kit, if the FARC had the need and could pay.

'We need doctors, medicine. We need all of that,' Carlos confirmed. But the number one priority had to be the weaponry. With the amount of equipment now being discussed, it might be better – more cost effective – to freight it by ship, he suggested.

Mike nodded, enthusiastically. 'You know, to buy a ship to carry a little stuff . . . You take to Suriname . . . and then you can fucking sink it. It's simple . . . It's costing nothing to do that . . . to carry two hundred tonnes of something. It's nothing.'

Carlos sensed it was time for the final piece of Curaçao theatre, as far as he and Ricardo were concerned. He reached into his pocket and pulled out an envelope. It contained $5,000 in cash – 'official authorized funds' in DEA parlance. He had been green-lit to pass it to Smulian, as a 'sweetener' on the sting.

Carlos slid the envelope across the table. 'You know, you make a big effort to be here today. This is just a token of our gratitude.'

Smulian glanced inside. He didn't know exactly how much was in there, but he could see a mass of $100 bills. It was like Christmas had just come very, very early.

The meeting broke up, Carlos and Ricardo heading off to hand over the precious tapes to the DEA team. But Mike wasn't done yet with the Curaçao play-acting: it was time for one final flourish.

He got Smulian into the hire car and drove him around the island. Curaçao was no more than fifty miles from tip to toe, so he could afford to take it slow and easy. They did the tourist hotspots – Caracas Bay, Fuik Bay and Spanish Waters – Smulian admiring the stunning beaches, the gleaming yachts cutting through turquoise seas, and the bevies of bikini-clad beauties gracing the sands.

Mike headed towards the island's highpoint, the 1,230-foot Sint Christoffelberg, the rocky cone of which is surrounded by lush forest, peppered with giant cacti. From the high ground the island rolled out before them, Willemstad to the south, the airport to the north, and the golden beaches plus the gorgeous expanse of the Caribbean Sea beyond.

'By God, but I could live here,' Smulian muttered.

'You know, Andrew, you could,' Mike told him. 'They like you. At your age, you don't attract a lot of attention. You can fly beneath the radar. They want you to base yourself here and in Aruba, and work for them pretty much fulltime.'

Aruba was the neighbouring island to the west, which together with Curaçao and three lesser islands makes up the territory of the Netherlands Antilles.

'You know, the way they're treating us here, it's amazing,' Smulian enthused. In truth, he was bowled over by the way the 'FARC' were throwing money around. 'These are serious people with serious resources.'

'Exactly. And all you'd need to do is go from here to London as a courier carrying messages; no drugs, not ever.' Mike remembered Carlos' words: *appeal to his greed.* 'They're looking at paying you $20,000 a month, every month. And I repeat; no drugs, not ever.'

Snow's words were like music to Smulian's ears. Carlos had actually mentioned earlier that maybe Smulian might like to live on Curaçao, but in the rush of things it had passed him by. From this highpoint, Smulian reckoned he could see his future stretching out before him, and it looked tantalizing.

Meanwhile, in Willemstad the DEA team was busy collating

their evidence. Wim was in charge of cataloguing the hours of recordings. He took the final batch of tapes off Carlos and signed, sealed and dated them. Gone were the worries and uncertainties of three days earlier. Lou Milione, the boss of the Operation Relentless team, could hardly believe how well things had gone. They had thrown out the bait and Smulian had gone for it big time.

'He bites it off,' Milione would remark later. 'In fact, he eats the whole thing. So, it was very successful.'

That evening Mike treated Smulian to a sumptuous meal. Neither man was much of a drinker, but he made sure to order a fine bottle of wine. There was much to celebrate: a deal to be signed and sealed, the first of many; serious money to be made; plus the option of Smulian becoming the FARC's 'man in Curaçao'.

His earlier call having failed to go through, Smulian sent Bout an email. It gave the Russian his travel itinerary – flying via Amsterdam to Copenhagen. He would arrive 'sometime 14/1/08 or the next day. Meeting here very good, and will explain when I see you.'

Bout responded by firing off an application for a multiple-entry visa for Andrew Michael Smulian.

The Moscow rendezvous was on.

CHAPTER SIXTEEN

ARU, THE CONGO, MAY 2002

The terrorist attacks of 9/11 brought intense scrutiny of Viktor Bout. After the World Trade Centre and Pentagon bombings, all eyes were suddenly upon the world's fleet of aircraft. The scrutiny of cargo lists and passenger manifests increased ten-fold. For Bout, this had unforeseen consequences, because some of the people that he had been dealing with were very much under the global spotlight.

Peter Hain, by then British Minister for Europe, took up the cudgels once more. Intelligence reports that he was privy to convinced Hain that Bout had been supplying the Taliban, and from early on in their meteoric rise to power. In a February 2002 interview with the *Sunday Telegraph*, he accused Bout's business network of 'supplying the Taliban and Al Qaeda'. He concluded it was high time that Bout was 'put out of business'.

At first, as Timur Edikhnov, one of Bout's long-standing bodyguards remarked, Bout wasn't overly worried about such adverse media attention. He wasn't particularly daunted by it. But, 'later he understood that the noose was tightening.'

Following 9/11, the 'leaders of the nations in which we worked began to cut off oxygen to Viktor's businesses,' Edikhnov explained. 'The President of the Central African Republic . . . turned us away. The President of Rwanda told Viktor not to come back. And finally . . . the Emirati authorities closed all companies associated with Bout.'

Little by little, the Russian businessman was starting to feel the heat.

Flint-eyed, intensely private and possessing a dizzyingly complex corporate structure to obfuscate his global web of operations, Bout remained an intriguingly enigmatic figure. He maintained a rigid silence in the media, and used a clutch of aliases when communicating about his worldwide business deals, including Victor Butt, Viktor Bulakin, Vadim Markovich Aminov and Boris.

Of course, discretion and confidentiality were the bedrock of the trade in which he excelled. He shied away from publicity, but in a sense this had proved a double-edged sword. Bout's invisibility only served to fuel curiosity and to grow the legend. Despite his global dealings, no one seemed to possess a recent image of the man, to put a face to the myth. The first photo passed to the press had been a grainy passport one, taken when Bout was in his early twenties.

But in the Congo, all of that was about to change.

For Bout the Congo represented the largest untapped source of natural resources in the whole of Africa. That was why he believed that wars there would be endless, and why he kept being drawn back, like a moth to the candle flame. In early 2002, Belgian journalist Dirk Draulands ran into him there, by chance.

The Russian passed Draulands his business card: 'Viktor Bout, Central African Airways.' Draulands, a veteran Africa hand, knew of the December 2000 UN report identifying Bout as a foremost sanctions-buster: he was intrigued to meet the man in the flesh.

The UN report concluded of Angola: 'Landing heavy cargo planes with illicit cargoes in war conditions and breaking international embargoes . . . takes an internationally organized network of individuals, well funded, well connected and well versed in brokering and logistics . . .' Viktor Bout was the head of the foremost such sanctions-busting operation.

Draulands secured permission for himself, and fellow Belgian Wim Van Cappellen, a photographer, to shadow Bout in the Congo. They would join one of the Congo's new would-be leaders – former rebel commander Jean-Pierre Bemba – as he toured the country, drumming up support for forthcoming elections. Bemba was visiting the north-eastern town of Aru, not so far from where Bout's fleet of aircraft had jetted in weaponry and personnel to the Second Congo War.

Fairly quickly, Draulands realized two things about Bout. One, he loved to be in the field. He preferred to camp in the bush than to stay in a hotel. Two, he could make just about anywhere the headquarters of his global business operations. His routine most mornings was the same: having made any necessary calls on his satellite phone, he would pull out his camera and start filming.

Bout loved to shoot video, and especially in such turbulent climes. He filmed Bemba – who would go on to be sentenced to eighteen years in prison by the International Criminal Court, for war crimes – promising electricity, a hospital and schools to the locals, should they decided to elect him.

Draulands had heard the stories about Bemba's horrific excesses during the Second Congo War: rape, looting and even cannibalism. Bout's relations to Bemba stretched back many years. When Bemba had been commanding his rebel fighters, his chief source of income had been a diamond mine that netted from one to three million dollars every month.

Bout had done business with Bemba, and now he foresaw a bright future in the Congo. With peace, he could build a mobile telecoms business, plus there were mineral riches to be mined and huge agricultural potential. Bout had even suggested setting up a free-trade zone around Aru, which sat at the nexus of three African countries.

Draulands found time to speak with Bout, and asked about the UN's naming him as one of the main sanctions busters in the region.

'I am not an arms trader,' Bout told him. 'It's possible that I have transported arms, but I am a businessman and I have lots of planes and I don't care what I transport because that is not my responsibility.' Bout had been present in every African conflict that Draulands mentioned, but he argued that he was there only in the name of making money.

For the Aru trip, Bout had with him bodyguard Timur Edikhnov. Edikhnov was fiercely protective of his boss. When he suspected that Wim Van Cappellen, Drauland's photographer colleague, was trying to sneak a surreptitious shot of Bout, he pulled out a bowie knife and made a slicing gesture across his throat.

But Cappellen – a veteran photojournalist – wasn't so easily intimidated. He realized that by fitting his widest-angle lens, he could maybe capture Bout in frame without Edikhnov realizing. If he aimed at a group of soldiers escorting Bemba, he might sneak Bout into the corner of the shot. Before long, Cappellen had captured half a dozen photos of Bout at work in the African bush.

Edikhnov was no fool, and he suspected what Cappellen was up to. He spoke to Bout and asked if he should confiscate the film. He felt it was 'bad taste' to take photos of someone secretly. But Bout told Edikhnov that he wasn't hiding, and that he didn't want his bodyguard to intervene or to worry.

Capturing Bout in action in Africa would play a key role in outing him, and upping his worldwide profile. 'The end was near, that was clear the moment the pictures were taken,' Draulands remarked.

Those images hit the international press, as did the story: 'Arms dealer Viktor Bout wanted in Africa.' In May 2002, the US public broadcaster PBS picked up the thread, screening a Frontline/World special, accompanied by a 'Gallery of International Arms Dealers'. Bout had the number one slot: 'Victor Anatoliyevich Bout: The Embargo Buster fuelling Bloody Civil Wars.'

The photo that illustrated the report showed Bout, sporting baseball cap and shades, and wearing a white polo shirt and slacks, standing next to a group of Congolese soldiers, with a nineteen-seventies-vintage Antonov 24 looming in the background.

The PBS Frontline news story, entitled 'Gunrunners', didn't pull any punches. 'Victor Bout is the poster boy for a new generation of Cold War international arms dealers who play a critical role in areas where the weapons trade has been embargoed by the United Nations. Now, as Frontline/World reports in "Gunrunners", unprecedented UN investigations have begun to unravel the mystery of these broken embargoes . . .

'At the heart of this unfolding detective story is the identification of a group of East European arms merchants, with Victor Bout the first to be publicly and prominently identified. The UN investigative team pursued leads that a Mr Bout was pouring small arms and ammunition into Angola, Rwanda, Sierra Leone and the Congo, making possible massacres on a scale that stunned the world.'

The 'Gunrunners' report cited Western officials claiming that Bout operated 'the largest arms trafficking network in the world'. The story went on to outline Bout's links to Afghanistan, citing sources that claimed Bout's arms shipments had found their way into the hands of Al Qaeda. Bout had made $50 million from the renegade Afghan militia, who had harboured Osama Bin Laden as he plotted the 9/11 terror attacks.

Those close to Bout found his newfound notoriety preposterous; laughable even. 'The first time I heard Viktor Bout called "The Merchant of Death" I thought the British Minister wasn't right in the head,' commented Sergei Bout, Viktor Bout's older brother and sometime partner in his global business affairs.

In defence of his brother, Sergei Bout cited the example of a taxi driver asking his passenger what was in his suitcase. 'It is not my bloody business what my customer has in his trunk. I am a taxi driver. I am a carrier. I don't know what I carry. Maybe I carry a nuclear bomb. No one is informing me about it.'

Of course, the counter argument was obvious: if a taxi driver sees a passenger load crates of weaponry into his trunk and is then ordered to drive across the border, he will very likely refuse the fare.

'The bogeyman was created,' bodyguard Edikhnov remarked, of the media portrayal of Bout. 'I heard so many expert opinions I almost died laughing. But the public isn't familiar with this industry and interprets smart talk as truth. But not all smart talk is truth. Viktor did not support the Taliban. He worked with

Massoud. So allegations of ties with the Taliban or Al Qaeda are absurd.'

Or, perhaps more credibly, as Brian Johnson-Thomas, a former UN arms investigator, put it: 'Viktor Bout is not *the* Merchant of Death. He is a merchant of some death, because on occasion his aircraft willingly carried guns for people who will use them to commit human rights abuses.'

Whatever the truth, US agencies rapidly moved Bout up their target list. By the summer of 2002, he ranked second only to Osama Bin Laden and his deputies on their list of most-wanted.

Even prior to 9/11, Bout had been hit by UN Security Council travel bans, along with Liberia's President Charles Taylor. It was Bout's role in Liberia – and by extension Sierra Leone – that had drawn such censure. The UN ban empowered any nation to stop Bout or Taylor, if they tried to enter their country. That was the theory. In practice, few governments ever took action and Bout continued to move around on business more or less at will.

But post-9/11 the travel restrictions would became onerous.

In the spring of 2002 a warrant was issued for Bout's arrest, by INTERPOL, the global policing organization. The INTERPOL 'Red Notice' was at the behest of the Belgian government. It charged Bout with laundering $32.5 million between 1994 and 2001, via a network of Belgian corporations.

When the authorities enquired of Moscow if Bout was in Russia, the Russian Foreign Ministry responded that he was not. But as it happened, at that very moment Bout was giving his first ever media interview at a downtown Moscow radio station. It made the Foreign Ministry's denial appear a little precipitate. The next day Russian officials admitted that Bout might be in the country, but they argued that they had seen no evidence of any crimes being committed, so were unable to act on the INTERPOL warrant.

By now, Bout had decided that silence was no longer an option. He realized he faced two choices: ignore the situation or fight back. He chose to do the latter. He broke cover to grant that interview to Echo Radio Moskvy, one of Moscow's most popular stations, guaranteeing him a considerable audience.

'One way to introduce our studio guest is "Viktor Bout, Russian Entrepreneur",' the Echo Radio interviewer announced. 'Or, as they say in the West, the biggest arms supplier to Al Qaeda and Osama Bin Laden.'

Typically, Bout, seated opposite the reporter in the studio, had his video camera running, keeping a filmed record of the interview. 'They also say I have twelve last names and fifteen passports and that I am hiding,' he told the reporter. 'I have never been in hiding. I have only ever had Russian citizenship.'

'The *LA Times* cites the National Security Council and calls your company "the world's largest illegal arms dealer",' the interviewer pointed out. 'Can there be smoke without fire?'

'When a customer leases an aircraft by the hour, the customer controls the plane's cargo, not the plane's owner.'

'Viktor, why were you singled out?' the interviewer probed.

'Maybe it was chance,' Bout declared. 'Maybe because we worked in certain parts of Africa and some people didn't like this work. They've made me into a scapegoat . . . They yell: "There goes the evil Viktor Bout! He has ties to every bad guy on the planet!" When it comes to Russia . . . they always attach the same labels: "Russian", followed by "mafia".'

Bout hunched his shoulders and swayed, bearlike, in his chair, spreading his arms wide. 'I should walk around smelling of Vodka and garlic – the Russian bear scaring the West. Be afraid!'

Everyone in the studio laughed.

When not playing the fool during the interview, Bout portrayed himself as the prey hunted by ravenous Western agencies. He likened them to a 'cowboy who rides around the African jungle, through prairies and deserts in Afghanistan . . . And every day I am amazed at this plot, like a thriller. What else will they come up with? Which terrorist organization have I not helped?'

He ended the interview seeming to throw out a challenge. 'They cannot catch Bin Laden. Naturally, they come up with another idea: here is Viktor Bout. Let's catch him.'

'Viktor did not feel guilty about anything,' bodyguard Edikhnov pointed out. 'He received gold statues from the Sheikhs of Sharjah for the development of the airport and the infrastructure. He saw himself as a legitimate businessman. He naively believed no one could spin a story around him.'

After that Echo Radio interview, Bout appeared to develop a taste for being in the limelight. It was as if the floodgates had been opened. Perhaps he had begun to believe his own myth; maybe he truly thought he was innocent of any wrongdoing. Either way, the message embodied in his interview acted like a red rag to a bull. *They cannot catch Bin Laden . . . Here is Viktor Bout. Let's catch him.*

He put himself bang in the sights.

CHAPTER SEVENTEEN

MOSCOW, RUSSIA, JANUARY 2008

The Russian immigration officer scrutinized Smulian's passport. 'Why you come to Russia?'

'Oh, you know, I've always wanted to visit Red Square.'

The official ran a sceptical eye over the figure standing before him, taking in his threadbare get-up and holey deck-shoes. Since leaving Curaçao, Smulian had yet to have an opportunity to refresh his wardrobe. Smulian wasn't quite geared up for Moscow in midwinter.

'Why you dress like this?'

'Um, I was visiting the Caribbean. I left in a bit of a hurry.'

The immigration officer shrugged. 'You will freeze to death, my friend.' With that he handed back Smulian's passport and wished him a warm welcome to Russia.

From Curaçao, Mike and Smulian had flown to Copenhagen and checked into the Best Western City Hotel. For Mike, it had been odd being back in the place where it had all in a sense begun, when he'd first met the agents from the DEA. But there had been little time for reflection.

Getting Smulian to Moscow had proved more difficult than they'd first imagined. There had been endless wrangles about his visa, which had forced him to fly to London and make an application from there. But finally he'd reached Moscow's Sheremetyevo International Airport, and a familiar figure was waiting for him at arrivals.

Viktor Bout was in the company of an imposing-looking individual – his bodyguard-cum-business associate, Mikhail 'Misha' Belozerosky. Both men seemed aghast at Smulian's get-up. Outside, it was minus 9 degrees centigrade. The immigration official had been right: Smulian would freeze to death on the bitter streets of Moscow.

'How can you come here like that?' Bout demanded, incredulously.

They bundled Smulian into Bout's black Mercedes and headed to a city-centre shopping mall. There, the Russian businessman treated his English friend – Babu; grandfather – to a smart new set of clothes, plus a thick overcoat. With Smulian thus attired, they headed for Red Square to grab a souvenir snap.

That photo – taken by Belozerosky – showed the two friends standing side by side, hands thrust deep into the pockets of their overcoats, with the centuries-old fairytale twisted spires of Saint Basil's Cathedral on one side, and the stark, angular mass of the Kremlin on the other.

Smulian's white-grey hair looked a little ruffled, and his moustache was still definitely pointing in the wrong direction for making deals with leftists like the FARC. Bout's, for that matter, was also turned down. But the tall Russian – dressed in a long brown overcoat, over a beige-striped woolly jumper – seemed happy to be reunited with his old friend.

In the background the clock on the Kremlin's tower showed two-twenty-seven in the afternoon. Bout and Smulian headed to a downtown café for a late lunch, after which Bout dropped Smulian at a nearby hotel. Over the past week Smulian had flown halfway around the world, from Tanzania to Curaçao, and halfway back again to Moscow, via a short detour to London.

It had been an exhausting merry-go-round.

Before getting some rest, Smulian took a quick snap from his hotel balcony, just as he had done upon arrival at the Curaçao Hilton. It was a very different scene that his camera captured now. The view was dominated by massive high-rise apartment blocks: slab-sided and bare, they were surrounded by ranks of grey leafless trees. The Moscow streets were clogged with snow, and the cars below his window were iced-in and immobile.

Bout and Smulian had agreed to talk business the following morning, but over lunch Smulian had revealed to Bout the identity of the 'clients' he'd met in Curaçao. That evening, while Smulian rested, Viktor Bout created a new file on his laptop. It was entitled simply 'Colombia'. He surfed the internet, beginning his research on the FARC.

Early the following morning Bout spent another thirty minutes checking on-line references to the Colombian terrorist outfit, before heading out to fetch Smulian. They drove to his home in Golitsyno, a town just to the west of Moscow, so they could talk in private.

After a brief family catch-up, Bout took Smulian into his study. It was cluttered with keepsakes from his global travels: statuettes of African deities, books on mysticism, model airplanes, plus souvenirs from an alligator farm in Asia. Bout was well-read, with eclectic tastes, and heavy bookshelves lined the walls. Indeed, a love of reading was something that the two men had in common.

Somewhat incongruously, on one shelf sat the DVD *Lord of War* – the 2005 Hollywood movie supposedly 'inspired' by Bout's life story. It starred Nicolas Cage playing a fictional Russian-American character, Yuri Orlov, the eldest son of Ukrainian refugees now turned amoral gunrunner.

In the ultimate irony, the makers of the film had actually hired one of Bout's aircraft to shoot some of the key scenes. 'The crew said that the plane ran real guns into the Congo the week before we were using it to film fake guns,' the film's director, Andrew Niccol admitted, when pressed on the subject by reporters. 'That plane has since crashed, running something described as suspicious cargo out of Uganda.'

Bout hadn't rated the film at all. 'It's cynical. Too bad for Cage though,' he remarked. 'He deserved a better screenplay.'

Adjacent to the *Lord of War* DVD sat a shoebox and some carrier bags stuffed full of video tapes: Bout's home movies, shot all over the world and covering two decades of his life in the airfreight business. As Bout's wife, Alla, brought in tea, and the snow fell softly outside, the two men began to talk.

Smulian related his meetings in Curaçao, first with Carlos, the moneyman, and then El Comandante, who represented the military side of the FARC. Bout's initial response wasn't encouraging: he warned Smulian that he didn't tend to do business with anyone who dealt in drugs.

Smulian had some work to do if the Curaçao negotiations were to bear fruit. He argued that narcotics were a necessary evil for the FARC: theirs was still an ideological struggle. As Carlos and El Comandante had explained, they were a left-leaning group fighting for their very survival. The Colombian government, their

US military backers and the right-wing paramilitaries were all waging war against them in the jungle.

Smulian argued that at the very least the FARC deserved a fighting chance. It had to be worth exploring some more, and especially the FARC's ideology. Then he began to itemize the weaponry that Carlos and Ricardo had told him they were seeking – starting with the humble AK-47 assault rifle, and concluding with the man-portable Strelas or Igla surface-to-air missiles (SAMs).

'Is Peter Mirchev still in the business?' he ventured, referring to the Bulgarian arms dealer that Bout had introduced him to in 1997.

By way of answer Bout picked up his phone and dialled a number. There followed a conversation in Russian, very little of which Smulian understood. Bout asked whoever he was speaking to how many 'sewing devices' he had available – 'igla' being the Russian word for needle. The speaker said he knew of one hundred that were good-to-go in the Ukraine.

Bout turned to Smulian and remarked: 'A hundred pieces available immediately.'

That, Smulian presumed, had to mean one hundred Iglas ready to be shipped to his Central American clients, in return for a suitcase or two crammed full of dollars.

'So, was that Peter Mirchev?' Smulian pressed, once Bout was done with the call.

Bout didn't answer the question. Instead, he began to wax lyrical about the specifications of the newest model Igla, which had a launcher tube that could be used repeatedly, as opposed to being just a one-use system. They went on to discuss other weaponry that El Comandante had ordered, before Bout mentioned that the cost of running tonnes of ammunition into Central America would be prohibitively expensive. The FARC should establish a manufacturing facility on the ground, he explained. He also confirmed that he could provide training teams to instruct the FARC in fighting in the jungle.

'The FARC told me their radio comms are monitored,' Smulian remarked. 'So they use couriers to carry messages. Is there some satellite system or advance radio comms system which they could use?'

Bout suggested there was a Russian satellite communications system that would be immune to intercept by the Americans. Smulian brought up the issue of End User Certificates (EUCs). Carlos had told him the FARC might have a problem securing usable EUCs. Bout's response was that anything was possible, as long as they had money.

Smulian remembered a comment that Carlos had made in Curaçao. He'd pointed out that the jungle in Colombia was so thick and impenetrable that it was impossible to use tanks or armoured cars. That was why the Colombian military – and the Americans – went everywhere by Black Hawk, and used Apache gunships as their 'flying tanks'.

He mentioned as much to Bout, whose response was that Russian helicopters were superior and those he could also supply. He mentioned that if the FARC were genuine in their political aspirations then it might be possible to provide covert 'political assistance' from the Russian government as well.

Bout pointed out that he had two aircraft sitting in the Congo, which he could sell to the FARC. They could para-drop weaponry into the jungle. The arms would be packed onto pallets and slung beneath giant cargo parachutes, enabling his aircrew to deliver them to a drop-zone with pinpoint accuracy.

He'd used a similar means to deliver arms to Savimbi and his UNITA rebels in Angola, so it was a tried-and-tested system. The arms deal should be priced separately from the costs of delivery: including aircraft and flight crew that alone would amount to some five million dollars.

But Bout sounded a note of caution. There was something of a glut in the arms market. Even if they went ahead and did the deal, they might not make their fortunes. In short, they shouldn't abandon their East African business ventures. For example, Bout was interested in importing cashew nuts from Tanzania, as a new moneymaking concern.

They'd been talking for approaching two hours, and Smulian decided it was time to drive the key point home, the one that had so impressed him during his time in Curaçao: the clients had cash to burn. This was an ongoing business relationship and money was no object. The FARC were also desperate enough to pay whatever price was asked to get their hands on sophisticated weaponry.

Moreover, it was more than simply arms alone that the FARC were after: they also had huge sums of cash they needed laundering. Container loads were sitting in Spain – the proceeds from drugs sales across Europe – all of which needed to be cleaned.

This aspect, Bout told him, could be easily addressed. With their help, the FARC could buy up an Eastern European bank. Once they owned their own bank, they could launder their money to their heart's content. Smulian asked what cut they should charge, if they were to help furnish such 'financial services'. Bout told

Smulian that it would cost the FARC forty per cent, at least in the short term.

Smulian's argument about mountains of cash burning a hole in the FARC's pocket seemed to be the clincher. The two friends ended the meeting agreeing that they should scope out the next stage. Bout asked Smulian to propose Montenegro – formerly part of the Socialist Federal Republic of Yugoslavia; now an independent country – as the ideal place for him to meet the clients.

Over a map of Montenegro, Bout sketched out a plan. Smulian and Carlos should head for Sveti Stefan – Saint Stefan in English – a five star resort set on Montenegro's stunning Adriatic coast. A playground for the rich and famous, it would be the perfect spot for the FARC's moneyman to await the forthcoming rendezvous in privacy and luxury.

Bout would catch a flight to Podgorica, Montenegro's capital. The three of them would meet up and head for the nearby town of Budva, where they'd rendezvous with Bout's people at a well-known seafood restaurant. There, he had excellent contacts to facilitate all that Carlos and his people might need.

Bout handed Smulian the map, to give to his 'FARC' people. He and Smulian would meet again the following day, to go over things in more detail. In the meantime, Bout warned, they should adopt basic security precautions. They should switch phones and SIM cards, if they were to speak about the proposed deal by telephone, and Smulian should discard all receipts from his Russian visit.

That evening Smulian put a call through to Snow to let him know that all was going well. A meeting should be on the cards soon, to seal the deal. Snow in turn told Smulian that Carlos had just flown in to Copenhagen, in case the meeting with Bout was on. They were ready to move at short notice, and he urged Smulian to push for a deal in Moscow.

DEA Agent Brown had also flown into the Danish capital. Agent Zach would follow on shortly, with Ricardo Jardeno, should the deal with Bout look like it was happening. As they had in Curaçao, the DEA team would stay in a hotel adjacent to the one where Snow et al were billeted.

But with Smulian away in Moscow negotiating directly with Viktor Bout, the DEA team sniffed trouble. Smulian would be pivotal to any successful prosecution, they reasoned, yet they had nothing on him; no way of compelling him to testify. With his immunity guaranteed – at Snow's behest – Smulian could simply walk away at the end of it all.

Wim and Zach explained to Carlos that they really needed Smulian to take the stand. If he faced gaol for trading SAMs to a terrorist group like the FARC – which carries a twenty-five-year mandatory sentence – he could be forced to cut a deal. He could be offered the promise of a reduced sentence in return for giving evidence against Bout.

But for that to happen they'd need to persuade Snow to drop his demand that Smulian be granted immunity, and neither agent could see a way to sway a stubborn beast like The Bear.

'Let me get this straight,' Carlos told them. 'If Smulian testifies, that means I have less to do in court, right?'

'Right,' the agents confirmed.

'How important is this?' Carlos pressed.

'It's crucial. Critical.'

'We need Smulian to testify. We need him in the dock.'

Carlos pondered this for a moment. The one part of being a confidential source that he hated was being grilled in court. In spite of having worked on over a hundred cases, he'd only ever had to give evidence three times. That was testimony to the power of the evidence that he gathered, which left most of those charged no option but to cut some kind of a plea-bargain.

There was another huge disadvantage to appearing in court: each time your real identity – name, biographical details, likeness – became more widely known. Court sketches were published in papers and shown on TV. In the Monzer Al Kazar case, his real name had made it into the evidence, and it had been quoted in the media. There were only so many times that could happen before your value as a confidential source became exhausted and you were too well known to pose as a genuine bad guy.

If you didn't know when to sensibly call a halt, you might go into a deep undercover role and get recognized. And the conse-quences of that could prove terminal. Make no mistake: keeping out of the courts was a key priority to Carlos, the King of Sting.

'Okay, leave it with me,' Carlos told the DEA agents. 'Give me a couple of days. I'll work on Snow.'

The Best Western Hotel was situated in Copenhagen's trendy docklands area. That evening Carlos took Mike to a local bar, one that overlooked the Nyhavn dock, which was chock-full of tall-masted Danish barges. To soften Mike up, Carlos shared with him some of his life story. He related how he'd gone from the son of a well-to-do Guatemalan doctor to drugs trafficker, to DEA undercover source. The pivotal moment had been when Carlos had been kidnapped by the Mexican police and his family had been threatened.

Mike had a wife and son. He could understand where Carlos was coming from.

Carlos explained that he had approached the high-ups in

Guatemala's Anti-Narcotics Squad – the Servicio de Analisis e Informacion Antinarcoticos; SAIA – with a proposal: he needed to move drugs from Colombia, through Guatemala and on to the USA. He needed help getting the shipping containers moving, in return for a handsome pay-off. The two top SAIA guys said they were on for the deal.

Next Carlos went to one of the chiefs of security at the Guatemalan ports. He told the guy he needed free passage for his containers of drugs. The fee for such 'protection services' was $1,000 per kilo of cocaine, Carlos was told. 'But please, once in a while let a small amount be captured,' the guy said. 'It looks good for our bosses and with the Americans.'

Carlos had got the first drugs shipments moving, and the first cash payments into the hands of the targets. The DEA decided they needed a ruse to lure them to the USA, so they could be put on trial. They acted as if there was an all-expenses-paid security course being run in Washington, and the targets were invited to attend.

The three big cheeses that the DEA were after duly flew to Miami, en route to the Washington 'security course'. Instead, a SWAT team descended upon their hotel and kicked in the doors to their rooms.

When the SWAT team seized the first SAIA guy, he started laughing. 'Oh yeah, cool! This is all part of the training, right? How to do a proper arrest?'

He stopped laughing once the SWAT guys shoved him onto the floor and slapped on the handcuffs.

After busting the three targets, Carlos and his DEA handlers had moved up the food chain. Above the targets were corrupt politicians, whose influence reached high into the Guatemalan government. But it was then that the US Embassy had stepped into the fray, halting any further action, claiming that Carlos's actions threatened to cause a serious diplomatic incident.

The moral of the story, Carlos explained, was that you never knew just who you could trust, which brought him around to the real purpose of tonight's little tête-à-tête.

'You know, Papa Bear, Smulian – I tell you something, he's not your friend. Not really your friend like you think he's your friend.'

Mike scowled. 'Fuck off. Andrew would never do anything against me.'

'You just wait and see.' Carlos paused, taking an apparently thoughtful swig of his beer. 'How about this: I show you. I show you he's not really your friend. But if I show you and you see what I'm saying is true, you gotta do something, okay?'

Mike shrugged. 'Yeah, okay. But it'll never happen.'

'We wait for him to come back from Moscow. I need one evening alone with him. Then I prove to you.'

'You got it.' Mike eyed Carlos, shrewdly. 'But you know something? Andrew keeps telling me that *you're* going to trick me.'

Sagstume chuckled. 'I tell you why. He's jealous of you. You're the big guy in the FARC. He's thinking: I've known Mike all these years, and never knew he was the big man in the FARC. How can he have kept a secret like that from me all these years.'

Mike didn't say anything.

'Like I say, he's jealous of you. Maybe he think he has more fuck of the dog than you. I need only a little time alone with him and I prove it to you.'

In Copenhagen, Mike had just agreed to Andrew Smulian facing a double-sting. He didn't know why exactly Carlos was gunning for him, but he had an uneasy sense that it wasn't going to end well. Meanwhile, in Moscow Smulian was facing other problems, as Viktor Bout began checking out their end of the deal.

It was midday on 21 January, and Bout had taken Smulian to his Moscow offices. Down a long corridor lined with military paintings and pictures of aircraft, they turned right into Bout's domain. There, the Russian proceeded to pull up photograph after photograph of the FARC's top commanders and political leaders.

Bout was logged onto the website farc.narod.ru, visiting the 'who's who?' page. He proceeded to scroll through the FARC gallery, repeatedly checking with Smulian if he recognized Carlos or El Comandante. It was reasonable enough to ask such questions. If Smulian's people were genuine, why wouldn't they be up there among the great and the good of FARC?

As Smulian gazed at the images, he realized he couldn't recognize either of the men. In fact Carlos and El Comandante had offered him no bona fides: no photographs of themselves with the FARC, or paper proof that they belonged to such a group. In fact he had nothing to go on, other than their word, plus the personal introduction from Mike Snow.

A seed of doubt had been planted in Smulian's mind.

Bout's research over the last twenty-four hours had been impressive. He told Smulian that the FARC had between nine and twelve thousand men and women under arms, a considerable fighting force. If Carlos and El Comandante *were* genuine FARC, their needs would be great. They'd require up to one hundred tonnes of weaponry, by Bout's calculations.

That represented a very significant arms deal, but only if these people were who they said they were. But if Carlos and El Comandante weren't FARC, then who were they?

Only two options made any sense. One: they were common-or-garden drugs traffickers, somehow posing as the FARC in an effort to impress. Or two, they were Western – British? Belgian? American? – agents, posing as the FARC to lure Bout into some kind of a trap. It was up to Smulian to prove which.

Smulian left Moscow feeling both closer to the deal, yet further from it than he'd ever been before.

CHAPTER EIGHTEEN

MOSCOW, RUSSIA, SPRING 2003

All the time that Bout was allegedly the world's most prolific and secretive arms dealer, he continued to shoot his home movies. Much of what he filmed documented his adventures, and misadventures, across far-flung regions of the world. Aircraft deliveries to conflict-torn capitals. Cargo deliveries to remote dirt airstrips. Camping out in war zones under the stars.

But there was also stuff much closer to home. One scene showed Bout rolling naked in the Russian snows, after a trip to a sauna. Another had him expounding on his 'theory of entropy' – the inevitable reversion to all-encompassing chaos being the ultimate law of the universe – as he and his beefy cohorts prepared traditional Russian *pelmeni* dumplings for dinner.

Bout had a self-declared aspiration to be a documentary filmmaker. He claimed a love of the environment and wildlife and he was fond of portraying himself as an accidental anthropologist – someone uniquely at home with Africa's myriad tribes. As his camera kept rolling, he seemed peculiarly oblivious to his growing notoriety, even as the walls were closing in.

What, if anything, seemed to define him was an unshakeable belief in his own invulnerability. His invincibility. It was almost as if he couldn't believe this was happening to him. He was hugely worldly-wise and business savvy, yet at the same time apparently incredibly naive. At one point he even applied for a tourist visa to visit the US. Needless to say, he wasn't granted one.

Bout's reaction to the lack of welcome extended to him by the United States – he stalked around the entire day in a sullen rage – had everyone mystified. What had he expected, his friends demanded? What the hell had he thought would happen, if he'd actually been granted entry to the USA? *Was he out of his mind?*

Bout's belief that he could, even now, cleanse his image – that he could prevent the dam of investigative reports and media exposure from bursting – was epitomized by a spring 2003 meeting held in an upscale Moscow hotel. After much toing-and-froing, he had finally agreed to give his first major interview to a foreign newspaper. It wasn't any old rag, either. He'd agreed to sit for a photo shoot with the *New York Times* Magazine.

It had taken journalist Peter Landesman – a veteran investigative reporter and specialist on international trafficking – many months and much chasing to secure the scoop. Even before Bout arrived at Moscow's Renaissance Hotel, Landesman had been warned. If he probed too deeply, one of Bout's people told him: 'They'll put you on your knees before they execute you.'

With Bout's arrival, the interview began with a surreal combination of the bizarrely humorous mixed with veiled threats. By way of introduction, Bout opened his blazer before Landesman. 'I don't see any guns,' he declared. His brother, Sergei, accompanied him. He also raised his arms: 'None here, either.'

'Maybe I should start an arms-trafficking university,' Bout quipped, 'and teach a course on UN sanctions-busting.' He and Sergei laughed.

Bout placed a thick folder of documents in Landesman's lap. 'I woke up after September 11 and found I was second only to Osama.' He patted the folder of papers. The truth, Bout explained darkly, was much bigger than his personal story alone. 'My clients, the governments . . . I keep my mouth shut.'

Later, he pointed to the middle of his forehead. 'If I told you everything I'd get the red hole right here.'

In his *New York Times* article, Landesman reprised Bout's mercurial past – evading reporters, UN investigators, plus arms-trade watchdogs such as Human Rights Watch. His one previous interview with an international news outlet – CNN, in 2002 – had ended prematurely, when Bout had walked out.

'The longer Bout has remained out of the reach of international law, the bigger his legend has grown,' Landesman wrote. 'In many ways, he is now the public face of a giant international criminal structure.'

Bout revealed to Landesman that recently he'd seized upon the chance to reinvent himself. He talked expansively about his aspirations. 'In the middle of nowhere, you feel alive, you feel part of nature,' he explained. 'What I really want to do now is to take one of my helicopters to the Russian Arctic North and make wildlife films for National Geographic and Discovery Channel.'

Bout seemed oblivious to the fact that it was very likely a little late for all of that.

Refusing to be blindsided, Landesman challenged Bout over his weapons flights to Liberia – the ones that had first brought his activities to the attention of the British, and to the desks of numerous US agencies. Bout denied that such shipments had ever happened. 'How do you think a plane can fly to Liberia, which is under UN embargo, without being tracked?' he protested.

By way of answer, Landesman placed before Bout documents obtained from intelligence sources in Europe, indicating that his companies had flown two Russian Mi-8Ts helicopters to the West African country of Ivory Coast.

In truth, that was just the cover destination. In reality, the Mi-8Ts had been destined for Liberia, along with four missile launchers and three bomb launchers. The price paid for the helicopters and weapons hardware was $1.9 million, plus $90,000 for the spare parts needed to keep them airborne.

Bout glanced over the documents coolly, trying to declare them a forgery. But gradually, the façade was starting to crack. Finally, he admitted that he had delivered weapons shipments. The question was, what was wrong with doing so?

'Illegal weapons? What does that mean?' he challenged. 'If rebels control an airport and a city, and they give you clearance to land, what's illegal about that ... Look, killing isn't about weapons. It's about the humans who use them.'

Bout's attempt to reinvent himself had just hit the wall. 'His wit and his insider's perspective on international geopolitics suddenly coalesced into the cynical visage of a drug dealer peddling crack in a schoolyard,' Landesman wrote. 'He was just a businessman selling his wares. Who was he to be the arbiter of good and evil?'

On their final night together in Moscow, Bout drove Landesman to a restaurant on the city limits that specialized in wild game. Bout seemed relaxed. He acted as if his and Landesman's discussions of his life and work had exonerated him, somehow. Set the record straight. But as far as Landesman was concerned, they 'had done neither, of course'.

After dinner, Bout drove the reporter down a dirt track into some woodland. They stopped at a walled compound. It turned out to be an exclusive private members club, and they were here to enjoy a *banya* – a traditional Russian sauna. They stripped, got pounded by a male masseur brandishing eucalyptus leaves, slipped into an ice-cold dunking pool, then lounged in the sweltering heat, with only towels draped over their private parts.

'Bout seemed the personification not of the world's inability to stop him,' Landesman concluded, 'but of its reluctance . . . If he was indeed the public face of arms trafficking and if he couldn't be caught, or stopped, what, I wondered, does this say about the . . . huge profits at stake for individuals and government alike?'

Landesman's *New York Times* article was published in August 2003. A photo of Bout filled the magazine's front cover, under the title 'Meeting Mr. Bout'. 'By most accounts the world's largest arms trafficker, Victor Bout is also a fugitive from justice,' the cover copy declared. 'So how does it happen that he's living in plain sight in Moscow?'

The glossy, professionally lit image had Bout posing in a tailored beige business suit and matching silk tie, looking more like Tony Soprano with a Cossack-style moustache, than any would-be environmental filmmaker. He sat sideways on to the photographer, jacket buttoned tight, his chin resting on one hand.

Comfortable, defiant, gazing directly into the camera, the look in the hooded grey-blue eyes seemed arrogant. Flinty. Dispassionate. Cold even. This was the image of a powerful man; a man secure in his invulnerability; a man of means, whose reach engirdled the world.

Finally, the man behind the myth had been given a face. Whether it was a fair representation or not was something of a moot point. There was no going back now.

As Sergei Bout would complain: 'They essentially created that pose. The one the photographer needed.' After the photoshoot, he'd said to his younger brother of the photographer: 'He totally used you. Didn't you realize that?'

Either way, Bout's strategy of going on a media offensive had backfired. The *New York Times* article was published under the title: 'Arms and the Man'. The powerful introduction sealed Bout's image, if not his fate: 'In Liberia and Congo, Afghanistan and Rwanda, bloody conflicts are more and more often fuelled by arms transported through vast shadowy networks run by traffickers like the notorious, mysterious and unstoppable Victor Bout.'

Notorious ... mysterious ... unstoppable: for the Western agencies tracking him, this was the proverbial red rag to the bull.

CHAPTER NINETEEN

COPENHAGEN, DENMARK, JANUARY 2008

La Sirene was a lucky discovery, as far as Mike Snow was concerned. A quaint and quirky Italian restaurant, tucked away in Copenhagen's harbour area, it had a fine ambience, plus the portions of lasagne al forno were to die for. But tonight, the atmosphere between the three would-be friends – Mike, Carlos and Smulian – appeared somewhat strained.

They'd rendezvoused earlier that afternoon, in Smulian's room in the Best Western, with Smulian fresh back from Moscow. It was then that the trouble had started. Smulian had waded right in, making it clear that he needed reassurances from Carlos that he and El Comandante were genuinely from the FARC.

He'd confirmed that Bout was willing to play ball, but only on one condition: 'What I must be sure of is that you are who you say you are.'

If Carlos and El Comandante did indeed represent the FARC, then the help from Bout and his people would be all the greater, Smulian had stressed. If the FARC were determined to rule Colombia with a leftist regime, then Russia could offer very real support.

'It means they will help you politically,' Smulian had explained. But first he needed Carlos to prove his bone fides.

'Well, what can I say?' the King of Sting had demurred. He gestured at Snow. 'You guys know each other for I don't know how many years . . . And he knows me.' Snow's connections with the FARC should give Smulian comfort that they were for real.

'The only thing is . . .' Carlos continued, as if mulling an idea for the first time. 'If you wanna go to the middle of the jungle . . . I can take you over there, no problem.'

Smulian shifted about uneasily. Going to check out FARC's operations in deepest darkest Colombia wasn't really his kind of thing. In any case, taking him to the Colombian jungle wouldn't help as the suspicion hailed directly from Bout.

'He's a little bit afraid that it might be a . . . a trap . . .' Mike tried to explain, as if attempting to be helpful.

'Yeah, naturally,' Smulian agreed. 'In his position . . .' He left the rest unsaid: in Viktor Bout's position you couldn't be too careful.

Carlos furrowed his brow. It was time to push back; play the reverse psychology card. Turn the tables. 'This is . . . what I don't understand,' he objected. 'Because . . . I don't know who the hell he is! And we are scared too . . .'

Smulian hadn't quite been expecting that.

'Because you say he cannot get out from . . . Russia.' Carlos was pushing harder now. 'And we are sure thinking – why he cannot get out from Russia? . . . so we don't know who he is.'

'Yeah . . .' Smulian conceded. There was suspicion on both sides.

'Because you know . . . it's very dangerous for us . . . to talk to the wrong person.'

'Yeah.' Smulian was on the back foot now. He began to talk about who Bout was, and why he had trouble leaving his homeland. 'But I've known him for a long time . . . He's restricted, but he has total protection of the boss.'

'The boss in Russia,' Mike added.

'In Russia,' Smulian confirmed.

'Yeah, but . . . How we know that it's real?' Carlos pressed. One last push, just to back Smulian into a corner.

'No . . . The guy is the real guy,' Mike interjected.

Carlos had Smulian in full retreat now, and he went in for the kill. He explained how the FARC's struggle had propelled them into the limelight, especially as they were fighting against the 'gringos'. You make war against the Americans, he explained, you make headlines all over the world.

Smulian nodded, sympathetically. 'He doesn't like gringos. Let me tell you, to the maximum.' Viktor Bout shared the FARC's antipathy towards Americans.

Carlos complained that the world's media were scrutinizing the FARC's every move. 'It's because maybe we use . . . a lot of drugs to fund . . .'

'Generate funds. Yeah,' Smulian said.

Perfect, Carlos told himself. It was great to capture on tape that Smulian knew the FARC's money came from drugs.

Smulian reiterated that he had no problem with Carlos or his FARC bona fides, or how they earned their money. Bout had left it up to him to make the call: if he was happy, Bout would be happy. Smulian moved on to Bout's proposition as to how the FARC should buy a Russian bank to launder their cash, the rake-off from which would be forty per cent.

Carlos laughed, dismissively. 'Normally, it's fifteen per cent that we pay . . . But forty per cent – never. Never. Never and never.'

It was Smulian's turn to laugh. 'Yeah, I know. Even I know that's stupid . . . But, um, it's for you to discuss with him. You know, I don't want to be in between.'

Smulian suggested they should move to the rendezvous with Bout in Montenegro, at the Sveti Stefan resort. He pulled out the map that Bout had given him. He explained that Bout had protection in Montenegro, which was why he had no problem going there. And he repeated what Bout had told him about the readiness of the shipment of Igla surface-to-air missiles.

'They've got one hundred pieces available immediately.'

Carlos glanced up from the map. 'Wow! Okay.'

'They will provide you with a team of twelve guys . . . even some speaking Spanish . . . who can train, everything.'

Carlos began to act excited now. He stressed to Smulian the need to sit down with Bout and talk, after which they needed to get the cash to wherever Bout was, to seal the deal. Plus they'd need some form of guarantee that having handed over the money, the arms would be delivered.

Smulian's response was to offer himself as security. He and Bout had discussed how he could remain with the FARC, as a kind of human guarantee. 'I can guarantee you,' Smulian explained. 'You can . . . keep me there with you until it's done.'

Smulian went on to outline Bout's plan to airdrop the weaponry into the Colombian jungle. 'See, they can put, uh, forty tonnes into a football field, on the dot.'

As Carlos knew well, a large cargo airliner fitted with internal fuel tanks could fly from Eastern Europe to Central America, and lose itself among the vastness of the Atlantic Ocean. It could reach Colombia undetected by Western intelligence agencies, which meant that Bout's proposal of an airdrop delivery made good sense.

Carlos agreed that it was all looking very positive, but he wasn't about to let the guy off the hook that easily. He wanted to bury Smulian's suspicions, and that meant driving home the message that he was the aggrieved party. He stressed to Smulian the need to be extremely careful when cutting such a deal.

Mike gestured at Smulian. 'It's all right for him saying it could be a set-up, it could be a fucking set-up for you as well.'

'Yeah,' Carlos agreed.

'And you know, sometimes people in trouble can catch other people who are . . . who are wanted,' Mike added. Bout – facing a whole range of problems – could have been put-up to ensnare the FARC. Mike mimed a pistol shot with his hand. 'And blow them, you know . . .' Then he smiled disarmingly. 'But you know me: I'm a good guy.'

'On this type of business we gotta be very careful,' Carlos added, 'because, like you say . . . he's scared that there's a set-up, and we're scared that it's a set-up.'

'A set-up. Yeah,' Smulian confirmed.

'Set-up. Uh-huh,' Mike echoed.

'And not just that,' Carlos added. 'We're scared . . . because they can steal the money and everything . . . We are very careful. We are very scared, very careful. We gotta be . . .'

Smulian nodded, sympathetically. 'Yeah. Of course. I understand.'

Got you, Carlos told himself. That was enough for now.

The three wandered over to La Sirene for drinks and a bite,

which lay three blocks east of the Best Western. They'd headed for the cosy interior, where fisherman's netting hung from the ceiling, weighed down with Sangria bottles. One entire wall was decorated with a colourful mural of Venice, complete with gondolas on an azure sea, and framed with bare-breasted mermaids – the siren, La Sirene, was the restaurant's theme.

After the earlier altercation, Smulian seemed to want to make peace. Once they'd ordered food, he related what he thought was an amusing tale from his Moscow visit. Before making his phone call to Snow, Smulian had explained to Bout that The Bear used two numbers these days. One was his South African mobile, the other a US number – the cellphone that the 'FARC' had given him.

Bout had glanced at Smulian. 'US number? Direct to CIA,' he had joked. 'Direct to CIA,' Smulian repeated, laughing. What a blast.

Mike and Carlos feigned amusement. Only, it wasn't really very funny. If you supplemented the acronym 'DEA' for 'CIA,' Bout had hit the nail on the head. And despite the apparent bonhomie, Carlos figured that Smulian was still quietly testing them. A smidgen of suspicion remained. That would have to be killed dead.

Mike was struck most powerfully by something that Carlos had told him, in Miami, a week or more back. In every case, the King of Sting had explained, there always came a time when the target should wake up and smell the coffee. The eureka moment. This 'direct to CIA' comment had been Bout's eureka moment – the point at which he should have got the hell out of the deal.

But, as with most such cases, greed had got the better of him.

'We got the cash to handle . . .' Carlos assured Smulian. 'We got to make an arrangement to sit with him.' The cash was ready to hand over, and cash would always compensate for any lack of trust.

It was during their first night in Copenhagen that Mike and Smulian had discovered La Sirene. A cold, bruising wind had whistled in off the Baltic Sea, a far cry from the balmy climes of Willemstad that they'd enjoyed the previous day. They'd stopped to admire a two-masted Baltic schooner moored on the canal. They'd turned away from the ship, to discover the warm stucco façade of La Sirene. It looked homely and welcoming, and the two friends had slipped inside.

Over dinner they'd talked about a book that Smulian had given Mike – *Beginning's End*, by Shaykh Fadhlalla Haeri. The Shaykh was a Sufi spiritual leader, Sufism being an esoteric, mystical arm of Islam. The book spoke of the widening gap between 'sustainable inner happiness and the ever-increasing outer frenzy' of modern globalized living. It was all about offering 'a challenge to our modern lifestyle that is out of balance'.

Though he was mostly self-taught, Mike loved to read. On his bookshelves at home works by Byron, Blake and A E Housman sat side-by-side with military memoirs, which lay cheek-by-jowl with texts on Zen Buddhism. Their shared love of reading and of acquiring knowledge was one of the bonds between him and Smulian.

As they had discussed the Shaykh's message, the waiter had paused at their table. 'Excuse me, but you are talking about Shaykh Fadhlalla Haeri?'

It turned out the waiter was from Syria, and he'd come to Denmark as a refugee. It was obvious that he'd found precious few people in Copenhagen with whom to discuss the Shaykh's message. He simply could not believe that in a corner of La Sirene he'd found two ageing Englishmen who knew the Shaykh's philosophies so well.

La Sirene was exactly Mike and Smulian's kind of place – hence bringing Carlos here tonight. El Mexicano fitted in well: he was in his own way a fellow seeker. Though Catholic of birth, Carlos was of Mayan ancestry – the Mayans being the ancient high civilization that ruled much of Central America. Carlos had read the 'Mayan Bible' – the Popol Vuh; the Mayan book of Creation – and he could discuss the Shaykh's philosophies with the best of them.

But tonight, they were here on very different business. The Bear and El Mexicano could sense that Smulian was still circling warily, not yet happy to dive back into the deal. Carlos set his recorder running. Time to push some more.

'I gotta jump on the plane tomorrow, go over there and . . . talk to him personal . . .' Carlos demanded a face-to-face with Bout as soon as possible.

Bout would understand why such deals needed to be done one-on-one. No one would hand over millions of dollars in cash for a consignment of weaponry, not at least until they'd looked each other in the eye and shaken hands. That was how such deals were done, and Bout would know that.

Smulian said that he understood Carlos' sense of urgency. But it was then that he related the incident in Bout's Moscow office, when the Russian had asked him to scroll through the Who's Who of the FARC.

'He showed me photographs of the senior officers,' Smulian

explained. 'He told me: "Identify the people you saw." And I said: "I can't."'

Carlos feigned laughter. This he hadn't been expecting. But in a sense he should have seen it coming. Why wouldn't a man of Bout's capabilities and intellect seek a simple and direct verification of the clients' bona fides? His mind raced. What the hell was he supposed to say now?

He found himself struggling for the right words. 'Yeah, because the people, the people on . . . on the news, and the people around that is . . . is the head – not the head, but it's the heads of the fronts.'

Smulian stared at him in confusion. Carlos wasn't surprised. What the hell was that bunch of gibberish supposed to mean? It would only arouse more suspicion.

He tried again. He tried explaining that the FARC's foremost leaders were based in the midst of the Colombian jungle, where they felt safe. 'They never go out from there, because they know if they go out from there, they get fucked up . . . That's the reason they use people like me . . .'

He was a middle-tier finance guy. As for El Comandante, he was only a commander of one of the FARC's several fronts. In short, they were too junior to have made it into the gallery that Bout and Smulian had looked at.

As far as Carlos could tell, Smulian seemed to have accepted the explanation. They finished their meal steering clear of the topic of the coming deal. It was then that Mike made his excuses. He was feeling under the weather and he needed to get some rest. He'd hurry on ahead.

Carlos kept his recorder running, as he and Smulian left the restaurant, pulling their coats closer against the chill. They turned left onto Nyhavnsbroen – the folding bridge that spanned the Nyhavn canal – and from there headed directly onto Holbergsgade, which would take them to the Best Western by a more sheltered route.

As they pushed along Holbergsgade, Smulian seemed relaxed and at ease. 'I'll tell you the name of my friend, so that you know,' he remarked. 'But this is just between you and me.'

Carlos nodded. 'Uh-huh.'

Smulian leaned closer. 'It's, uh, Viktor Bout.' He spelled out Bout's name – 'B-O-U-T' – and explained that he was wanted by the world. 'They call him "The Merchant of Death",' Smulian added.

After all that Smulian had told them about his much-vaunted weapons supplier, it was almost inconceivable that the FARC wouldn't have realized who he was by now, but it was a relief not to have to play that little game any more, and of course it was fantastic to have it all captured on tape.

As they were alone and having such an apparent heart-to-heart, Carlos was tempted to raise the issue of the jealousy and resentment that he suspected Smulian felt for Mike Snow. He figured that was the real reason The Bear had left the restaurant early, to give him the chance to do so.

'You know, my friend, I notice something,' he ventured. 'You have been very different since you come back from Moscow.'

Smulian looked surprised. 'I have? Like how?'

'After you come back you seem very different . . . in front of Mike. You're not open in front of him, like you were before. What's going on? What's worrying you?'

'Ah. That.' Smulian paused. 'Well, you see the trouble is . . .

Mike's son works for the CIA. And that makes it . . . hard to totally trust him.'

'Well, we trust Mike. He's been working with us for many years. Very loyal.'

Smulian shook his head. 'Mike . . . well, let's just say you can't trust Mike . . . He does weird stuff. The amount of shit I've had to put up with, because of Mike. You wait and see . . . he'll blow everything. That's just Mike for you.'

'No, no, we know Mike,' Carlos remonstrated. 'We've done deals with him, many times. He's no like that.'

'Well, he may be fine now, but he'll get bored and he'll turn to bad. He'll burn you. And I tell you something else: my friend in Russia – he doesn't trust him, either.'

Carlos eyed Smulian. 'That – that may be a problem. If your friend doesn't trust Mike, how he gonna do the deal?'

'Exactly. My friend just doesn't want Snow a part of what we're up to. He'd like him kept out of it completely.'

'I see.' For a moment Carlos acted as if he was deep in thought. 'I tell you what. If you say so, we take Mike out of the deal. He gets paid anyway, but not from this side. Important thing is – we want you and your friend to be happy.'

Smulian nodded. 'It's just safer that way.'

'Okay,' Carlos confirmed, 'if you say so, we take Mike out.'

Carlos said he'd talk to El Comandante, and get Mike moved sideways out of the weapons deal. It might take some time, but they could sidetrack him into some aircraft purchases that the 'FARC' were planning. Carlos' hunch had been proved right: Smulian *did* resent Snow. Having secured all that on tape, Carlos now needed to choose his moment to present it to The Bear.

They reached the hotel to find that Mike was still awake. He'd apparently got a second wind. The three of them headed for Smulian's room. Barely had they stepped inside when Smulian's phone rang. He checked the caller ID, excitedly: 'It's him. It's him.' He answered the call. 'Yes. Can you hear me? Yeah, I'm okay. And you?'

Bout said something on the other end.

'Yeah. Okay, we're ... talking ... It's just a question of ... a suitable venue. That's, that's the thing.'

The conversation went back and forth a little, as various suggestions of possible places to meet – Romania, Ghana, Morocco and Montenegro – were fired at Smulian by Carlos and Mike, and by Bout on the other end of the call.

'Morocco would be okay?' Smulian checked with Bout. 'All right. You call me Friday. Okay. Anytime. You call me anytime ... All right. Okay. Bye.' Smulian ended the call. 'Okay, he's going to go and check ... He's going to check now.'

'He hasn't got his private jet any more?' Mike queried.

Smulian confirmed Bout didn't have his Gulfstream any more.

'Romania is very close ...' Carlos suggested. It was the DEA's favoured option for the sting, and for a whole variety of reasons. 'I want him to feel safe, but we gotta feel safe too ... I going to give you a few countries that he feels safe, everybody feels safe, and we'll have a meeting.'

Smulian said they'd get it sorted, but that right now Montenegro was Bout's favoured venue. 'You know, when I arrived in, uh, the airport ... it was freezing cold,' he added. 'I didn't have anything, and he took me immediately to the biggest supermarket and he buys me six hundred dollars of clothes ... Because I just went with the clothes from Curaçao.'

Carlos chuckled.

'No, he's a good man . . .' Smulian added. 'Really, he's a good man.'

The three went their separate ways shortly thereafter. Carlos hurried off to the nearby Marriott to deliver the new batch of tapes to the DEA team. Mike headed to his room and logged on to the internet, to find he had a new email from Agent Zach.

The DEA agent explained that he was worried that Bout might have messed with Smulian's phone, turning it into some kind of bugging device. He urged Mike to be cautious. He also warned Mike that he might have to go to Montenegro, on behalf of Carlos, to do a first face-to-face with Bout.

No way could the 'FARC' team agree to such a rendezvous, for there would be no arresting Bout in Montenegro. He enjoyed top-level protection there. Instead, they would have to try to lure him to a country where they could grab him. But Mike fronting up to a first meeting might help with that process, being a twitch on the thread.

Mike knew that if he did head for Montenegro, he would be going in alone and unarmed. The DEA had made it clear that when operating outside the USA, no one – agents or sources – was allowed to carry weapons. Regardless, Mike was in too deep. He was hooked on the hunt. If the DEA sent him, he would go.

If he did head to Montenegro, Zach explained, he should try to lure Bout to a follow-up offshore, either on the Adriatic or Baltic seas. El Comandante had experienced just such cat-and-mouse negotiations – including various mid-ocean rendezvous – during his real-life career as a drugs and arms dealer. It went with the territory.

Agent Zach also pointed out that Bout's suggested forty per cent cut for money-laundering services was laughable. They needed to push back on that hard. If the FARC agreed to something that exorbitant, they'd lose all credibility.

Bout would realize they had to be either cops or spooks, and the game would be up.

CHAPTER TWENTY

BAGHDAD INTERNATIONAL AIRPORT, IRAQ, NOVEMBER 2003

As the fierce early morning light cut across Baghdad's International Airport (BIAP), DHL flight OO-DLL, operated by European Air Transport – a Brussels-based company wholly owned by Deutsche Post DHL – clawed into the dawn skies. It was en route to Bahrain International Airport, some six hundred miles away.

Today, the Airbus A300 had a thirty-eight-year-old Belgian, Captain Eric Genotte, at the controls, with fellow Belgian and First Officer, Steeve Michielsen, plus Scot Mario Rofail, the Flight Engineer, making up the rest of his crew.

After takeoff, Genotte executed a steep climb to 8,000 feet, in an effort to reduce exposure to ground fire. Barely six months after the Iraq War proper had been declared 'over', the country remained a hotbed of unrest, with various insurgencies targeting both Coalition forces and each other. It wasn't uncommon for Baghdad Airport to come under fire.

The US military – embroiled in a post-war anti-insurgency campaign, plus fevered reconstruction efforts – required daily deliveries into Iraq to replenish its supplies. Some thirty-odd airfreight shipments were shuttling in and out of BIAP daily, carrying tents, televisions, generators, medical equipment, frozen food, uniforms, body-armour, ration packs, boots, blankets, vehicles, building supplies and sacks bulging with mail.

Refuelling crews ran hoses out to waiting aircraft, as private military contractors paced the perimeter, scanning for any insurgents lying in wait to ambush aircraft upon take-off or landing. Several times a week mortar crews got close enough to lob a few hurried rounds over the airport's perimeter. Fortunately, they generally couldn't shoot for shit.

But today's attack would prove very different.

On a road running through some scrub not far from the main runway, a group of men had staged a breakdown. Their vehicle – a bog-standard white sedan – was parked at the roadside, its bonnet very noticeably raised. As flight OO-DLL thundered into the dawn skies, three individuals broke away from the sedan, making a beeline for the deserted scrub.

Two had Arabic-style scarves wrapped around their faces, obscuring all but their eyes. A third brandished a video camera, to shoot the film of what was coming. One of the masked men hefted a weighty object on his shoulder: it was the long form of a Strela-3 anti-aircraft missile system, the direct forerunner of the Igla.

With the business end pointed skywards, the masked insurgent let rip. A thick cloud of dust and smoke engulfed the figures, and an arrow-like form streaked away, climbing almost vertically. Moments after being unleashed, the missile's vapour trail traced a sharp change in direction, as the warhead homed in on the hot exhausts of the Airbus.

An instant later there was the flash of an explosion, followed by a hollow boom at altitude.

As the insurgents raced for their car, slamming down the bonnet in preparation for their getaway, fire was already engulfing the A300's shattered left wing – the point of impact. The missile had punctured the aircraft's left fuel tank, which was full of aviation fuel. Already gallons of the stuff were gushing into thin air, and flaring into angry, boiling gouts of flame.

Captain Genotte had just lost around one third of his left wing. Three metres of one flap were missing completely, and another dangled uselessly, a mangled mass of scorched metal hanging loose in the slipstream. What remained of his twisted outer wing was warped and peppered with shrapnel.

His aircraft was on fire and he'd also lost all hydraulic pressure, which meant that his flight controls were no longer functioning. The Airbus, Captain Genotte realized, had suffered a catastrophic hit and his only option was to try to put down at BIAP.

Flight OO-DLL was thrown into a violent phugoid – a roller-coaster motion that pitched the aircraft upwards in a series of desperate climbs, each of which was followed by plunging into an accelerating descent. The only means Captain Genotte had to try to stop the wild gyrations was engine thrust, all other controls being lost to him.

Captain Genotte worked out that by varying thrust, he could still turn his aircraft. As Flight Engineer Rofail executed an emergency 'gravity drop' to lower the landing gear, Genotte tried to steer a course back towards the airport from which they had just taken off. Getting the wheels down was crucial, for the drag should reduce airspeed and help stabilize the crippled plane.

Genotte set up for approach to BIAP's runway 33R. But the damaged aircraft veered right. Genotte was forced to switch to runway 33L, the shorter of the two. At 400 feet of altitude turbulence hit the crippled plane, throwing one wing violently earthwards, but by using thrust alone Genotte managed to correct it.

The Airbus touched down, and Rofail triggered full reverse thrust, to try to bring them to a standstill.

Instead, the Airbus careered off the asphalt, ploughed into soft, rough ground in an explosion of dirt and sand, tore through a razor wire barrier and eventually came to a smoking halt sandwiched between a taxiway and the adjacent runway. The aircraft had taken 3,000 feet to come to a standstill, and amazingly, none of those aboard was injured.

They evacuated using the rear emergency slide, the front one having been torn to shreds on the wire.

Flight OO-DLL had been ferrying materiel into BIAP on behalf of the US military. That evening a US Air Force caterpillar was able to extricate the Airbus from the wreckage and tow it away, dumping it in an aircraft graveyard on the far side of the terminal. The damage the aircraft had suffered as a result of the missile strike was so great it would never fly again.

The video of the attack was passed to the media, and responsibility was claimed by the *Fedayeen*, an Iraqi militia fiercely loyal to the former President, Saddam Hussein. The crew of Flight OO-DLL received several awards for their astonishing feat that day, including the Flight Safety Foundation's Professionalism Award. The Foundation cited the crew's 'extraordinary piloting skills in flying their aircraft to a safe landing after a missile strike'.

The near-catastrophe suffered by the aircraft and her crew underlined what a dangerous place BIAP was from which to operate. As the insurgents stepped up their attacks, any number of airfreight companies baulked at doing business in Iraq. But there was one, in particular, that bucked the trend – and it would draw US and allied forces into the mother of all scandals.

Iraq in 2003–4 had become the site of the largest US government airlift since the iconic Berlin Airlift of the late 1940s. The US Department of Defense (DOD) had a marked shortfall in long-haul capacity airframes. There was a mass of cargo needing to be flown and not enough military aircraft to carry it. Accordingly, the DOD had turned to the same private companies that had flown their supplies into Bagram Airbase, in Afghanistan, over the two previous years. Mostly they were Eastern European, and based in the Middle East hubs of Sharjah and Dubai.

The companies had to be approved by RAMCC – Regional Air Movement Control Centre – the US military's air command headquarters. DHL had been one of the very first operators to set up office in the bombed-out shell of BIAP, and pretty soon their flights were streaming in, often using Russian crews and planes. They corkscrewed down, spiralling from altitude directly over the airport, to avoid exposure to anyone positioned to either side of the runway.

During delays caused by mortar strikes, the Russian crews slung their hammocks in the shade beneath their aircraft's wings, dozing through the blistering heat. There was business to be done, and as long as there was money to be made they would fly. The pace was hectic. Some crews would land during the morning, unload, depart shortly thereafter, and return with a second load just prior to sunset.

Then on 17 May 2004 a story broke in the *Financial Times*,

making sensational allegations: Viktor Bout's airfreight companies were back in business. Not only that, but they were 'delivering goods to US forces in Iraq'.

'US and British officials . . . deny any knowledge of Mr Bout's alleged activities in Iraq,' the *Financial Times* reported. But at the same time the paper accused the US and Britain of resisting pressure by the UN to freeze the assets of those associated with Charles Taylor's bloody Liberian regime, implying that some kind of murky deal had been done with Bout.

By the time Washington awoke to the news, several hours after the story's 17 May publication in London, the shit had already hit the fan. The phones were red hot in Washington. Urgent calls were made to the US civilian authorities and military command in Iraq, demanding answers. Were the allegations about Bout's aircraft true? If so, how could this have happened?

Enquiries confirmed the fears were well founded: Bout had pulled off the ultimate coup. What had made his fleet of rugged Russian planes so indispensable to African warlords, made them equally useful to the Coalition forces in Iraq. Whether unwittingly or not, they'd hired his aircraft to haul in hundreds of tonnes of much-needed supplies.

Within hours of the story breaking, the Coalition Provisional Authority (CPA) – Iraq's transitional civilian administration – and the US DOD realized they had a public relations nightmare on their hands. The man accused by the *New York Times* of being a 'fugitive from justice', the 'notorious, mysterious and unstoppable Victor Bout', had aircraft flying on a daily basis under official US government contracts.

The main company involved was called Irbis – Russian for Snow Leopard. Registered in Kazakhstan, Irbis had been brought in as a subcontractor, flying supplies for private companies working for the US Army and the US Marines, and for the US Air Mobility Command, a key component of the US Air Force.

'Somehow, this guy was on the payroll of the US government when he should have been blacklisted,' Jeffrey Oster, a former Marine general and the CPA's chief operating officer pointed out. Oster figured that Bout's companies could only have been hired in the midst of the proverbial fog of war. 'We have an old saying in the Marine Corps: If you want it bad, you get it bad.'

The day after the *Financial Times* story broke, Senator Russell Feingold, a Democrat from Wisconsin, raised the issue during a US Senate Foreign Relations Committee hearing. 'Is Viktor Bout or any firm associated with Viktor Bout, providing airfreight services for coalition forces in Iraq?' he demanded.

No one seemed to have any answers. The situation was beyond bizarre: it was incomprehensible. On the one hand the US government was leading the hunt for Bout: on the other, he now seemed to be working for them. But it wasn't the US alone that was culpable.

Amazingly, Jet Line, a Moldovan-registered company also associated with Bout, had flown cargo into Iraq on behalf of the British government. In March 2004, Jet Line had delivered armoured cars to British forces operating in Basra. Jet Line had also been hired by Britain's Department for International Development – its foreign aid agency – on a contract that was suddenly cancelled, when officials realized the company was linked to Bout.

Peter Hain was horrified. The MI6 case officers who'd headed up Task Force Bloodstone were equally appalled. The British government had seriously taken its eye off the ball. By then Hain was the Leader of the House of Commons – a senior role in Cabinet – and he tried to apply pressure to halt the use of Bout's planes, but there was little interest in pressing the Americans to act.

Through the weeks that followed the controversy snowballed. The Irbis flights became the repeated targets of exposés in the US – the *Los Angeles Times*, *Newsweek* and *Mother Jones* running with the story. In the UK, the British government's use of Bout's airfreight companies made headlines in the *Guardian*, *The Times* and the *Evening Standard*.

Flight records obtained by the *Los Angeles Times* revealed that Irbis planes had landed 92 times in Baghdad during the first few months of 2004. The US Department of Defense was even refuelling Bout's airfreighters. The DOD's own records revealed that Bout's aircraft had refuelled 142 times at their Baghdad facility between March and August 2004.

Charging $60,000 for a round trip from Sharjah to Baghdad, Bout's fleet of battle-worn cargo aircraft could undercut most rival carriers. But even at such bargain basement rates, Irbis had netted tens of millions of dollars before the scandal was uncovered. And it wasn't just Baghdad that Bout's aircraft were servicing. They had also flown into Balad Air Base, in northern Iraq, a hub for F-16 fighter jets, and Al Asad, a Marine Corps facility. At times, they had called at all three airbases in the same day.

In December 2004 a *Los Angeles Times* reporter reached Bout's Moscow cellphone, and was able to ask him about the flights. He was given short shrift. 'You are not dealing with fact, you are dealing with allegation,' Bout snapped. 'Don't call me any more.'

In the US, the schizophrenic attitude towards Bout's air-operations persisted. While the CIA began a probe into the Iraq flights, and the US State Department pledged to support international efforts to end Bout's activities, his airfreight companies continued to fly on DOD contracts. The State Department warned all US overseas posts 'to ensure that contracts with freight forwarders preclude any use of entities connected to Bout'. But was anyone listening?

As the story ran and ran, the possible legal implications of continuing to use those airfreight companies became clear. US Air Force officials began to revoke fuel allowances and terminate contracts, but the US Army continued to argue that it bore no responsibility for second-tier subcontractors like Bout's airfreight companies.

The situation appeared to have reached a stalemate. While one arm of the US administration hunted for Viktor Bout, for another it was still seemingly business as usual. There were allegations from some quarters that elements of the US government had done a secret deal with the Russian. As the US military needed him so badly, they'd agreed to turn a blind eye to his 'wanted status', if he continued to fly their cargo.

Russia expert and lawyer Lee Wolosky – who had led the National Security Council's pre-9/11 efforts to nail Bout – had proved dogged and innovative in his efforts to track the Russian. He found Bout's rehabilitation by the US military puzzling, to put it mildly.

'It befuddles the mind,' Wolosky remarked, 'that the Pentagon would continue to work with an organization that both the Clinton and Bush White Houses actively fought to dismantle.'

How could this supposed 'fugitive from justice' be working for the US government, earning millions of dollars of US taxpayer's money? It just didn't add up. Either way, by the summer of 2004 the *New York Times* Magazine's characterization of the 'fugitive' Russian appeared to have been borne out.

Viktor Bout did indeed appear to have become 'notorious, mysterious and *unstoppable*.'

CHAPTER TWENTY-ONE

BUCHAREST, ROMANIA, JANUARY 2008

Carlos had justified the move to Romania because that was where the FARC's money was supposedly stashed. They had cash sitting in Bucharest, the nation's capital, with which to get the deal under way. And since Romania was a former Soviet Bloc country, it should give Bout a certain sense of security. It made sense to head there for the next stage of the deal.

The truth was somewhat different.

Romania was where the DEA had planned to ensnare Syrian arms dealer Monzer Al Kazar, a year earlier. Kazar had cried off at the last moment, but the fact remained that the DEA worked well with the Romanian National Police and the Prosecutor's Office, and they could get legal clearance for bugging and phone-taps. There were also few impediments to extraditing suspects to the US, a crucial consideration in a case like Bout's.

With the sting drawing ever closer to biting deep, Wim and Zach decided both 'FARC' confidential sources needed to be wired for sound. That way, if either one got separated during the action, the DEA should still be assured of capturing on tape the vital evidence they needed to build a watertight case.

Lou Milione could not believe the quality of evidence coming out of Operation Relentless, especially when he'd heard the recording of Smulian revealing Bout's name – 'B-O-U-T' – followed by his less-than-edifying moniker, 'The Merchant of Death'.

'He spelled it out for them,' he would remark, incredulously. 'We marvelled that Smulian would do that. But it was just great evidence.'

That was the kind of material that he needed Carlos and Ricardo to keep drawing out of the targets, as they drew closer to the final chapter: *capture*.

Carlos had flown out to Bucharest first. His story was that he needed to link up with El Comandante, to brief him on the coming deal. After the success of Moscow and Copenhagen, the DEA team was convinced that Operation Relentless had truly found its 'fuck of the dog'. They were gathering for what they intended would be the final stage of the sting.

From the get-go, Mike Snow hated being in Bucharest. It was 26 January 2008, and he found the place cold, frozen, grey, bitter and grim. The city seemed to be staggering along, surviving on life-support. He and Smulian caught a taxi from the airport to the Grand Hotel de Boulevard, which certainly had the right ring to it. It lay bang in the city centre and was one of Bucharest's oldest.

With its glittering chandeliers and fine marble floors, it had certainly looked the part on the internet. Unfortunately, the rooms turned out to be anything but grand. Everyone here seemed to want to rip you off. Mike had asked for a bag of laundry to be done. He was quoted the price of $100 dollars. Eventually the laundry woman had agreed to do it for $10.

At first Smulian wasn't particularly bothered by Bucharest's shortcomings. Carlos had slipped him another $3,000 – more

DEA 'official authorized funds' – to cover his expenses, and he sensed that he was moving ever closer to hitting the jackpot. But he worried that the FARC were running out of time.

The afternoon of their first day in the city, he emailed Viktor Bout. 'Please call me, urgent ... They need to speak as soon as possible, due to time problem.' Carlos had told Smulian that the FARC had moved €5 million into Bucharest, as a down-payment on the arms deal, but they couldn't hold it there indefinitely.

That evening, Carlos and Ricardo turned up at the hotel. In a mixture of Spanish and English, they proceeded to ratchet up the pressure on Smulian. Having complained about how 'mucho frio' – freezing cold – it was, they went over Bout's favoured option one more time: the planned rendezvous in Montenegro.

El Comandante acted as if the very idea got his back up. Why didn't they meet here in Bucharest, he demanded. 'We have the stuff here and it's very much more viable.'

Smulian looked troubled. 'I know, I just think that he can't come here. That's the problem.'

Ricardo's face darkened. 'We have money here, but it's not money we can keep here for ever ...' If Bout couldn't make it, they'd be forced to turn to a rival weapons supplier, he warned.

At the mere suggestion that the FARC might do such a thing, Smulian looked crestfallen. Carlos pressed him for an answer as to why Bout couldn't simply fly to Bucharest, shake on the deal and collect his cash. 'What's the problem?' he demanded. 'Why?'

Smulian glanced at his 'FARC' friend with a hangdog expression. Bout was worried he'd get arrested in Bucharest, he explained. By contrast, in Montenegro the Russian enjoyed protection.

El Comandante gestured angrily; while he spoke little English he could understand almost everything. 'Explain to him that in leaving my country I'm running the risk of being arrested . . . two blocks away from my house! Explain to him!'

Things were in danger of turning ugly. The act was becoming all too real again; spinning out of control. It was time for Mike to make his intervention. He whipped out a gleaming new cellphone – a fancy-looking Nokia, with a silver front and white and blue metallic sides – and presented it to Smulian.

'So that's a brand new phone,' Mike announced. 'We just brought it on the way here.' As part of FARC's security protocol, he explained, Smulian needed to hand back his Curaçao mobile. Switching phones and SIM-cards helped fox the watchers.

In truth, this was the phone on which the DEA had secured authorization from the Romanians to tap calls. Mike suggested that now might be a good time for Smulian to put his new phone to use, and call Bout. The deal had reached a critical juncture: either Bout showed some flexibility, or the 'FARC' would likely turn to an alternative source of supply.

Smulian made the call. 'Yes? Can you hear me? Okay, look, um, we need to do something quickly, so you think it's possible you can *habla Español* with the um, the top guy? He's sitting here with me . . . They're desperate, because they . . . they need to move urgently . . .'

Bout said something in reply.

'Just talk to him, okay?' Smulian handed the phone to El Comandante, explaining that it was 'Viktor'.

Ricardo took the phone. '*Alo? Buenas tardes. Cómo está usted?* Hello? Good afternoon. How are you?

Bout's answer – in serviceable Spanish – was that he was fine.

'My understanding was that I was coming here . . . to finish up the negotiation . . .' Ricardo began, knowing how crucial it was to lure Bout to Romania. 'Just the fact of me coming here is very complicated. Having money here is even more complicated. I want us . . . to settle this as soon as possible. Because I need what you have. Do you understand?'

Bout confirmed that he knew what constraints the FARC were operating under, but he stressed that he was facing his own challenges too.

Ricardo explained that the countries Smulian and Bout were proposing were impossible for the FARC. 'I'm going to ask you the question – what would two Latin guys be doing in a country like, I don't know, Armenia or Montenegro? Tell me, what? . . . I have no infrastructure, no money, I can't do anything there. I can do it here. I can do it here. I have money here, I have people here . . . You understand?'

Bout said he understood, but he would need time to get his Bucharest travel sorted.

While Ricardo and Bout were talking, Carlos and Smulian had been having a side conversation. Smulian mentioned that Bout had some form of airfreight operation already under way, in the Central American country of Nicaragua.

'If he can go to Nicaragua, we can go to Nicaragua,' Carlos exclaimed. He turned to Ricardo and explained in Spanish that Bout could get to Nicaragua. Nicaragua was a country in which the DEA were happy to operate.

'He's telling me you might also be able to get to Nicaragua,' Ricardo related to Bout. 'We have very good relations right now with Nicaragua . . . So I need you to clear this up right now. Is it impossible here? Because . . . the money that I have here, I need to get it out of here. If I'm not going to do anything here, I have to move it.'

Bout confirmed that he'd try to get to Bucharest, but they needed to give him time.

'Then, my question is, how much time do you need?' Ricardo demanded.

Bout asked for a few days in which to organize his Romania travel.

'Okay, perfect, because I need to move away. Do you understand? If I don't come to an agreement with you, I've got to move away quickly. Okay? Okay, all right. Goodbye. Be well.'

Ricardo handed the phone back to Smulian, who signed off the call. Bout would check immediately on his travel options, Smulian explained, and phone later with an update. But he didn't feel overly positive about the way things were going. Caught between El Comandante's urgency and rush, and Bout's horrendous travel constraints, he could feel the deal slipping away.

It was time to slip into salesman mode. Show them the goods. Keep them onside. Smulian grabbed his laptop and flipped open the screen. He pulled up some images of the kind of weapons systems they were offering the FARC. He scrolled through to find a photo of the Igla then beckoned Carlos and Ricardo over.

He gestured at the screen. 'For Igla, eh, tiene agora . . . Para Igla agora cien,' he tried a few words in Spanish; *for the Igla, he now has a hundred available.*

'Perfect!' Ricardo declared, gazing at the image of the sleek anti-aircraft missile. 'What are we waiting for? Tell him to get a move on . . . I have the money. What does he want?'

Smulian flicked through more images on the laptop. 'He says . . . he can supply to you special helicopter . . . which can wipe out their helicopters.'

Ricardo gestured dismissively. 'Tell him I already knew that.'

The talk went back and forth about the various types of weaponry that Smulian could supply, as he pulled up further images on his screen.

Finally, Carlos fixed him with a look. 'Okay, this is the problem. How we going to move the money?' They needed Bout to come to Bucharest, so they could marry him up with the cash.

'Yeah,' Smulian agreed; he'd work on Bout.

'And, and it's very dangerous. The money's danger . . .' Carlos continued. 'It's not just a little box with two dollars. It's a lot; it's a lot of money.'

'Cash, cash,' Ricardo interjected, in English.

Play to his greed.

Sensing how near he was to the money, Smulian dug deeper into the weapons deal. The arms were manufactured in Bulgaria, he explained, at a company called KAS. He spelled out the name: 'K-A-S'. The boss of KAS was Bout and Smulian's friend Peter Mirchev. The KAS complex actually consisted of nine separate factories, which manufactured every type of arms imaginable.

'Carlos, repeat this to him,' Ricardo declared. 'I want them. I need them . . . Doesn't he . . . Don't they want the money?'

Carlos translated.

Smulian gave a half-embarrassed kind of shrug. 'Yeah, of course. Oh, everybody wants money.'

Ricardo adopted a suitably revolutionary pose. 'Explain to him I have no use for money . . . For my interests, money has no use.'

Smulian had caught the gist of the Spanish. 'Yeah. It's okay. I understand.' He paused, before turning to his 'friend' Carlos. 'You know, I would like very much for this thing to work, because . . . they don't like him, and they don't like your friend.' 'They' – the Americans – didn't like Bout a great deal, and they wouldn't warm to his 'friend' El Comandante, a guerrilla leader in the FARC.

The meeting broke up, with Smulian agreeing to work on Bout regarding a Bucharest rendezvous. Carlos and Ricardo exited the hotel and made their way direct to the DEA's lodgings. In addition to the new batch of tapes, there was also Smulian's Curaçao phone to hand over. Carlos would pass it to agent Brown, who would bag and tag it into evidence – sealing it with date and time, and signing it with his own name. If Operation Relentless ever got to court, it would be a key exhibit at trial.

Mike, meanwhile, was giving Smulian a stiff talking-to. 'You need to be very careful, my friend. This what we're doing here – it's highly bloody illegal. All we should be doing is taking our commission on the deal. We're better off knowing as little as possible about who's buying what or selling what to whom.'

Their role was purely to make the introduction – the 'FARC' to Bout – he explained. 'But you – you're getting yourself deeper and deeper into the arms side of it. Leave it to them to do the negotiations. Otherwise, you're only incriminating yourself.'

It wasn't the first time that Mike had given his friend such a warning. He'd said as much in Curaçao, but he figured that Smulian wasn't listening. He seemed to be playing an act – increasingly that of the full-blooded arms-broker – as if he was irredeemably hooked.

The day after this crunch meeting, Bout called Smulian. It was a bad line, but the two friends were just about able to make each other understood. Little did they know it, but the entire call was being captured and recorded on tape.

'Look, tomorrow I'll try to arrange . . . that we can come directly to where . . . you are now . . .' Bout told Smulian. Having spoken to El Comandante, Bout realized why coming to Bucharest made such sense.

'Okay . . . So call me, please, when you have the news,' Smulian told him.

Bout signed off the call: 'Sure, sure, sure.'

True to his word, the Russian called again a few hours later. 'I have to receive . . . some answer tomorrow by noontime, when the travel doc ready.' Bout should have his visa to visit Bucharest by then. 'And I'll let you know, uh, when I show up.'

'Okay . . . All right. Bye. Bye.'

The minute the call was done, Smulian phoned Carlos and informed him of the developments: Bout was expected in Bucharest maybe as early as tomorrow evening. At last, it all seemed to be coming together nicely.

Mike and Smulian decided to move into a nearby Bucharest apartment hotel. It was marginally better than the 'Grand', but only in the sense that the bedrooms were at least passably clean. It lay in a Victorian-looking corner block on a busy road junction, with piles of snow lying in dirty, frozen heaps.

The snow was especially thick and unpleasant around the bus stop at the foot of the stairs. People caught-short clearly peed in the snowdrifts. The entire place reeked of stale urine. That and vodka. It was a cliché, but it did indeed appear to be true: on the streets of this bitter city people slugged back cheap alcohol in an effort to keep warm.

The apartment was served by an ancient-looking stove. It was covered in green tiles and packed full of firebricks to eke out the heat, but it never seemed to get the place properly warm.

That evening Bout called Smulian again. If anything the connection was even worse. He'd checked out the logistics of the

Romania rendezvous, and it wasn't looking too good. Applying for a visa would involve a degree of official scrutiny, and who knew what that might throw up. Romania was now a part of the EU, which meant a whole different set of rules applied.

'Check with the friends,' Bout told Smulian, over the badly distorted connection, 'if we meet in . . . Moldova, Chisinau, early next week . . .'

'Where?' Smulian asked. He could hardly hear properly.

'It's nearby from Bucharest. It's, uh, Chisinau, in Moldova . . . It's very easy. I can be there next day . . .'

Smulian promised to see if Bout's new suggestions might meet with the 'FARC's' approval.

Chisinau is the capital of Moldova, the former Soviet Bloc state that shares a 200-mile border with Romania. As it wasn't an EU member state, Bout was free to travel there with little scrutiny. Indeed, he'd based several of his airlines in the country. Chisinau was a little over a 200-kilometre drive from Bucharest, which made it the perfect place to meet, as far as the Russian saw things.

But Smulian was worried. Twenty-four hours earlier, Bout had promised to make the Bucharest rendezvous. He doubted their 'FARC friends' would be particularly happy at this change of plan.

He, Carlos and Mike gathered at the chilly apartment for a talk. Sure enough, Bout's abrupt volte-face didn't go down well.

'We're getting fucked . . .' Mike declared. 'I'm getting fucking pissed off, man.'

Smulian nodded, morosely. 'Yeah, me too.' He explained that it would take three days for Bout to secure a Romanian visa, hence suggesting the alternative rendezvous.

Mike seemed to brighten a little. 'Well, that's okay – three days.'

'If he's serious . . . three days is good,' Carlos confirmed. 'I can tell El Comandante to wait. Better than nothing.'

Mike nodded. 'We're come a long fucking way . . . Me, I've been nearly twenty-five days from home.'

Carlos stressed that a change of plan wasn't on. 'Believe me, if I go tell El Comandante that, he's going to say: "I'm leaving."'

'I reckon if he don't come here, we fuck off,' Mike declared, bluntly. If Bout didn't show in Bucharest, he was done with the whole thing.

Smulian gave a slow, hangdog shrug. 'I sort of feel the same way, you know.'

Carlos reiterated that if they tried to push El Comandante to move to Moldova, he would blow a fuse. 'The first thing he's going to think is that this is a lie and somebody wants to steal the money . . . And, uh, he's going to get upset . . . He's going to get upset with Mike . . .'

'He won't get upset with me,' Mike exploded, 'because I'm going to fucking disappear!'

Smulian could see the deal falling apart before his eyes. He tried to calm things by promising to speak to Bout, and to push for a Bucharest RV. It was late, everyone was tired and fractious: they agreed to revisit it in the morning.

It wasn't just the undercovers who were feeling the heat. Locked in their Bucharest hotel rooms 24/7, for fear of bumping into the undercovers on the streets, the DEA agents were going up the wall. Mike put a call through to Agent Zach, to get a heads-up. They ended up bawling each other out. The roller-coaster, on-again-off-again ride was getting to everyone.

Making his excuses to Smulian – he needed a change of scene – Mike caught a cab direct to the DEA's hotel. He figured he needed to clear the air right away. Carlos met him in the lobby, and the King of Sting could sense how tense things were. Operation Relentless felt like a pressure cooker poised to blow.

Carlos knew the team needed a boost. They were desperate for a lift; for some good news. Which meant that now was perhaps the time: the time to break out the 'Smulian tapes' – the ones wherein he'd told Carlos to cut Mike Snow out of the deal.

Carlos led Mike to one of the DEA's rooms. Inside, Wim, Zach and Lou Milione were waiting. Carlos had given them prior warning about what he was up to. As he and Mike stepped inside, the agents eyed them expectantly. So much was hanging on this moment.

But Carlos was saying nothing. He was giving nothing away. Instead, he sat Mike down at a side table, placed the headphones on him and coolly set his machine playing. 'Listen to the tape-recordings, my friend.'

Four sets of eyes were glued to Mike's features as the tapes began to play. The Bear's expression grew increasingly dark. The recording came to an end, he scowled angrily and thumped the headphones down on the table. Mike shook his head, as if trying to clear it. He was trying to process what he'd just heard. He'd never have believed it, if the King of Sting hadn't captured it all on tape.

He turned to Carlos, anger burning in his gaze. 'Fucking take him. He's yours. Fucking do him.'

Fists punched the air, euphorically. The DEA agents were on their feet instantly, scrabbling for a phone. They placed a call there and then to the Prosecutor, in New York, to relay the good news: Andrew Smulian's immunity was over. He was to be roped in with Viktor Bout, when – *if* – the arrests were made. Surely, Smulian would be forced to turn state's evidence – to cut a plea bargain – which meant that Operation Relentless had truly found its fuck of the dog.

But for Mike this was a bitter and conflicted moment. From the very start he'd never once intended to drop his friend in the shit. But that was entirely the point: it seemed as if he'd misjudged Andrew Smulian. He wasn't much of a friend, after all.

When he returned to the apartment, Mike found Smulian making a round of toast and marmite for the two of them. Mike found it almost impossible to look his old 'friend' in the eye, knowing what he now knew.

After Carlos' entrapment of Smulian, Mike set upon a new name for the Guatemalan. He was 'the silver-tongued one', or whatever the equivalent was in Spanish. Carlos told him it was 'Lingua Plata'. From now on, Carlos was Lingua Plata as far as The Bear was concerned.

But he was worried. How was he going to share his every waking hour with Smulian, after what had happened? Never one to mince his words, this was going to be some kind of a challenge.

Mike didn't doubt Smulian's motive in selling him out. If he was cut out of the arms deal, Smulian could argue to take the full five percent. With the kind of shipment they were putting together, it would be tens of millions of dollars, and Smulian's cut would be a cool one million or more.

As always, it boiled down to greed.

Late that night Smulian managed to reach Bout by phone. The Russian had been in meetings all day, and he'd been hard to get hold of.

'Okay, look, it seems to me they can't get there,' Smulian began. Moldova was a non-starter. 'And they say, please, if you can . . . apply for a visa and come here – it will solve everything.'

'But the problem these bastards . . .' Bout began, angrily, 'asking for five to ten working days to get the visa. Shit!'

Carlos and El Comandante were worried that Bout was 'playing with them', Smulian explained. The whole thing was in danger of falling apart. It was Bucharest or bust.

Early the following morning Smulian and Bout spoke again. Bout seemed more upbeat. He addressed Smulian as '*habibi*' – Arabic for 'my dear' or 'my friend' – and confirmed that he was going to make the Bucharest rendezvous after all. 'Hundred per cent. Hundred per cent sure. Wait me. Max ten days I'm there . . .'

Smulian communicated the good news to everyone in turn: the Bucharest RV was back on.

CHAPTER TWENTY-TWO

SHARJAH AIRPORT, UNITED ARAB EMIRATES, SUMMER 2004

The tide in Bout's fortunes began to turn in the summer of 2004, with President George W Bush's signing of the EXORD – the Presidential Executive Order. Prior to that, the supremely intelligent and astute Russian businessman had continued to fox the US administration – and especially the American military – with seeming ease.

In Sharjah, the authorities had genuinely tried to ground his fleet of ageing Russian transport aircraft. But Bout's response was to continually reinvent himself, registering new firms to new countries with lax or non-existent enforcement regimes. Shell companies established in Moldova and other former Soviet states applied for operating licences, before the authorities were able to discover who their real owners or controllers might be.

On the ground at Sharjah, the US military air controllers were on six-month rotating contracts. In essence, by the time one had worked out just who he was dealing with in terms of airfreight contractors, he was on his way out. As a result, Bout's aircraft had continued to ship US military cargo into Iraq with something close to impunity.

'He was working for the Americans because he was willing to fly stuff into anywhere regardless of how lunatic the situation was,' remarked Mark Galeotti, 'which made him very useful. He was the supplier of last resort.'

'It is a constant fight, because the military want to fly stuff and the new people are under pressure,' commented one US official closely involved in the hunt for Viktor Bout. 'Tracking aircraft ownership is, frankly, not a priority.'

The word from Europe echoed the American sentiments. 'He doesn't go away,' remarked a military intelligence official. 'He just keeps changing his aircraft and registrations, hoping he will outlast the interest in following him. So far, he is right.'

One of the most active trackers of Bout's Iraq flights was a British blogger and aircraft enthusiast called Alexander Harrowell. Under the blog-name The Yorkshire Ranter, Harrowell made it his business to track Bout's labyrinthine corporate structures, and the way his fleet of aeroplanes was quietly serving US and British military interests.

Pulling together a global network of like-minded individuals, Harrowell had launched 'Operation Firedump', a worldwide effort to name and shame Bout's airfreight empire. 'It's time to find these aircraft and demand their seizure,' declared Harrowell. 'All bloggers are invited to mirror this and help land [Bout planes] on the fire dump, which is where most . . . will end up given their age and general condition.'

Unbeknown to Harrowell, a carefully crafted strategy was being put into place in the US, designed to ensure Bout's airfreight businesses would end up exactly where the Yorkshire Ranter wanted them – bang on the fire dump. It was primed to launch in the spring of 2004, and its aim was to strike at the one place where Bout might be vulnerable: his finances.

The strategy was masterminded by Andreas Morgner – middle-aged, sandy-haired and refreshingly impassioned – who'd spent ten years in the CIA working as a counter-narcotics specialist. From there he'd moved to the US Treasury Department's little-known Office of Foreign Assets Control (OFAC), and it was there that Viktor Bout had first come onto Morgner's radar.

OFAC had become increasingly important in anti-narcotics work, because it had the power to 'designate' an individual as a danger to the United States, and freeze their assets. Of course, OFAC had to pass numerous legal thresholds to get such a 'freezing' order granted, but it could do so relatively quickly: often, it had to freeze drug traffickers' assets and cash in the US, before they could flee the country.

Morgner had taken up his new office in the spring of 2001. Tracking drugs traffickers meant he had to keep tabs on the aircraft they used, and in the process he'd stumbled across photos of Bout's fleet of planes lined up on the taxiway at Sharjah. As his interest in Bout's air-operations grew, he began to wonder if OFAC might build a case to seize the Russian's assets.

The closer Morgner looked, the more convinced he became that Bout was a legitimate target for such a measure. 'Viktor Bout supports people who absolutely slaughter people,' he concluded. 'No one else has the ability to put that kind of stuff into wars. He is a vulture, basically profiting on other people's misery. And what is galling is the sheer volume of it.'

In early 2004, Morgner, assisted by a tight circle of OFAC attorneys, began to build his case. The United Nations had already targeted Bout with sanctions, and their in-depth research was used to bolster OFAC's legal arguments. When the US courts quietly ruled that they would accept the UN's reports as definitive fact, Morgner knew they'd chalked up a game-changing breakthrough.

'They had summaries, narratives and source documents,' Morgner noted. 'This was golden. The decision to take the UN documents as fact . . . was vital.'

But every step of the OFAC process required extreme confidentiality and caution. If Bout got a sniff of what was in the offing, Morgner worried that he would further obfuscate his bank accounts and his airfreight companies, in an attempt to put them beyond anyone's reach.

By the summer of 2004 OFAC's case against Bout was ready. On 22 July the US government fired its broadside. President George W Bush signed Executive Order 13348, 'Blocking Property of Certain Persons . . .' In the EXORD, Bush identified those 'linked to the proliferation of and trafficking in illegal arms, which perpetuate the Liberian conflict and fuel . . . other conflicts throughout West Africa.'

Bush declared such arms sales 'an unusual and extraordinary threat to the foreign policy of the United States'. At the top of the list of targeted persons was 'BOUT, Viktor Anatolijevitch, aka BUTT, aka BONT, aka BUTTE, aka BOUTOV . . .' Along with his list of aliases, Bout was described as being a 'Businessman, dealer and transporter of weapons and minerals'. His main passport number was detailed in the EXORD, along with three 'alternative' passports.

President Bush's EXORD came into legal effect at 12.01 a.m. eastern daylight time on 23 July 2004. OFAC – the chief agency charged with implementing the EXORD – targeted thirty Bout companies, including Irbis, Air Bas and Transavia Travel. Some $3 million in Bout-controlled bank transfers were seized, as the sanctions began to bite.

Citing Bout's arms deals to Liberia as the key reason to go after him, OFAC listed Bout as a 'Special Designated National'. This meant that any business dealings between Bout and US citizens were now prohibited, and any of Bout's assets within the jurisdiction of the United States were fair game.

In the aftermath of such seizures, Juan Zarate, the NSC's counter-terrorism expert, spoke about Bout's alleged connection to the Taliban, 'which was problematic at the time, given their sponsorship of Al Qaeda'. Zarate pledged that the State Department would work with the Pentagon to ensure all DOD contracts with Bout airfreight companies were wound up. His days flying US military supplies into Baghdad International Airport were over.

At OFAC, Morgner continued tracking Bout's global operations, as names, planes and registrations kept shifting like a miasma. It reminded him of trying to keep tabs on the drugs cartels, which had been his chief role at the CIA. 'They keep trying new things and you have to adapt,' he remarked.

The summer of 2004 proved the watershed in Bout's fortunes; the US administration had truly gone in for the kill, hitting Bout where it hurt – in his pocket.

US authorities continued to strike hard against Bout's interests inside the US. His longtime business associate in the States was a Syrian-born naturalized American and former US Army sergeant called Richard Ammar Chichkali. For months a secret grand jury investigation had been tracking Chichakli's activities, and especially his links to Bout.

Treasury and FBI agents raided Chichakli's Richardson, Texas home, plus his accountancy practice. They seized his computers, bank records, flight journals, a copy of one of Bout's passports, plus assets worth in excess of $1 million, including a stash of diamonds held in Chichakli's safe and two gleaming Mercedes sports cars.

Even as Federal agents boxed up and carted off Chichakli's records, so the man himself was speaking long-distance to Viktor Bout, and his brother, Sergei. Shortly after the raid Chichakli quietly slipped out of the USA, before he could be brought to court.

The US government would go on to file charges against him for conspiracy to commit money laundering, conspiracy to commit wire fraud, and six counts of wire fraud. In essence, he was accused of assisting Bout in purchasing aircraft, evading sanctions and laundering his funds. But by then Chichakli had flown the coop.

He'd managed to purchase an airline ticket using frequent flier miles, as all his US bank accounts were frozen. He flew to Moscow, where he published an open invitation via the internet. Deliberately provocative, it challenged 'the United States government to meet with Victor Bout in Moscow anytime they want, just call my attorney or drop me an email. Victor is ready, so how about you?'

That September, the Nicolas Cage movie the *Lord of War* was released. In it, Yuri Olov, the character supposedly modelled on Bout, remarks: 'There are over 550 million firearms in worldwide circulation. That's one firearm for every twelve people on the planet. The only question is, how do we arm the other eleven?' Needless to say, the movie's release caused something of a stir.

According to Richard Chichakli, the global targeting of Bout's operations amounted to nothing less than a witch-hunt. 'It's out of the question that my gentle friend Viktor, who wouldn't hurt a cat, could have smuggled weapons on a grand scale . . .' Chichakli complained. 'He just wanted to retire in Africa, near the rainforest, to raise his daughter. They didn't get the man but they sure killed his dream.'

Either way, Bout's attempt to reinvent himself had failed. His media offensive had only served to raise his profile and his notoriety. US agencies ranked Bout up there with Osama Bin Laden on their list of most-wanted. Even Bout referred to himself sardonically as being 'second only to Osama'. With US sanctions starting to bite, outside of Russia there were few places left where he could hide.

Cue Operation Relentless – supposedly the endgame in the hunt for Viktor Bout.

CHAPTER TWENTY-THREE

BUCHAREST, ROMANIA, JANUARY 2008

The Operation Relentless team had waited for over a week – and a week in Bucharest in the dying days of January wasn't exactly a blast. For much of that time Smulian had brooded in the apartment, head stuck in his laptop researching weaponry. He kept presenting his findings to Carlos: eye-candy, to keep him and El Comandante onside.

For their part, Mike, Carlos and Ricardo had filled the days with tales from their wildest years as narcotics and arms traffickers, or in the bush-flight business. The most memorable was the story of El Comandante's 1989 arrest in Holland, and subsequent escape from the clutches of the DEA.

Back then Ricardo had been based in Amsterdam, running drugs into Europe. He'd been awaiting a 1,000-kilo shipment of cocaine – worth some $77 million on Amsterdam's streets today. He'd been making so much money he couldn't launder it fast enough. He'd taken to buying Rolex, Cartier and Patek Philippe watches – the more gold- and gem-encrusted the better – as a way to try to clean his cash. He had a pair of suitcases stuffed full of the loot, which he'd parked in the walk-in wardrobe at his luxury penthouse apartment.

The night before the 1,000-kilo dope cargo was due into Amsterdam docks, Ricardo went out to celebrate. It was a little premature perhaps, but he had few doubts that his ship was coming in. He drank a little too much, and decided to steal a bicycle. Cycling home, he'd been arrested by the Amsterdam police for being drunk-in-charge of a bicycle, and thrown into the cells.

So far so straightforward, except that the DEA had been watching the entire thing. Their agents had been tracking the dope shipment for months, and they were poised to bust Ricardo. But right now the sting was going to rat-shit, and all because the target was locked in the cells, facing charges of being drunk-in-charge of a pushbike. It was hardly the kind of bust the DEA agents had in mind.

They had a quiet word with the Amsterdam police and managed to get Ricardo released without charge. Sure enough, he headed to the dock area and took delivery of the massive shipment of drugs. He was thrown into prison for a second time in twenty-four hours, only now he faced a massive narco-trafficking charge.

Ricardo briefed his lawyer, and they worked out what must have happened: he must have been sprung from prison the first time at the behest of the DEA. His lawyer decided to make that the key plank of his defence. When Ricardo's case came before the Dutch courts, he pointed out that just twenty-four hours before the arrest on narcotics-smuggling charges, his client had been arrested for being drunk-in-charge of a pushbike. He could only have been let off and freed at the behest of the DEA.

The Dutch judge became incensed. She accused both the Dutch police and the DEA of acting as if they were above the law. 'How did you let this man go free without charge, and without any authorization from the courts?' she demanded. 'A judge has to authorize such a release, especially when the accused is to face no charge.' Neither the police nor the DEA seemed able to offer any explanation.

'Holland is not a colony of the USA,' she had declared. 'This is a free country and the courts are free. Case dismissed.' That was how Ricardo had escaped both charges scot-free. Even so he fled Holland right away, leaving behind everything he owned, including the two suitcases stuffed full of fine watches.

Mike remarked that in Holland Ricardo had truly lost his dog fuck. He'd lost the drugs, the money and his suitcases full of glittering loot. In short, it was a right royal fuck-up. Ricardo had retorted that the only royal he knew anything about was the British queen.

'And you wanna know what I know about her?' he'd challenged Mike.

'I'm sure you're going to tell me anyway.'

'She love her Corgis. You know why she love her Corgis? Because they lick her private parts.'

Mike shook his head in disgust.

Carlos shuddered. 'You know – that's just Ricardo. He's a little evil, you know.'

Mike nodded. 'Yeah. He'd fuck a frog if he could only stop it from hopping.'

Undoubtedly, Ricardo could prove rude, crude, provocative and combative, but that went with the territory. It was what made him so effective in the role that he was playing – the battle-worn, jungle-hardened commander of the FARC, hustling arms deals on the streets of Eastern Europe. And as January bled into an equally bitter February in Bucharest, El Comandante decided it was time to turn up the heat on Smulian and Viktor Bout.

The 'team' met on the evening of 2 February, at the Café Bistro Vilacrosse, a bar in the city's banking quarter. The polished wooden floors and wooden-framed wall-mirrors of the Café Bistro reflected the wealth that flowed through this part of town. The restaurant was renowned for its massive portions of Romanian goulash, served in a hollowed-out loaf of bread the size and shape of a small pumpkin. The four 'friends' placed their orders, and then El Comandante got right down to the business of tightening the screws.

His top people were losing patience, he cautioned, and for very good reasons. FARC were planning a big new military offensive – a guerrilla spectacular – and for that they were in urgent need of weaponry. 'What I don't want to do is waste my time,' he warned.

Mike turned to Carlos. 'You're not fucking translating here!' he snapped. The pressure was getting to everyone.

'No more time,' Ricardo repeated. 'No more, uh, talk. Start!'

'You understand that?' Carlos demanded of Smulian.

Smulian nodded wearily. 'Yeah, yeah.'

Bout had to come to Bucharest, Carlos explained, to cut the deal, 'grab the money and go'.

Smulian nodded. Of course, Bout would be happy to grab the money and go, if only he could get there!

A pretty young Romanian waitress arrived with their orders.

'You put some olive oil on the spinach,' Mike counselled Carlos. 'It's nice with olive oil and, uh, salt.'

'Salt, yeah.'

Mike turned to the waitress. 'Are you married?' The young

woman looked flustered. 'You come with me, I'll give you my son,' Mike continued. 'You can marry my son.'

The waitress tittered, not quite knowing whether Mike was joking or not.

'They have a new thing against helicopters,' Smulian ventured, cutting through Snow's overtures on behalf of his son, and getting back to the job at hand.

'Hmmm?' Carlos asked.

'They have a new thing against helicopters,' Smulian repeated. He'd been researching all sorts of hardware, much of which he felt sure the FARC might need. Ricardo confirmed that they were willing to consider any type of anti-aircraft weaponry that might secure them an advantage.

Mike, meanwhile, was still trying to woo the waitress. 'He will love you,' he declared of his son. 'I will tell him.'

'The Americans have also developed some new stuff,' Smulian ploughed on. He cited the M307, a 25-millimetre weapon that was computer controlled, using infrared beams to measure distance and bearing to target. It was able to shoot through walls, blasting a target on the far side.

'You understand it, Comandante?' Mike queried. He mimed a fist punching through a wall formed by the palm of his hand. 'It's . . . like this, in here, pow!'

Smulian boasted that Bout had promised to equal or outgun any American hardware. 'What . . . is patience in Spanish?' he ventured.

'*Paciencia,*' Carlos told him.

'*Paciencia,*' Smulian counselled; you just need to have patience.

'We've been drinking paciencia every night,' Carlos growled.

'I have patience,' Ricardo added, darkly. 'What I don't have is time . . . Right now I'm working on something very big in my country. I need them ASAP.'

By now the guys had dug down to the lowest reaches of their bread loaf goulashes, and the evening was drawing to a close.

Ricardo fixed Smulian with a look. 'Andrew, right now in my country, the, uh, Americans are coming in . . . with helicopters.. That didn't used to happen. Now it does . . . We no longer see where they're coming from. Do you understand? . . . Do you understand?'

Smulian spread his hands in a gesture that craved patience. In a few days Bout would be there, he promised, and all El Comandante's dreams would come true.

If only.

In truth, the full extent of Bout's predicament was about to be revealed. It was 1.54 p.m. on 4 February when he called. The connection kept breaking up, but one thing was clear: Bout was burning up with frustration. His Romanian visa was proving so problematic that he suggested a radical alternative: he would hire a private jet to fly the 'FARC' to Moldova, complete with their cash.

'The question is, if it's urgent for them, why not do it this way?' he reasoned. 'Because it's very stupid what you're trying to arrange now . . . We need one day, everything is finished . . .'

Smulian didn't sound convinced. 'What they say is they want me to stay with them once they . . . hand over the stuff, you know? Then they have . . . some security . . .'

'Okay, it's no problem . . . Andrew, we're no, uh, crooks.'

Bout called again a few minutes later. He'd thought of an alternative, in case the FARC baulked at taking his VIP flight. 'Look, the best, uh, available option – most safest and most reliable –

you put these bastards in a good car or two. Just drive . . . It's visa-free for them and for you . . . You tell me it's okay, tomorrow you going there, I'm also going tomorrow there.'

'Okay. All right. I'll tell them when they come here. They'll be here just now.'

'But, uh, it's quickest and it's smart option, and it's safe for everybody.'

Smulian reiterated that he'd speak to their 'FARC friends' and see what was possible.

A short while later Carlos arrived at the apartment. Smulian outlined Bout's newest suggestion: they could hire a car, fill the boot with cash, drive the two hundred kilometres to Moldova, and enter the country, no visas required. Bout would be waiting for them. What was not to like?

'Okay, you know the problem . . .' Carlos began. His mind was racing, as he tried to come up with a reason; a viable objection; anything that might explain why this option wasn't doable. *Cash*, he told himself. Conjure up images of heaps of bank notes. Piles of cash from dope sales. El Comandante counting thick wads of dollars – or rather euros, this being Europe. *Play to their greed.*

'Problem is the money . . . Even the Comandante in the apartment is five million euros. And that's the reason he don't wanna move from there. The money's right there . . .' Ricardo was sitting in his Bucharest apartment with five million euros in cash. It was no surprise that he didn't want to leave.

'Money. Yeah.' Smulian understood: shifting huge heaps of cash was the issue.

'The Comandante's with the money right there . . .' Carlos repeated. Plus there was this: El Comandante had decided that either Bout made it to Bucharest by Friday, or the FARC were out of there. Gone.

Smulian explained that the Russian feared he couldn't make Bucharest at all. Would the guys look to a future date to meet at an alternative location?

Carlos looked doubtful. He and El Comandante would have to return to Colombia, to check out the next steps with the FARC's high command.

'I'm sorry, Carlos, I'm responsible here . . .' Mike interjected, 'so if you ask my advice . . . if this don't work we fuckin' leave it. Because . . . this fucking operation has cost a fortune.'

'That's true, that's true, my friend,' Carlos agreed. 'But . . . Let's wait, let's talk, lets see . . . I gotta go and sit with everybody and explain . . . But, uh, I don't wanna say no. I don't wanna say yes. But maybe.'

Smulian got the message: the deal was hanging by a slender thread. Later, he got on a call with Bout. He explained that the entire proposition was falling to pieces, and for no other reason than that the two sides weren't able to meet.

'But they're not eager to move at all?' Bout queried.

'No, not at all.'

'Fucking shit, you know . . .' Having looked into it, Bout explained, the risks associated with flying into Bucharest were unacceptable.

'Yeah, yeah, I understand.'

'So they will sit there and wait until I come. Correct?'

'Yeah, yeah.'

'Oh, shit. Fucking shit. You know, it's so stupid . . . waste of time, and . . . a stupid idea . . .'

'Yeah,' Smulian confirmed. The line was terrible, but Bout sounded pissed off and close to desperate.

'Look, try to talk with them and find out exactly why they can't move, because . . . Because I'm trying real . . . hard myself, but you know, they also must do some steps from their side.'

'Yeah, yeah, yeah.' Smulian promised that he would try. But in truth, he felt jaded and close to exhausted. He sensed it was all slipping fast through his fingers.

Thirteen minutes after that call, Bout was on the line again. He'd been thrashing about trying to find a solution, and he figured he'd cracked it.

'I've got idea . . .' he declared, excitedly. 'Most quickest way to avoid this shit with the visa is come with a private flight . . .'

At first Smulian misunderstood what Bout was suggesting. 'You know, uh, the problem is . . . they can't move from here . . .'

'No, I understand. But I mean I will come with a private flight, but then, bloody hell, you know, it cost a arm and leg . . .'

'Oh, okay, okay.' Smulian got what Bout was driving at now.

Being a former pilot, he understood what Bout meant. Generally speaking, aircrew don't require visas to fly into a country. They enter on a 'Gen Dec' – a General Declaration – which allows them ten days on the ground. The aircraft would need over-flight and landing clearance, which would involve declaring the names of the captain and crew, but passports were rarely checked.

In theory, Bout could fly into Bucharest posing as aircrew and under an assumed name, and no one would be any the wiser. Finally, they'd hit upon what had to be a workable solution from both sides.

Smulian signed off the call and immediately phoned Carlos. He outlined Bout's suggestion. El Mexicano confirmed that the

'FARC' would be up for this. All they needed was a price for the private aircraft hire, and it was game on.

Unless the cost was exorbitant, Carlos felt certain the private jet hire would be covered from the Operation Relentless budget. He double-checked with the DEA agents. They'd need to run it past headquarters, but it would be a small price to pay to nail the notorious, mysterious, unstoppable Viktor Bout. And as a bonus, they would have tricked him into flying right into their clutches.

At the apartment, Smulian dropped some more weapons specs onto a zip-drive, along with the most recent photo of Viktor Bout that he had been able to find. He'd give it to Carlos, so he and El Comandante would be able to recognize Bout the moment he stepped off the plane.

With Relentless having seemingly found its fuck of the dog once more, the four plotters converged at the Café Bistro Vilacrosse. It wasn't quite La Sirene, but it was about as good as it got in Bucharest. Mike, Carlos, Ricardo and Smulian ran through the proposal, trying to determine if there were any holes. There were none, as far as they could ascertain.

From both sides it seemed like the 'perfect' solution. There was a decidedly upbeat feeling to the gathering, this 5 February evening, over their giant bread rolls filled with the thick and spicy goulash that was the Café Bistro's speciality.

'Let me ask you something . . .' Carlos ventured, as if out of idle curiosity. 'You are British, no?'

'I'm born in Britain,' Smulian confirmed, 'but I moved when I think I was eight years old.'

'And you don't like the . . . the Americans, the gringos?'

Smulian nodded. 'Because they lie, and they . . . think they're better than everybody else.'

'That's the reason that we want to kill everybody,' Carlos declared.

He turned to Ricardo and translated what Smulian had said. 'I asked him why he doesn't get along with the gringos . . . And he told me they're liars and they're cold. And I said to him: "That's why they all have to be killed . . ."'

Ricardo's eyes narrowed. It made perfect sense to him.

Carlos turned back to Smulian. 'It's like I told you in the beginning – we are not fighting against another country. What we got is an internal war. So why they wanna go and be in our country? Why?'

'Have you got oil there?' Smulian queried.

'Yeah, but it's not much.' As long as the Americans stayed in Colombia, they were legitimate targets, Carlos declared.

'I don't care if you kill gringos or not . . .' Smulian told him. 'I'm not thinking about the gringos. I'm thinking about your people. So, you have to work for the good of your people. If you . . . kill gringos – let's say you shoot down ten helicopters, or whatever – how does it help your people?'

Carlos thought about that for a second. 'Okay, what is going to happen is they, every time that they go fly to the jungle, they get . . . one shot down . . .'

If the Americans kept losing helicopters, Smulian explained, the American public would quickly lose the appetite for further intervention in Colombia. They'd be forced to withdraw.

'Ah, okay.' Carlos nodded. 'Okay, now without . . . the gringos in our country, we can go back to the table.' Carlos meant the negotiating table, around which the FARC could cut a deal with the Colombian government.

'And you can help us on that . . .' he continued. 'I know that you

want to help us. I know that, that you've . . . got good intentions.'
Carlos gestured at El Comandante. 'But right now, if you talk to
him, you only going to hear fight. And kill . . .'

'You know, I've been in many wars,' Smulian remarked. With
the upbeat atmosphere and the food and drink, he was getting
somewhat carried away. 'You know, when I was . . . eighteen years
old I was killing people already . . .' Smulian boasted that while
he hadn't shot any gringos, when serving in the South African
military he'd spent time 'mowing blacks down like wheat'.

In truth, this was pure beer talk. Smulian had never killed
anyone in his life. In fact he'd never had the need to fire a weapon
in anger. But this close to the deal going through – with Bout
poised to fly in on a private jet – he felt the need to big-up his
credentials; to show that he knew what he was talking about; to
prove that he was the man.

Bout called the following day. Smulian was expecting to hear
good news. 'Yeah?' he answered, excitedly.

'Alo. Yep.'

'Okay . . . if you can get a private fight here, they can get somebody to meet the aircraft outside and bring you through.'

'Um, there is a political problem with this . . .' Bout announced.

The problem, he explained, was all about him; his wanted
status and the worldwide travel bans. He'd been passed a warning
from contacts in Bucharest. They'd told him that he'd be crazy to
travel to Romania, no matter what form of ruse he might employ.
No ifs, no buts – Bucharest wasn't happening.

In a series of further calls and texts, Bout seemed to vacillate
between trying to keep the deal alive and kissing it all goodbye.
At one point he assured Smulian: 'On my side we now fully
ready . . . get the full list of what they need . . .' But a few minutes

later he said that maybe they should cut their losses. 'Or just . . . let's forget it. That's all.'

Smulian was inclined to do the latter. He'd played long-distance piggy-in-the-middle for far too long. He'd been squeezed between the two sides, wrung out, and hung out to dry. He felt deflated, jaded and most of all, dog tired.

He relayed to Carlos the dispiriting news: Bucharest was a non-starter and maybe the whole deal had hit the buffers. The King of Sting gathered the DEA team at their hotel. He explained what had happened.

Supervising Agent Lou Milione knew what they had to do. They'd been chasing Bout for months now, and they'd got so very close, but this was the time when they had to step away. If they were genuine FARC, they'd be busy people with multiple projects to attend to. They couldn't afford to give the impression that they were happy to wait for ever.

It was a tough call, especially as they knew that the President of the United States was taking a personal interest in their mission. George W Bush had signed the 2004 EXORD, signalling that the US was getting serious over Bout. Just a few months of his presidency remained, so time was running out to get his man.

Carlos agreed with Lou's take on things. It had reached the stage where if they waited any longer it would seem suspicious. They needed to head home, regroup and look for a country where they as the 'FARC' and Bout could both travel. That rapidly became the focus of their discussions: where to plan an alternative rendezvous.

'Why don't we shoot for Japan?' Mike ventured.

'No way,' said Agent Zach. 'They're far too correct over there.'

'Plus it'd take years to extradite him from Japan,' Lou explained.

'Well right now it's all moving slower than a barmaid's fart,' Mike growled. 'So someone better come up with something.'

'Why don't we go for a mid-ocean meet?' Carlos suggested.

That presented its own set of challenges. They'd have to get Bout to somewhere outside of any nation's territorial waters, for the US authorities to be able to arrest him, and even then they could be accused of an act of kidnapping on the high seas. No one else seemed to have any bright ideas.

Mike glanced dismissively around the Relentless team. 'Just realized what DEA stands for: Defining Extreme Apathy.'

Several of them objected: that was way below the belt.

Then someone threw out the suggestion of Thailand. It had several big plusses. One, Russians didn't need a visa to get there. Two, it was seen as something of a tourist and party destination, so unlikely to arouse suspicion. And three, the DEA had excellent working relations with the Royal Thai Police. Maybe that was the answer. Maybe Thailand was it.

They agreed to propose Thailand, and to see if Bout would bite. To that end, Wim and Carlos worked on setting up an undercover email address, for future communications with Bout. It would be routed via a server in Colombia, so if the Russian had the ability to trace or interrogate its source, it would appear genuine.

On 6 February Carlos met with Mike and Smulian for the last time in Bucharest. The King of Sting passed Smulian the email address they'd just created for all future communications. He asked Smulian to call Bout, so they could have one final conversation before going their separate ways.

'Hello, my friend. How are you?' Carlos began, in Spanish.

'Oh, very well. Very well. And you?'

'Good, good. I'm a little bit sad here, because we were not able to see each other. But, uh, what I want to tell you is that, uh, our organization always needs friends like you . . . And I don't want to close the door with you . . . So, we can keep in touch . . .'

'Yes, yes, yes, yes, yes, yes,' Bout confirmed.

'We can . . . come to an agreement to see if we can meet.'

'Okay. Okay . . . It's a good plan. Let's do it like you're saying.'

Carlos reiterated that from their side, they were still very keen to do the deal. They agreed to stay in contact via the 'secure' email Smulian would pass to Bout.

Carlos handed the phone back to Smulian.

'So just, you know, be good with them and keep line open,' Bout told Smulian. 'I think it will work . . . Because, what he told me, they're very excited and this most important. Okay?'

Smulian agreed to Bout's suggestion and killed the call.

But when Carlos was gone, he seemed to sink into a dark morass. It wasn't the first time that Mike had seen him like this. Smulian complained that he'd had more than enough. He was utterly fed up, because after all the hard work they'd hit a brick wall. The deal was dead in the water, as far as he saw it.

Mike decided to play along. 'Yep, we've wasted more than enough fucking time. If Viktor ever was serious, he's not going to make it happen now.'

After Smulian had betrayed him, Mike really didn't have a great deal of sympathy. More to the point, he feared that Smulian was right: the deal was dead in the water. The Bucharest debacle had proved that much. Thailand was a decent enough idea, but he didn't rate its chances. Barring some kind of miracle, no one was about to lure the Russian out of Moscow any time soon.

In truth, Mike felt a crushing sense of disappointment. It was as if another SAS mission or bush flight had just got canned, except that this time he was on his own, with no buddies with whom to share his sense of disillusionment. He caught a flight back to Africa feeling a hollowness setting in.

Right at this juncture, Bout seemed beyond anyone's reach and utterly immune to capture.

CHAPTER TWENTY-FOUR

MOSCOW, RUSSIA, FEBRUARY 2008

On 12 February 2008 Viktor Bout opened a new email account: agregatum@gmail.com. He was in Moscow at the time, and over the next few days he would check it several times: once on the thirteenth, from Kaliningrad, once on the fourteenth from Leningrad and once on the fifteenth from Moscow again.

This signified several things. One, that Bout was busy. Two, that he was travelling a lot within Russian territory: in four days he'd covered some 2,000 kilometres. Three, that he was keen to receive a response to the four-line email that he'd sent from his new account.

Six days after he and Carlos had signed off on their Bucharest phone call – agreeing that, for now at least, the arms deal was a dead duck – Bout had sent an email to the 'secure' contact address that Carlos had given him: bogotazo@yahoo.com.

It read:

Buenos Dias!
This is e mail we can use for communication.
Best regards
Friend of Andrew

Bout's message popped into the Yahoo inbox, and Carlos and Agent Brown were watching. They realized immediately that it very likely signalled that Operation Relentless was back in business, but Wim reckoned that they had to play it cool. Somehow, they had to turn the bullshit-fest of Bucharest into triumph in Thailand.

He and Carlos would not reply at first. Instead, they'd let Bout sweat a little. Five days after receipt of his email they drafted a carefully worded response. It was written in Spanish, for obvious reasons:

'HOLA MI AMIGO! COMO ESTA? PERDON POR LA TAR-DANSA . . .'

'Hello, my friend. How are you? Sorry it took me so long to get back to you, but I wasn't in a good place to be able to get in touch. I don't know if you'd rather that we write to each other in Spanish. I hope to be able to talk to you very soon. Your new friend.'

The baited-hook had been thrown in the water: now to see if Bout would bite.

Agent Zach got in touch with Mike Snow, to warn him that Relentless might be back on. 'We emailed MOD . . . yesterday but we're waiting to see what the response is.' 'MOD' – short for Merchant of Death – was their agreed code for Viktor Bout. Smulian was also chasing Carlos, Zach told him, as the parties circled each other warily.

Zach attached to his email an audio file of a phone conversation between Bout and Smulian, recorded the day the DEA team had bailed out of Romania. 'Take a listen and see if you can make sense of it. The end of the call clearly deals with our guys and our deal . . .'

Mike double-clicked on the WAV file, turned up the volume

on his home computer and settled down to listen. The recording was surprisingly clear.

'They left this morning, early I think,' Smulian explained to Bout – referring to the 'FARC' team's departure from Bucharest.

'But I think we talk very good yesterday,' Bout replied, 'and I understand they hook up to idea . . . so let us organize the rest of it . . .'

'No, no, no. It's okay. I made like I was upset but it was just to, you know . . .' Smulian suggested his down-in-the-dumps act at the end of the Bucharest visit had been just that – a bit of theatre to guilt-trip the 'FARC' and to keep them onside.

'Okay, but good. At least you explained well and they really hook up to this,' Bout enthused. 'I am already doing the shop, you know, preparing everything. No problem in two weeks to finish everything . . .'

During the endgame of Bucharest it seemed both sides had been playing mindgames. Bout – and Smulian with him – had been playing hard to get. Of course, the DEA had the one big advantage in all of this: they had Smulian and Bout wired for sound, to help unmask whatever public face they might try to present.

As Mike contemplated yet another chapter in the hunt for Viktor Bout, he felt an odd mixture of emotions. On one level, ever since his tutor, Foot, had told him that he'd never amount to anything Mike had had a pathological hatred of failure. His life had been defined by the need to prove himself; to succeed. Plus he figured he owed it to the brother and sister from the N'Djilli Airport explosions to help put a stop to the work of a man like Bout.

But on another level there was absolutely no guarantee that

Bout would make it to Thailand. There was one undeniable upside: Thailand was sunny, the Thai people were friendly and the food was to die for. Plus a part of Mike was still caught up in the buzz of Operation Relentless: the thrill of the hunt.

On balance, he figured they might as well give Bangkok a whirl.

Things began to move swiftly now. Carlos and Bout spoke by cellphone, both seeming to agree that Thailand was a good and workable option.

'I'm going to be travelling . . . and I'm not going to have my phone in Mexico,' Carlos explained. He wasn't, of course: he would be taking it easy in sunny Florida. This was just more 'FARC' theatre. 'But I'll be able to communicate through . . . the phone number in the country where I am . . . I'll call and give it to you . . . so that we can meet on Thursday.'

'Okay, okay . . . Thursday is the eighth?'

'Uh, it's the sixth, right?'

'Yes, yes, yes, yes . . . I have to travel on the fifth. So on the sixth I'll be there . . .'

'Okay, my friend.'

'See you soon.'

They were on for a rendezvous in Bangkok on 6 March 2008. Once the call was ended, Carlos spoke into the recording device that he was using to capture any calls made from home. 'This call was to Viktor. The time is 11.50 a.m. and today is 29 February 2008.'

Then he sat at his laptop, loaded up the audio file and emailed it direct to Agent Brown.

In Moscow, meanwhile, Bout was busy doing his home-work. He pulled out a black plastic loose-leaf file, to collate any printed research, and began downloading documents to his desktop. He logged onto a story by the US news network PBS about the FARC's war in Colombia. The PBS Newshour Special defined FARC's mission as to 'overthrow the State and establish a communist-agrarian' rule.

'The FARC finances its operations through kidnapping and ransom, extortion, and narcotics trafficking. It also targets anyone suspected of conspiring with the military . . . According to . . . analysts, the FARC earns between $250 and $300 million through criminal acts, of which 65 per cent comes from the drugs trade.

'The FARC's . . . weapons include explosives, landmines and bombs camouflaged as necklaces, soccer balls and soup cans. They have also orchestrated prison revolts, attacked against police and military personnel and regularly set up roadblocks to "protect" villages . . . According to reports, the FARC forcibly enlists any persons between the ages of 13 to 60 to work coca or poppy plantations . . .'

Bout logged onto a YouTube video, which explained how the FARC had learned to mix 'adhesive, gasoline drums, sulfuric acid and ACPM (diesel oil)' with certain explosive chemicals, resulting in 'fire bombs that would adhere to the victims . . . and burn them in seconds.' Basically a DIY version of napalm.

He downloaded a March 2005 US Department of Justice (DOJ) press release, announcing the extradition to the US of four FARC luminaries – chief among them Rojas 'Sonia' Valderama – on drugs-trafficking charges. The DOJ also accused the FARC and its members of 'the kidnapping and murder of US citizens'.

The entire case had been masterminded by none other than the DEA. 'The . . . extradition of the FARC commander known as

"Sonia" has shown the FARC for what it is,' a DEA spokesperson commented, 'murderous drugs profiteers terrorizing their fellow citizens. Sonia's extradition is a victory not only for the people of Colombia and the United States, but for the rule of law.'

This was perhaps the moment at which Bout should have started having second thoughts about Thailand. But apparently he did not. Perhaps the idea of the DEA using the reviled FARC as cover to lure in the bad guys just seemed too farfetched. Either way, not even a warning by Bout's long-time friend and body-guard, Timur Edikhnov, seemed able to sway him.

'We met . . . to discuss the trip,' Edikhnov explained. 'He said: "I'm flying to Thailand. I have a buyer for helicopters and I might be able to sell a plane." I said: "Don't go. Your situation is unstable and in Russia you are safe. Let me go instead of you and offer the planes." But he thought this meeting might be crucial and he wanted to go himself. He said he hadn't been to Asia for ages . . .'

In Moscow at least, the die was cast.

Mike was the first to jet into Bangkok. Several years ago he'd set up a business flying consumer goods – colourful silks and rattans – from Thailand to Africa, and he had fond memories of the country. He made his way to the five-star Sofitel Silom Hotel, a glittering edifice of glass and steel towering thirty-eight floors above the city's teeming Si Phraya Road, in the heart of Bangkok's commercial district.

Mike had stayed there before when on business in the city, and he'd even taken Margaret there for their thirtieth wedding anniversary. It was something of a home-from-home. He'd grown to like the Thai people. He knew that beneath the gentle Buddhist façade they were likely to take your balls off in any business deal, but still there was something wrong with you if you didn't fall in love with the locals' welcome and grace ten times before you reached your hotel.

Shortly after his arrival the DEA team jetted in – Carlos, Ricardo, Wim, Zach and Lou Milione. It was time to split up: from now on DEA agents and confidential sources would be strictly segregated. Carlos and Ricardo would join Mike at the Sofitel, while the DEA agents would remain secreted in the nearby Silom Plaza.

Today was 4 March, and by coincidence it was Mike's sixty-first birthday. He and Carlos had struck up a genuine friendship and they headed out into downtown Bangkok. Snow took the Guatemalan on a tour of the temples that line the Chao Phraya River – the River of Kings – the city's main waterway.

They ended up visiting a traditional Thai fortune-teller. There was nothing particularly surprising foretold about Mike Snow's future: apparently, he would live to a grand old age. With Carlos Sagastume it was somewhat different. The wrinkled old Thai took the Guatemalan's hand, and studied it for a few seconds, before glancing at Carlos, a touch of surprise burning in his eyes.

'You – you work for American government,' the fortune-teller announced.

He glanced back at the hand. When he looked up again, his eyes were wide with astonishment. 'You with the CIA. You work here in Bangkok with . . .'

Carlos reached over and gently placed his hand over the old man's mouth. *Be silent.* With his other he palmed a $100 bill into the fortune-teller's pocket.

'Something for your wife and kids,' Carlos told him. 'And . . . not another word . . .'

He removed his hand. The fortune-teller gestured at the

tiny room in which he worked. 'Nothing ever leave these four walls.'

Carlos insisted he and Mike jump in a cab for the return trip to the hotel. Once inside, Mike was practically doubled-over with laughter. 'You look like you've just seen a ghost! Hey, Lingua Plata – you just lost all your fuck of the dog!'

Carlos grimaced. 'You know, Papa Bear, that could have been very bad moment, if the wrong guys listening.'

Mike shook his grizzled head. 'No way were we fucking followed.' He paused. 'Anyway, what did you expect? It's like I told you: thoughts become things . . .'

Neither Smulian nor Bout were expected for another twenty-four hours, so in typical DEA style – Drunk Every Afternoon – the team decided to head out that evening and paint the town red. The Bear's birthday needed to be celebrated, and at the risk of tempting fate they'd also raise a glass or two to the coming sting.

Come nightfall, the streets around the Sofitel transformed themselves. The hotel was only a five-minute walk from Bangkok's infamous Pat-Pong red light district, and street-vendors had set up stalls on every corner, hawking delicious-smelling Thai delicacies. If the team were going to hang out and wait for Bout, this wasn't the worst of places to do so.

It beat Bucharest in January, that was for sure.

After feasting at the roadside stalls they returned to the Sofitel, whereupon Carlos disappeared to his room. He was back again a minute later, bearing a bottle of Ron Zacapa 23. He'd brought it especially to celebrate Mike's birthday. This was no ordinary rum, he explained. Produced in Guatemala from the first-pressing sugar cane juice, it was the finest in the world.

Mike glanced at the label: 'The balance of bouquet and unique flavors is derived from a blend of aged rums originating from the "Systema Solera" aging process . . .'

'Very nice,' he remarked. 'Trouble is, I don't drink rum.'

Carlos grabbed the bottle. 'Ah, but Papa Oso, you will this. You have to try a Cuba Libre. Just one, my friend.'

Somehow, Carlos persuaded the Sofitel's barman to mix a round of Cuba Libre cocktails – rum, Coca-Cola and fresh lime-juice poured over ice – using his bottle of Ron Zacapa 23. He presented the first to the birthday boy.

'You like this, Papa Bear, I tell you a funny story,' Carlos promised. 'Real funny, this one.'

Mike took a swig. He had to admit, the drink was like liquid gold.

After a few rounds of Cuba Libres, Carlos began to tell his tale. 'You remember a year back we got Monzer Al Kazar? When I flew out of Spain I didn't realize they had routed me via Ceuta, the Spanish enclave in Morocco. And when you transit through Ceuta, you have to clear customs . . . Big problem.'

Carlos explained how he had entered Spain for the Kazar sting without getting an entry stamp in his passport. The immigration guy at Ceuta airport had searched and searched, trying to find one. Finally he'd popped the question: how had Carlos entered into Spain without any record of having done so?

Carlos argued it had to be Spanish immigration incompetence. It wasn't his fault if they had failed to give him a stamp. All the while he was worried about the mass of bugging and recording equipment that he had disassembled and stashed in his luggage. If this got serious, it could get well out of hand.

The officer called the head of immigration. He asked Carlos

the same questions all over again. Finally, noting that Carlos was supposedly a Guatemalan, he ventured: 'So, tell me, what is the best rum in the world?'

'There are two,' Carlos answered. 'Ron Botran and Ron Zacapa.'

'Yes, but which is the best?'

'Ron Zacapa. Has to be.'

The immigration guy let Carlos go, on the strength of his Ron Zacapa bona fides. Only a true Guatemalan would know such a thing. Carlos signalled for another round of Cuba Libres.

'So what do we do when – if – Viktor gets busted?' Mike asked.

'You run. You get out of the country as soon as you can. You run.'

Mike bridled. 'Why the fuck would I want to do that? I ain't done nothing wrong.'

'No, no, no. Of course, you done nothing wrong.' Carlos turned serious for a moment. 'But still – is the most dangerous moment of any operation. You're still in the country where the bust is made. In Thailand, anything can happen. Viktor may still have associates here. You can even be killed. Wiping out the witnesses . . . So make no mistake, Papa Bear – you run.'

'I ain't running from anyone. It's not in my DNA to run.'

Carlos fixed The Bear with a look. 'Trust me, my friend, when the moment comes you will run. Along with the rest of us.'

Through his Cuba Libre-induced haze Mike suddenly understood. This wasn't theatre any more. This was deadly serious.

The following day – 5 March 2008 – the partygoers were surprised at how modest were their hangovers. It was testament to the quality of the rum they had consumed – Carlos's bottle had been drained dry. It was good that minds were more or less in order. Smulian was due in that evening, and Viktor Bout himself the following morning, assuming he went ahead and boarded his nine-hour flight, Moscow to Bangkok.

That afternoon Lou Milione called a meeting of the team. The DEA's regional director in Bangkok, Tom Pasquarello, joined them. He would play a crucial role in planning things here on the ground, in what would be a citywide operation. He'd liaise with the elite Thai police unit that was going to lead the takedown.

Wim and Zach briefed Carlos and Ricardo on exactly what they needed to secure on tape. They needed Bout to agree the list of weaponry that he would supply to the 'FARC', and the terms of the deal – namely numbers of arms, prices and the means of delivery.

Of crucial importance was to nail down the provision of the Igla surface-to-air missiles, the ultimate prize for terrorists worldwide. They were also to agree how the cash for the deal would be delivered into Bout's hands. And at some point they had to make crystal clear that the entire package of weaponry was to be used against the Colombian armed forces, *and* US pilots flying helicopters in the country.

The DEA had booked a room on the twenty-fifth floor of the Sofitel, in which to establish an operations room. They'd base themselves there, along with a contingent of Royal Thai Police (RTP) from the elite Crime Suppression Division. Oddly, RTP officers weren't actually issued with any standard firearms. Instead, they had to buy their own weapons from commercial suppliers. Popular pistols were the Colt M1911, and the Austrian-made Glock-19.

Having to fork out hard-earned cash for their weaponry, RTP officers were known to seek value for money. They were not averse to using lethal force, where necessary. Indeed, Taksin Sathon, the commander of the RTP unit tasked with the takedown, was reputed to have killed an armed assailant in a shoot-out just a few days before.

Carlos and Mike were to lure Bout to the twenty-fifth floor of the Sofitel, where the business centre was situated. Ricardo would meet them there, as if he'd been busy on other FARC business. They were to hire a private conference room, which would help optimize the quality of the audio recordings. Meanwhile, the DEA team and their RTP counterparts would be lurking close by.

At the end of the briefing, the DEA agents turned their attention to the moment when the guys with guns showed up. Carlos and Ricardo would need to be arrested along with Bout and Smulian. That way, neither target would know if the 'FARC' were for real or not, leaving them with the impression that they had been cutting a genuine deal, which was crucial if Smulian was to be persuaded to turn state's evidence. If the targets believed the 'FARC' were for real, it would also help safeguard Carlos and Ricardo as they got the hell out of the country. And because knowledge is power, the less the targets understood about what had happened the more strength to the DEA's arm.

But in Africa, meanwhile, Operation Relentless had very nearly crashed and burned, and for a whole different set of reasons. Shortly before catching his flight to Bangkok, Andrew Smulian had phoned Margaret Snow. Margaret thought Smulian a charming English gent, which meant she could largely forgive him his roguish ways.

Smulian had told her that he was about to leave for Bangkok.

'Are you excited, Andrew?' Margaret had asked him – meaning are you excited to be this close to nailing Viktor Bout. Incredibly, she didn't know that Smulian wasn't in on the sting, because her husband hadn't told her.

There was a moment's awkward silence, before Smulian answered. 'Excited? No, I'm actually really quite nervous.'

Smulian sounded like a worried man. Margaret knew that he'd been to Moscow solo, playing what she presumed was a 'Postman Pat' role on behalf of the DEA. It didn't make sense for him to be feeling so anxious right now. Fortunately, she didn't pry any further and Smulian didn't think to do so, either. Instead she wished Smulian luck, assuring him it would all be okay.

Nine and a half hours later, Smulian had flitted east across the Indian Ocean and touched down in Bangkok, on a flight booked and paid for by Mike Snow, using DEA funds. He made his way to the Sofitel and linked up with Carlos and Mike, in the hotel's plush mezzanine lounge.

From the outset, Smulian seemed ill at ease. Carlos sensed he wanted a quiet one-on-one. He suggested he help Smulian get settled in his room. Smulian used his plastic key-fob to swipe open the door and Carlos fetched a couple of beers from the minibar. Barely had he cracked them open, before Smulian began to unburden his concerns.

'The system he was suggesting that we use, I see that . . . you people have used it before. And . . . that's a worry because that means . . . the guys supporting the government, they know about these things.'

Smulian had discovered that the parachute delivery system proposed by Bout had been used to deliver arms to the FARC on previous occasions. It was known about, including by the Colombian government and their US advisors. In which case, did it really make sense to utilize the same system again?

Carlos suggested that perhaps they should send the weapons by ship to Paramaribo, the capital city of Suriname. From Paramaribo they'd transport them onwards to Colombia by smaller boats, each taking a separate parcel of weaponry.

'Yeah, maybe we have to do that,' Smulian agreed.

He went on to outline what lay at the heart of his worries right now. In recent weeks a top FARC leader, Tomás Medina Caracas – revolutionary name 'El Negro Acacio' – had been killed in a Colombian military operation. During the two-year hunt, Caracas – the mastermind of the FARC's narcotics business – had escaped numerous attempts to nail him.

But on 1 September 2007, he'd been trapped on Colombia's border with Venezuela and hit in an air assault. The US authorities had been seeking Caracas for years, citing his shipments of cocaine and heroin to America as the key reason. He was also charged in US courts with kidnapping and holding to ransom two American oil workers, until a million-dollar ransom had been paid.

Smulian's worry seemed to be that Caracas' death must have been the result of an 'inside job' – someone within the FARC betraying his whereabouts. He was nervous that the FARC had grown leaky, with obvious ramifications for the kind of business they were about to conduct here in Bangkok.

'No, no, no, no, no,' Carlos insisted. 'There's no leaks.'

He had to grip this now. The last thing they needed was the Englishman going flaky on the deal: Bout was due in the following morning. Carlos explained this wasn't the first time that a FARC leader had been hit: it pretty much went with the territory.

'What happened is that they know almost where is . . . all the bases and everything . . . What happened is they cannot go there with troops because we are prepared, and it's very difficult to get there. What happened is they went on the chopper and they went on the plane . . .'

Carlos made a whistling noise, like bombs falling from the heavens, while miming with his hand a helicopter swooping in to attack.

'Yeah. Yeah . . .' Smulian acknowledged.

'Now . . . you see, the gringos are the one who's fucking everything up, so we gotta stop that.' All the more reason for the FARC to take delivery of some top-notch weaponry, he explained.

'Yeah.' Carlos' fighting talk seemed to be settling Smulian's nerves.

'It's like what happened with, uh, Vietnam . . . So, what we going to do is everything that fly, we gotta take 'em down.'

'Yeah,' Smulian enthused.

'Like they move troops . . . on those choppers, on the, uh . . .'

'Black Hawks,' Smulian filled in for him.

'Black Hawks. So . . . we need to take them down . . . Because the Black Hawks that they are using over there, they are gringos. They are no . . .'

'No locals.' There were no Colombians at the Black Hawks' controls: it was all American pilots.

The US aircrews would be taken by total surprise, Carlos explained, for no one would know that the FARC had acquired surface-to-air missiles.

'Yeah. No, that, that's good,' Smulian agreed. 'I, I just hope we can get it all together. Yeah, it will be excellent.'

Carlos' tape-recorder was capturing every word. Smulian was totally screwed by now, of that the King of Sting had no doubt.

With his immunity waived, the DEA had everything they could possibly wish for to force Smulian to testify.

Carlos and Smulian finished their Bangkok 'heart-to-heart' at about the same time that Bout would be heading to the Moscow airport, to catch his flight. *If he was catching his flight.* Either way, Carlos felt certain he'd put enough steel in Smulian's backbone to get him through the next forty-eight hours, whatever they might bring.

If Bout flew into Bangkok, they should have him banged to rights. The US prosecutor dealing with the case, which was filed in a New York court, had already drafted a warrant for the Russian's arrest. But the DEA wanted a clear, tape-recorded admission from Bout that he knew the weapons he was selling would be used to kill Americans. That would be the icing on the legal cake, as it were.

But in truth, this was Bangkok that the Operation Relentless team was working in, and that was a very long way from New York. In truth, anything could happen. And whether Bout actually stepped onto his Bangkok flight – that was in the lap of the gods.

Already Operation Relentless had proved one of the most costly missions ever undertaken by the DEA. Admittedly, much of its budget had been funded out of the rake-off from the Copenhagen money-laundering sting, but still the bottom line was the bottom line, and Relentless needed to deliver.

Yet all the Bangkok team could do now was wait.

CHAPTER TWENTY-FIVE

BANGKOK, THAILAND, MARCH 2008

At shortly after 1000 hours on 6 March 2008 Lou Milione took the call. A Royal Thai Police officer was phoning from the airport: Viktor Bout was in-bound.

The Russian had stepped through Arrivals at Bangkok's Suvarnabhumi Airport with a *Lonely Planet* guide to Colombia stuffed in his suitcase, and the familiar hulking figure of Mikhail 'Misha' Belozerosky at his side. The morning air in Bangkok was already hot and sticky: Bout was dressed for the climate, wearing an orange polo shirt, khakis and sneakers.

'It was just unbelievable . . .' Lou Milione would remark of the moment. 'You know you kind of hang on as you climb up the mountain, at different parts of the investigation. This was one where I believed, and the other investigators believed, not only are we in the game . . . we've got him.'

Working closely with the Royal Thai Police, the DEA had planned the surveillance operation of Bout with painstaking care. Presuming he would be very much on his guard, they had eschewed the blunter forms of spycraft. There would be no tail placed on Bout's taxi. Instead, RTP officers in plainclothes were stationed along the route – in tollbooths, at a broken-down vehicle, and staking out the Sofitel itself.

Bout's taxi took a good hour to nose through Bangkok's chaotic downtown crush. In the mezzanine lounge of the Sofitel, Mike, Carlos and Smulian lingered anxiously over the remains of breakfast. Bout reached the hotel shortly after 11.30 a.m., checked into room 1420, then made his way towards the mezzanine.

As soon as Carlos got word that Bout was heading their way, he flicked on his hidden recording gear. He and Mike had chosen a quiet corner of the mezzanine lounge, where a pair of matching blue sofas were arranged facing each other. Right now, they felt a strange mixture of wired, knife-edge tension, suffused with pure adrenalin. It gave them a strange sense of clarity and calm – as if they were in the very eye of the storm.

Bout stepped into the space, with Belozerosky shadowing him. The Russian's eyes swept the area and came to rest upon . . . Mike Snow; the guy he'd repeatedly asked Smulian to keep away from the deal. There was a beat between them, as The Bear and the Russian bear eyed each other.

Bout took a step forwards: 'Mike, how are you?'

Mike rose to greet him. 'Gospodin, how are you? Huh?' *Gospodin*: Russian for 'mister'.

The two men did a noticeably stiff bear hug, complete with obligatory backslapping. They stood back to survey each other.

'Yes, a long time,' Mike declared. It was a decade or more since they'd last met.

Carlos stepped forwards, forcing a broad smile. '*Amigo, mucho gusto*,' he said. My friend, nice to meet you.

'*Mucho gusto*,' Bout echoed, his expression a fraction warmer now.

Smulian swept an arm across the sofas, urging all to take a seat. Carlos settled in one, with Bout seated beside him. Smulian took the seat opposite, with Belozerosky next to him and across from Viktor Bout. That left no space for Mike.

'I'm going to get myself a chair,' he announced. He dragged one over and perched at Carlos' far left, so closest to the target.

Mike eyed Bout. 'The last time I saw you was, uh, in Johannesburg in the airport. You were on your way to Dubai. Hmmm . . . That was a long time ago.'

Bout nodded. 'Yeah, it's about ten years ago. More than ten years.'

'Uhm, you wanna drink? Eat?' Carlos ventured.

The atmosphere was tense, and Lingua Plata needed to smooth things over and mellow everyone out. The last thing he needed was an upset right now, and Bout crying off at the last minute. The Russian said that maybe he'd take a little something, and Carlos signalled for menus.

'A lot of things have changed since then, my friend,' Mike declared.

Bout nodded, guardedly. Where was Mike's last air operation? he queried. Wasn't it the Congo?

'Yeah.'

'Just one – only the one plane?'

'We had two planes. But, uh, there was a big explosion at the airport – I'm sure you know, eh?'

'Oh, yeah, yeah, yeah, yeah. Big explosion,' Bout confirmed, in his slow, heavily-accented English. When he spoke the words seemed to rumble up from deep within his chest, each vomited out like a boulder.

'They stored the explosives at the domestic terminal . . .' Mike remarked, referring to the N'Djilli Airport catastrophe. 'And people were sitting on top, uh, cooking fucking food . . .' He paused, before adding, 'Yeah. Yes. Boom!'

Bout nodded. 'Bada-boom, bada-boom.'

'One hundred and forty-five people was killed, one Antonov 12 was burned completely, and a lot of Antonov 28s . . . The pressure wave from the explosion twist the tail like that . . .' Mike made a snapping gesture with his hands. 'The Congolese, they just dig a big hole, throw the people in, cover it. It's finished. No insurance, nobody cares.'

'No, no, no, no, no.' Bout chuckled. 'They dance and eat . . .'

Mike and Carlos forced a laugh.

The waiter arrived and Bout ordered tea, hot, with lemon. He turned to Carlos and asked how he was coping with the jetlag. Flying from Colombia to Thailand really threw your clock out of sync. It was an 18,000-kilometre trip, involving twenty-four hours of travel, and the time difference upon arrival was plus-twelve hours.

It was tough both on body and mind. 'Especially when you travel from your zone to here . . .' Bout pointed out. 'When you go there it's very easy, but come back, you pay the price.'

'So . . . you have him all over the world,' Mike declared, nodding in Carlos' direction. 'Fucking waiting for you in that shithole . . . Bucharest. Becoming fucking mad . . . It's a terrible place . . .'

'No, first of all, it's, uh, not friendly place,' Bout objected. 'And . . . even to get visa is disaster . . .'

Mike nodded. 'Me, I don't trust them people there. I don't trust them.'

'Where?' Smulian interjected.

'Fucking Bucharest.'

307

'No, uh, they're big friends of the gringos.'

'Yeah, yeah, yeah, yeah, yeah,' Bout agreed.

'Yeah?' Carlos queried.

'Yeah,' Bout repeated; *Bucharest*.

Carlos feigned puzzlement. 'Hmmm . . . We never have problems in there before. We doing—'

'No, 'cause you – you pay plenty of money . . .' Mike cut in.

It was a timely intervention. Bout seemed edgy over the Bucharest connection, and Carlos had been in need of Mike's on-the-hoof improvisation. Working with The Bear sure was a rollercoaster ride, but on one level he was a dream undercover partner. His brash, blunt exterior concealed a razor sharp intellect, combined with a real animal cunning. They made a great tag team.

'Nah, but . . . we pay everybody over there and they're happy,' Carlos declared, picking up on Mike's lead.

Bout explained that he had an air operation running out of Romania, and it was his people there that had warned him that Bucharest wasn't safe. They had persuaded him not to travel to Romania, by any means.

Mike eyed the Russian doubtfully. 'Fuck that. You got an airline – you, in Romania . . . ? Oh, no. Fuck you.'

Bout countered that he had 'friends' working for him in Bucharest – good people – but that the country as a whole was a nightmare. It was a big centre of operations for the Americans.

'But, uh . . . we've been doing a lot of business from that area . . .' Carlos insisted.

'From where?' Bout challenged. 'From Romania?'

'Romania . . .' Carlos echoed. 'We deal with a lot of people of different countries and, uh, every country is different . . . like we do business in Greece, and they're different people than, you know, Romanians . . .'

'The Greeks is all right,' Mike remarked. 'Just don't go in the shower with them . . . And drop the soap . . . And be in trouble . . .'

Everyone cracked a smile. It was hard to risk a joke when you were as uptight and on edge as all were now, but the atmosphere seemed to ease just a little.

'Let me ask you this: how do you know?' probed Carlos, jokingly. How did Snow know about Greek males' habits in the showers?

Mike said he'd read about it in the papers.

'Oh, okay. I'm a little concerned . . .' Carlos continued. 'If you know all these stories, then 'cause maybe you got a little experience . . .'

Everyone laughed.

'Yeah . . .' Bout remarked. 'There's two kinds of people: those who know but they never speak and those who . . .'

'Who speak and don't know,' Mike completed the sentence for him.

'Those who got a little bit of experience,' Carlos repeated, to more smiles. He turned to Belozerosky. 'You speak English?'

Belozerosky shrugged. 'So-so.'

'But he's listening . . .' Mike added.

'Yeah. He's just listening,' Bout confirmed.

The waiter arrived with the drinks.

'Tea?' Carlos offered.

Smulian tried cracking a joke, paraphrasing Shakespeare – badly. 'The tea or, or not to tea.'

A little laughter, but it sounded forced. Nervous still. The chat

309

moved on to South Africa, and the high levels of violence being experienced there, especially in urban areas.

'Me, I live in the Congo for ten years,' Mike declared. 'I never heard of one person murdered . . . Yes, they steal your cellphone, maybe do that sort of thing . . . But they never kill anybody . . .'

'Not like my country . . .' Carlos volunteered.

'No, your country is a bit different . . .' Bout confirmed. 'Very different. How come? What is situation now . . . I don't know what's happen exactly right now . . .'

The FARC, Carlos suggested, were in danger of losing their way. The 'white gold' – cocaine; heroin – had made them rich, but they needed to refocus on what mattered in Colombia: the armed struggle.

'Uh, I'm very sorry to what happened . . . few days ago,' Bout remarked. 'Is very serious.'

He was referring to events of five days earlier, when FARC had been struck a hammer blow. Luis Edgar Devia Silva – better known by his revolutionary name, 'Raúl Reyes' – had been killed in a military assault. Reyes had been the FARC's spokesperson, and number two in its seven-person ruling council. He had forced through the expansion of the FARC's drugs trafficking globally, and he'd orchestrated the killing of hundreds of people who had tried to stand in his way.

Reyes had been convicted in absentia for the deaths of thirteen policemen and for eighteen kidnappings. He stood accused of dozens of prominent murders, including a judge, serving and former Colombian government ministers, a congressman and his mother, local governors and councillors and even a Catholic priest. Most of his victims had been kidnapped before their deaths.

The US State Department had offered a $5 million reward for information leading to Reyes' capture. In February 2008 – while the Operation Relentless team had been trying to lure Bout to Bucharest – another DEA team had been busy tracking Reyes. They'd picked up a satellite phone call made by Reyes to the then Venezuelan president, Hugo Chávez. No surprises there, bearing in mind how deeply the Venezuelan administration was mired in the drugs trade.

That call had been traced to a jungle encampment a mile beyond Colombia's border, in neighbouring Ecuador. At 0025 hours on 1 March 2008 the helicopter gunships had gone in. Reyes had tried to flee the camp, but he'd trodden on one of the FARC's own landmines, and blown himself to pieces.

The government of Ecuador – also accused of complicity with the FARC – had lodged a formal diplomatic complaint with Colombia, for the armed incursion into its territory. As for Venezuela's President, he had denounced the strike on Reyes as 'a cowardly murder'. He'd threatened that any similar action on Venezuelan soil would be seen as an act of war.

Unsurprisingly, Reyes' killing was headline news. Bout had read about it during his pre-departure research into the FARC. He explained that he was surprised to see the same tactics being used in Colombia as the Americans had employed in Africa, when hunting down their enemies there.

'If they keep going for the main guys,' Mike pointed out, 'it's 'cause somebody is telling them where they are . . .'

That was all the more reason for the FARC to secure the kind of weaponry that Bout could offer them, Carlos suggested. 'Let me explain in Spanish,' he continued. '*Yo soy parte del Secretariado General . . .*' He described how he was a member of FARC's ruling secretariat, but it was El Comandante who called the shots on the weaponry. Carlos was there to negotiate the money side only.

'*Esta bien.*' Very good, Bout confirmed. 'But soon. Because, uh, we have to prepare the . . . work. You understand? Start the work . . .' They had to move quickly, for there was much to be done. Bout turned to Smulian. 'Andrew, where we gonna sit and discuss?' They needed a private room in which to talk business.

Just then Carlos' cellphone rang. He checked the caller ID. It was DEA Agent Wim Brown. He had two choices: either reject the call, which might trigger Bout's suspicions, or take the call and play along.

He pressed answer. 'Yes, yes . . . Uh-huh. Well, I'm sitting here. Everything's fine, but we're going to figure out where we're going to meet. Okay? Okay. So, I'll . . . I'll let you know where . . .'

Cool as a cucumber he signed off the call, turned to Bout and indicated that he'd just been speaking to El Comandante. Bout suggested they should check for a conference room in which they could talk. Mike said he could go and sort a room. He wandered off to ascertain availability on the business level.

Once he was out of earshot, Bout turned to Smulian. 'Andrew, what we do with Michael?'

It was Carlos who answered. 'No, no, no . . . Mike is going . . . Don't worry.' He gestured at Smulian. 'He explain to me that you don't trust him. So I say: "Okay, he's going to be out."'

Bout shrugged. 'Because, he just . . . he's good friend.'

Carlos made an appropriate gesture. 'He . . . he's crazy.'

Bout smiled. 'Uh, all those . . . African bush pilots, they become crazy . . .' He glanced in the direction that Snow had gone. 'Mike, you are crazy.'

Carlos laughed. *Not half as crazy as you might imagine, Mr Bout.*

A minute later Mike was back again. 'They got one. But I'm going to check it out, 'cause . . . I know these fuckers, there'll be somebody there . . .'

Bout turned to Belozerosky and uttered a few words in Russian, asking him to check out the meeting room. Mike led Bout's body-guard towards the Sofitel's lifts. Now it was just three remaining on the blue sofas: Bout, Carlos and Smulian. It was Bout's turn to be interrupted by a call, one that he signalled he had to take.

'Pash, we'll talk later,' he told whoever was on the other end. 'Igorek will come over now . . . There will be a letter, they'll do the registration themselves . . . As agreed, they will pay? No problem, no problem. Agreed. So long.'

Once Bout was done with the call, Carlos moved the conversation on to his key area of responsibility: finance, and specifically the FARC's need for money laundering. He nodded at Smulian. 'Now, on my side he was telling me maybe you can help us – we got sometimes a lot of cash . . .'

'Where?' Bout demanded. 'Which . . . where is place?'

Carlos said they had cash in Romania, Greece and Spain right now.

'What is amount? In Spain we can help you, if you can bring everything in Spain . . . ?'

'We can produce around forty million euros . . . every month.'

Bout looked surprised. 'Truth? We can find you the way to . . . do it properly . . .'

Carlos gestured at Smulian, explaining that their proposed percentage rake-off was too high: Bout's forty per cent cut was taking the piss.

'Usually, in Europe, if it goes to this level . . .' Bout shrugged: forty per cent wasn't unreasonable. 'Like in Switzerland they charge you up to fifty . . .' He switched tack, highlighting the dangers of moving hot money internationally. 'If you work in the dollars, everything goes to US . . . They have computer program . . . everything in the OFAC list. You know OFAC?'

'Uh-huh,' Carlos confirmed. He knew OFAC all right – the Office of Foreign Assets Control – the body that had seized Bout's assets in 2004, at the behest of the Bush administration.

'But usually, we suggest you work through . . . Russia, Venezuela and Belarus . . .' Bout continued. 'You know what I would do on your place? I would go and purchase a bank . . .' Bout explained that the bank would launder their cash and wire the 'clean' funds wherever and whenever they needed it.

Just then, Mike and Belozerosky returned, having checked out the business suites.

'We can, uh, *vamos a discutir los pormenores*,' Bout suggested, switching into Spanish; let's go discuss the details in private.

'When you want them not to understand something it's better if you speak to me in Spanish,' Carlos advised, with one eye on Mike. 'Because they don't understand . . .'

'Oh. Yes, yes, yes. Sure, sure. Vamos.' *Let's go.*

Bout got to his feet. He signalled Belozerosky to lead the way. The hulking bodyguard uttered a few words in Russian. He didn't sound overly happy. It turned out that he hadn't understood a thing about what had been arranged with the meeting room, because it had all been discussed in English.

'*No este bien?*' Carlos checked with Bout. Is everything all right?

'*No, si, si, si. Esta bien.*'

'It's just a normal outside boardroom,' Mike announced. What was not to like?

Bout studied Mike for a long second. 'Michael . . . you get local cards here?'

'SIM cards?'

'Yeah . . . Arrange me one, because I gonna need it this afternoon very much . . . You need money?'

'No, no. I don't need money . . .'

'Put fifty bucks, put fifty bucks. Please.'

Mike headed out to a 7/11 store that he knew of nearby. He realized why Bout had sent him on this SIM-card buying errand: the Russian wanted The Bear out of the way. Not a bother: he'd use the stroll through the busy Bangkok streets to calm his frazzled nerves.

Back in the Sofitel, Bout and Carlos made for the lifts, dragging Belozerosky and Smulian in their wake. As they waited for the lift, Carlos tried to get his heartbeat under some form of control. They were so close, and at this vital juncture the King of Sting truly needed to hold his nerve.

He heard Bout make an enquiry about politics in Colombia and the level of popular support the FARC enjoyed. Carlos was glad of the excuse to fill the tension and silence. He began to talk, explaining that the country was divided: there were people backing the FARC, and people backing the government.

'In any case . . .' Bout ventured, 'you don't trust the gringos. Whenever they're, uh, in negotiation, later they always kill those same people . . .'

'Right now, we have to show the gringos and everybody that we are an armed force and we can defend ourselves,' Carlos replied, picking up on Bout's anti-American sentiments.

'The gringos ... yes, they're more armed, they have all the technical means available ...' Bout continued. 'But they don't have morale to fight. Because they don't have mother country ... They don't have national ideal. They don't have anything. Only have money ...'

'I told ... Andrew,' Carlos said. 'I was telling him ... They're, uh, a force with airplanes, intelligence, but soldiers—'

'Zero,' Bout completed the sentence for him. 'Yes ... of course. Like always.'

'That's why they use a lot of helicopters,' Carlos added, resentfully. 'And ... we don't have anything right now to defend ourselves with.'

'Okay, do you have your people near the military bases?'

'Uh, yes. Of course.'

'Do you have ... all the info of when they go out ... ?'

'That's another thing ... the Comandante is going to ask you for,' Carlos suggested, by way of answer. 'It's sights for sharpshooters, because we want to start to blow the heads off ...' He explained that the Americans were training the Colombian soldiers, and they needed to start killing Americans.

'Snipers?' Bout queried.

'Uh-huh. We want to start to use a lot of snipers ... But ... why don't you talk to the Comandante ... I call him and tell him to come there.'

Carlos pulled out his cellphone, and dialled Ricardo's number. 'Hello? Hello ... Go up to twenty-seven and wait on twenty-seven ... You're going to wait for me in front of the lift. We're going up right away.' He killed the call and turned to the tall Russian at his side. 'Let's go. My friend's on his way ...'

'*Si, si, si. Vamos* ...' Yes, yes, yes. Let's go. They stepped towards the elevator doors. '*Ah, la guerra . . .*' Ah, the war, Bout remarked, wistfully.

'*Como siempre.*' Like always, Carlos replied, as they moved into the cramped confines of the lift.

Carlos had switched to more modern technology for this chapter of the sting: he was using two recording devices, disguised as a watch and a key-fob. He wondered if they'd captured enough? During their chat on the blue sofas and waiting for the lift, had Bout said enough about arming the FARC to kill Americans? He still wasn't certain.

They stepped out of the lift on the twenty-seventh floor, and Ricardo was waiting. Dressed in a white T-shirt, jeans and desert boots, he looked every bit the rough and ready guerrilla leader fresh out of the jungle. Unsophisticated, raw, excitable. Carlos' role had been to suck Bout in and put him at ease.

Now it was El Comandante's job to nail him.

CHAPTER TWENTY-SIX

The tension was getting even to Carlos. He realized he needed a toilet break, and at such a crucial juncture. Fortunately, there still seemed to be some confusion over which conference suite they were to use and he figured he had the time.

He handed Bout over to Ricardo, introducing him as, 'My friend, El Comandante.'

While Carlos took his pee-break, Bout's bodyguard got busy checking out the conference suite. He made a show of giving it the once over, searching behind the door, around the window frame, under the chairs and even beneath the table, before apparently concluding that it was 'clean'.

Carlos meanwhile, finished up in the bathroom and hurried over to the meeting room, where he found Belozerosky standing guard by the door. The big Russian moved aside to allow him in. Before Carlos lay a long, rectangular conference table of dark polished wood, complete with high-backed leather chairs. Each place was set with a Sofitel notepad and pen, bottled water and glasses, and there was a fancy arrangement of white lilies at the centre.

Bout was sitting on one side, with his attaché case before him, and Ricardo opposite.

Carlos had barely taken his seat, when Mike reappeared. Belozerosky had tried to keep him out, but there was no stopping The Bear. He handed over the Thai SIM card that he'd purchased for Bout.

'You don't need me?' he queried, glancing around the gathering.

'No, no,' Carlos confirmed. He was amazed at how calm and collected The Bear – the supposed amateur on the Relentless team – seemed to be.

'Okay, I'm going to my room . . . I'll see you later.'

Mike knew he wasn't wanted – or needed much – right now. After the months of bluff and counter-bluff, the takedown couldn't come soon enough, as far as he was concerned. But they'd likely need several meetings to nail Bout, and in truth he was feeling dog-tired. The days and weeks of acting out multiple roles had taken their toll. He'd head for his room and channel surf TV.

'Let's take it out,' Bout announced, once Snow was gone, unzipping his case with a flourish.

Smulian – seated beside Bout – and Ricardo laughed.

'At that rhythm, sir . . . Perfect,' Ricardo remarked, noting Bout's speed with the zip. He was surprisingly fast for such a big man.

Bout removed a map of South America and unfolded it, spreading it across the table. Carlos took the seat next to Ricardo – facing Bout and with Smulian diagonally across the table.

'I have a lot of questions,' Bout announced, before moving on to make a quick apology about his Spanish, which was nowhere near as good as his Portuguese.

True to form Ricardo jumped in, going right for the kill. 'Tomorrow I can give . . . money. But I need it to be right away. Do you understand? Do you know what I mean? . . . before, the

American government, the gringos, would go to Colombia and advise ... They provided training ... they taught how to patrol and things like that from their experience in Vietnam.'

'Uh-huh,' Bout confirmed.

'Not now!' Ricardo declared, hotly. 'Now these sons-of-bitches go themselves ... !' As he said that, his fist pounded the table. 'With their helicopters.'

'They're flying,' Carlos interjected. 'They're flying their Apaches ...'

'How can we defend ourselves with a rifle against a Black Hawk or against an Apache?' Ricardo demanded angrily.

No one had coached him to act like this. From his experience this was how such people – Latin American drugs-and-arms dealers – behaved.

'I need ... anti-aircraft protection,' Ricardo continued. 'But what's essential, essential, is that it's portable ... You understand? We don't have a base. We have to move ...'

'Yes, yes, yes, yes,' Bout confirmed. 'That's why the Iglas we talked about.'

'Iglas. Exactly.'

'Uh, portable.'

'It's portable,' Ricardo echoed. 'Easy to handle ... There are lots of things ... Viktor. But what's important to me right now are the anti-aircraft weapons. I'm interested in missiles, I'm interested in grenade-launchers, I'm interested in fragmentation grenades and all that.'

Ricardo went on to explain that most of the FARC's weaponry, which was mainly of Russian or Chinese origin, was hopelessly outdated. He needed ammunition and spare parts, and a great deal of both.

Bout pulled his Sofitel notepad closer. 'Okay. So . . . let's make list of your needs.'

'What are you offering me?' Ricardo countered. 'I need anti-aircraft defence – missiles that I can operate against . . . Apaches.'

'How many?' Bout queried. 'For example . . . the Iglas . . . It has the base . . . And it has the, uh, the missile . . ' Bout started to sketch a diagram of the Igla on the Sofitel notepad. 'Each base can shoot . . . close to three.'

'Three. I know . . ' Ricardo confirmed. He'd actually seen the Igla in action at first hand. 'Which Igla do you have? The . . . Zero-nine?'

'It's the . . . Nine-three . . ' Bout explained, adding that he'd source the missiles in Europe.

'Can you deliver them on the coast for us?' Ricardo asked, leaning over the map to point out where he sought delivery. 'Here. Suriname.'

'With a plane I can. With a plane, yes . . . So, then, I also have cargo parachute systems . . ' Getting the paperwork in order to facilitate the weapons delivery would be key, Bout explained. They'd need to secure the End User Certificates (EUCs) to allow an over-flight of the Colombian jungle in which the FARC operated, and that would entail a great deal of work.

'I have to leave my country . . . convince the Minister of . . . Defence, to sign the paper . . . to do the contract, have to officially pay part of the money . . . then I have to organize, uh, the plane . . . leave, take care of things with a certain country and then . . . get rid, uh, of all things—'

'How much money do you need?' Carlos cut in.

'I don't know. I don't know.' Bout spread his hands. 'A mistake, but I don't know.'

Carlos looked askance at the Russian. Finance was his department, and what was Bout's point in being here, if he didn't know his prices yet?

'*El dinero, eh . . .Tranquilo . . .*' Ricardo cautioned. The money, eh . . . Calm down: Carlos was always getting antsy about the money.

'But I've understood the situation well,' Bout reassured them. 'Very urgent, because they're killing your people and you don't have—'

'That's a lie!' Ricardo cut in, aggressively. 'That's a lie! They say that . . . a patrol came in. That's a lie. They fired shots from . . . American helicopters.'

Ricardo was referring to the mission that had killed Raúl Reyes. It wasn't soldiers on the ground that had got him. It was a US-backed air strike.

'Yes, yes,' Bout agreed.

Rage flashed through Ricardo's eyes. 'We want to knock down those Americans sons-of-bitches!' He flailed his arms about violently. 'Kill them and kick them out of my country . . . They don't care where they go any more. They go here, they go there. They go wherever they want. Why?'

'Yes, yes, yes,' Bout agreed. 'They act as if . . . it was their home.'

'Exactly. Why . . . ? Viktor, we are waging a real war . . . The FARC has been fighting for forty-six years . . . I was a baby when this started.' He grabbed at his chest, as if feeling it deeply in his heart. 'Now, Raúl Reyes was a great man, he was my teacher . . . We men die and live . . . We make the decision that we could die and it doesn't matter. Because it's for . . . our people. But we don't want any more gringos in our mother country. Now we're going to fight . . .'

'We're going to do it,' Bout confirmed.

'How can I shoot a . . . Black Hawk, an Apache, with a rifle? How? With what? . . . I won't do anything to them . . . What . . . can you offer me?'

Aside from the Iglas, Bout proposed they should consider the ZU-23, a twin-barrel 23mm anti-aircraft cannon accurate up to a two-mile range. It was a weapon that Carlos and Ricardo knew well, but it was designed to be towed behind a vehicle, which made it too cumbersome for the FARC's needs. In the deep jungle, the key requirement was that it be lightweight and portable.

'We also need the Dragunovs,' Carlos remarked, picking up on this point. The Dragunov – the semi-automatic Russian sniper rifle – weighed in at under five kilos.

'Sharpshooters . . .' Bout confirmed.

'We don't only need weapons,' Ricardo added. 'We need . . . the world to know what is going on . . .' For the FARC, winning the propaganda war was also vital.

'Very important,' Bout confirmed. 'Presently the mission is speaking well of the FARC.'

By 'the mission' Carlos and Ricardo presumed Bout was referring to the Russian government. It all went back to Smulian's promises of support on the 'political' level. Bout said something in addition, but it was clear that Ricardo hadn't caught it.

'I'm sorry . . . he's deaf in one ear,' Carlos explained. 'Sometimes he can't hear, because of an explosion . . .'

Bout shrugged. 'I'm the same . . . Artillery. With the explosion, two or three years later I couldn't hear too well.'

Bout explained that they could send a group of twenty people – Russian army and Secret Service veterans – to train 'subversive action groups', so as to undermine the Colombian government and the Americans from within.

'Don't . . . don't worry about money,' Carlos advised, as if excited by what he was now hearing.

'Yes, of course,' Bout confirmed. 'We're going to prepare and start . . . a job.'

'Long,' Carlos affirmed; they were looking for a long-term relationship.

'Long,' Bout echoed. 'But urgent.'

'Urgent,' Carlos confirmed.

Ricardo pointed out that they'd need bulk quantities of AK-47 assault rifles. What kind of numbers could Bout provide?

'For sure, we can start with five thousand . . .' Bout noted down the figure on the list he was compiling, with Carlos making similar notes from his side. He pointed out they'd need to get the paperwork sorted, for a major shipment of this kind might attract unwanted attention.

'That's why it is necessary to always come up with a scenario,' he explained. 'A simulation – that there's a country that is buying that weapon . . . Also, uh, we need an official who will go . . . to sign the contract to . . . make a payment, to take out your things. Uh, it's a job that is a bit political, a bit, uh, commercial, and a bit intelligent, you know?'

Carlos understood what Bout was driving at. They'd need someone from the country officially importing the arms to sign a contract with the supplier, to make it look totally legit.

'If not, we're going to create . . . scandal and the gringos will block . . .' Bout smiled. 'That is why I have same problems with the gringos . . .'

Carlos, Ricardo and Smulian laughed: the two DEA agents

because they were capturing every extraordinary word that Bout was saying on tape; Smulian because he believed he was on the verge of sealing a historic, and hugely lucrative, deal.

'Yes.' Bout nodded, sagely. 'Plus they say that seven years I am the number one list of . . .'

'Sure,' Carlos assured him. 'I'm right there after you. Don't worry.' Bout might be top of the US most-wanted list, but the FARC luminaries weren't far behind.

'Yes, yes.' Bout glanced from Carlos to Ricardo. 'We're together.'

More laughter. Everyone seemed happy now.

'I must be on the same list . . .' Ricardo ventured.

'Yes, yes, yes,' Bout confirmed. 'And we have the same enemy.'

Got him, Carlos told himself. Bout had just put his head in the noose, as far as the DEA undercovers were concerned.

'How many of these do you think you can give us?' Carlos demanded.

'How many AK-47s?' Ricardo queried.

'For the AKs he already said five thousand,' Carlos shot back at him.

'No, we start with five thousand,' Bout clarified. 'But . . . we're going to create twenty, thirty . . .' Supplying twenty to thirty thousand AK-47 assault rifles was Bout's long-term aim.

'How many Iglas can you give me?' Ricardo gestured at Smulian. 'He said something to me about you having a hundred.'

Bout said they could start with one hundred of the surface-to-air missiles, but seven to eight hundred could be provided over the longer term. *Seven to eight hundred surface-to-air missiles*: the figures they were capturing on tape were staggering.

'What prices?' Carlos queried.

Bout suggested each Igla would cost between 120 and 180,000

dollars. The price would depend on the kinds of numbers they were ordering.

'Okay,' said Carlos. That made sense. Bulk discount. The more they were buying, the cheaper the price was likely to be.

For the AK-47s, second-hand would be one hundred dollars per weapon, Bout explained. New ones were three to four hundred dollars apiece, and all sourced from Bulgaria. Dragunov sniper rifles were between two and three thousand dollars each. Bout could supply the whole package: the Dragunov itself plus sniping scope, and night-vision sights to use during the hours of darkness.

They settled upon an order of 250 Dragunov sniper rifles – also called the 'SVD' – with one hundred night-vision sights. Bout added that to the list scribbled on his notepad: 'SVD – 250 (100 Miras Nucturas)'.

Twenty thousand fragmentation grenades were added to the list, plus ten million rounds of AK-47 calibre ammunition. An order of this magnitude constituted many tonnes, which led around to the means of delivery. Bout smoothed out the map and began to explain what he had in mind.

He suggested that the FARC should run a supposedly commercial airfreight operation, flying from Nicaragua to Manaus in Brazil. The route would take the aircraft directly over the area to which they needed the weapons delivered.

'The route passes . . .' Bout pounded his fist on a spot on the map over southern Colombia, 'through here . . .'

'Through El Yari,' Ricardo clarified.

'Through El Yari,' Carlos echoed. El Yari is a remote part of Colombia and a stronghold of the FARC.

'Uh-huh . . .' Bout confirmed. 'But you have to tell me where the American radars are . . .'

Ricardo glanced up at Bout. 'I can find that out for you.'

If the radar stations could be identified, Bout could plot a route to fly around them. Ricardo leaned closer, tracing a circle with his finger around a patch of Colombian terrain. 'You have to go through here.' All of that territory belonged to the FARC.

Bout explained that he had the parachutes to execute the cargo-drops, and would do so via anything from an Antonov 32 – a mid-size Russian transport aircraft with a 10,000-kilo cargo-capacity – up to an Ilyushin 76.

'I don't know if you know the 76?' Bout slid something across the table. It was a booklet on the IL-76, complete with glossy photos. One showed a BMD-1 – a Russian light tank – being loaded aboard, and then parachuted from an IL-76's open ramp. Another showed a long column of parachutists jumping out of the aircraft.

With its fifty-tonne cargo capacity the Ilyushin 76 was the ultimate workhorse, Bout explained. It could carry three battle tanks, or four hundred people. He'd executed five thousand air operations from the IL-76. When it landed in Manaus having dropped the weaponry, they should load up sacks of flour or crates of fruit, to make it appear like any normal commercial flight.

'And the Americans can't, uh, determine, during night-time, what they were ... doing,' he explained. The parachute-drops would be executed under cover of darkness, to doubly hide them from any watchers.

'Hmmm. Okay. Perfect,' Carlos confirmed.

'Perfecto,' Ricardo echoed.

They pointed out a drop-zone that was an area of flat terrain devoid of any mountains. All four of them leaned closer over the map, as Ricardo and Carlos attempted to describe the type of vegetation found there.

'It's not jungle,' Carlos tried. 'This is a . . .'

'Savannah,' Smulian suggested.

'Savannah,' Ricardo confirmed.

'Savannah,' Bout echoed. Dry scrubby grassland, with the occasional trees. Perfect for making such a drop.

There were two options for the provision of the Ilyushins, Bout explained. One, he had second-hand IL-76s presently in Africa, which he could provide at a cost of two million each. Or the new ones, like those shown in the brochures, were four million.

The FARC should form a 'genuine' airfreight business, as cover. They'd start the airline in Nicaragua, using Russian planes. They'd need a warehouse right beside the runway, in which to store the weaponry, plus they'd require tight security while loading up the arms for the overnight flights across FARC territory.

Carlos asked if Bout could also provide C4 plastic explosives, for use in their gas-tank bombs – their DIY napalm. Bout suggested five tonnes of C4 wouldn't be a problem. 'I saw on YouTube . . . the gas-tank system. Congratulations. Genius. Genius. Genius.'

Everyone laughed.

Bout explained how he'd also learned about the FARC manufacturing 60mm mortars from regular steel waterpipes, and with training provided by the IRA. That in turn led them onto the FARC's need for professional mortars. Bout could provide 60mm, 90mm and 120mm calibre mortars.

Ricardo pointed out that the 120mm would be too heavy for the FARC, but the others would be very useful. He shoved back his chair and went to join Bout. He jabbed a finger at the Russian's notepad, indicating he'd like two hundred 80mm and four hundred 60mm mortars. Bout made a note of his needs.

'And mines?' Bout queried. Did the FARC need landmines?

Carlos explained that they only ever used mines for planting around their deep jungle dope-labs, to protect them, so they wouldn't need so many.

'Viktor, how many can we start with?' Ricardo asked.

'Mines,' Carlos clarified.

'Anti-personnel . . . ?' Bout queried. 'Uh . . . we have to make a place for manufacture . . . They're not being sold right now . . .'

'In other words . . . there's a world ban on them,' Smulian explained.

He was right. In 1997 most countries had signed the Ottawa Treaty, banning the manufacture, storage, export and use of landmines. If their export was banned, why didn't the FARC manufacture their own, Ricardo suggested, just as they made their DIY napalm and mortar tubes?

'Yes. Why not?' Bout confirmed that it would be far simpler to make their own landmines.

Carlos asked what kind of down-payment Bout was looking for? He tapped the Ilyushin brochure: 'Because I know it's eight million for this . . . How much money do you need to start moving . . . ?'

'At least fifteen, twenty million,' Bout ventured. 'I don't know, but to do the job quickly . . .'

One hundred Iglas alone would cost as much as $12 million, so this didn't seem like an exorbitant sum.

'But the thing is that I have money in, uh, certain places,' Carlos explained, 'and I need to know how much money so I can start moving it. The other day we had ten million euros in Romania waiting to be delivered to you . . . Where is a good place to deliver money? Spain?'

Bout nodded. 'Spain. That's possible . . .'

'Do you have people over there we can deliver to?'

Bout indicated his bodyguard. 'Yes, of course. My friend . . .'

'Okay. I can go with him to Spain.'

'Viktor, let's prepare a framework . . .' declared Ricardo. He leaned forwards excitedly. 'I want to finish off those gringo sons-of-bitches . . . ! That's it. They're not going to kill us in our sleep any more! That's what happened. They've caught us asleep at the wheel . . .'

'Listen,' Bout replied. 'We . . . we have a policy, uh, gringos are enemies . . .'

'It's now two of us who want to kill them . . .' Ricardo agreed, feigning heartfelt emotion.

'It's not, uh, business. It's my fight . . .' Bout declared. 'I'm, uh, fighting the United States . . . for ten to fifteen years . . . One person's resistance.'

For a moment the conference suite was filled with laughter.

'You're not alone, because you have the FARC's full support,' Carlos assured Bout.

At that point all four figures got to their feet, to shake hands. There were smiles all around.

'The missiles are first,' Ricardo reminded Bout.

'More urgent,' Bout confirmed.

'The most urgent thing for us is the missiles,' Ricardo repeated.

'What about, uh, RPGs?' Smulian interjected. Hadn't they forgotten the rocket-propelled grenades?

'Oh, yeah, yeah. The RPG-7s,' Carlos confirmed.

For a few minutes they discussed various options regarding the rocket-propelled grenades. Then the Russian turned a page in his Sofitel jotter, and began to sketch out an odd-looking type of aircraft. 'Another issue I was thinking about ... Very small two-engine planes for two people. Ultralight.'

'Ultralight,' Ricardo echoed.

'Yeah. Ultralight.' Bout sketched a pair of rectangular weapons pods, one on either leading edge of the wings, explaining how they would equip the ultralights with grenade-launchers. 'It's very good to bring down helicopters.'

'Wouldn't they be too slow?' Ricardo queried.

'Yes. Slow,' Bout confirmed. 'But helicopters are not any ... faster.' He could also offer unmanned aerial vehicles (UAVs) – drones with a range of two to three hundred kilometres. They were great for covert aerial reconnaissance.

'We can use whatever help you can give us . . .' Ricardo assured him. 'We're done with words. Now we're doing it like this!' He drove one fist into the palm of his hand. 'Fighting! And that's what I need all of this for . . . all that stuff you can offer us . . . With money we can't injure anyone . . . You understand? I can't throw money at anyone.'

'Sure, sure. And you have revolutionary responsibility . . .' Bout pointed out. 'And you have, uh, the objectives of . . . the people who are suffering there . . . And the gringos who are . . .'

'Enemy . . .' Smulian finished Bout's sentence for him.

'You . . . see the troops,' Carlos explained. 'You see, uh, the helicopters landing and the Colombia troops getting off, but the pilot . . .'

'American . . .' Bout confirmed.

'And we want to start . . . killing American pilots,' Carlos declared, with finality.

'That's the reason for the . . . the anti-aircrafts and for the Dragunovs,' Ricardo added.

'Yes, yes,' Bout confirmed. 'We're . . . we're going to prepare everything.'

'Viktor, listen,' Ricardo announced, with intensity. 'Whenever we kill two, three, four American pilots, they're going to think about it. They're going to think: why? Because we're going to have proof that they're there . . . If they say it – "They're killing our pilots" – the world is going to come down on them. "Hey, why are you involved there?" . . . As soon as we kill just two, three, four pilots . . .'

'Yeah, we understand,' Smulian interjected.

Just then, there was the sound of heavy footsteps in the corridor. Bout glanced at his bodyguard: 'Is everything all right there, Misha?' he demanded, in Russian.

'There is some movement,' Belozerosky warned. He listened intently, but the footsteps appeared to die away. 'We seem to have reached an agreement?'

'No, that's it, I'll be done in a moment . . .' Bout reassured him.

'*No hay problema?*' Carlos queried. Is there a problem?

Bout told him that everything was okay. Carlos, Smulian and Belozerosky would travel to Spain the following day, to collect the 'FARC's' down payment. They would all then move to a second meeting, scheduled for Nicaragua, to usher in the first weapons deliveries.

Carlos eyed the big Russian bodyguard. 'He knows we're going to Spain, to deliver the money in cash?' Was Belozerosky happy to accept such a large volume of euros?

'No problem . . .' Bout explained that Belozerosky had flown in from Málaga, in southern Spain, so he was familiar with the country.

'So, is it a done deal?' Carlos pressed.

Bout thought for a moment, before adding that in all paper-work that came out of this meeting his name should be recorded differently. Carlos had proposed getting Bout a forged passport, either as a Panamanian or a Nicaraguan national. It would help circumvent any travel bans, which would be crucial to facilitating the coming deals. With the FARC's connections, getting one shouldn't prove a problem.

'Yes. With what name?' Carlos asked. What name did Bout want to be used?

'Alejandro,' Bout suggested.

'Alejandro? No problem,' Carlos confirmed.

'That's very Latin, yes. Alejandro,' Ricardo added.

The three of them settled upon a code to use for future com-munications, and with that decided they were pretty much done.

'But . . . the most difficult night will come to an end . . .' Bout declared, quoting an old saying. 'The biggest road ahead always starts with small . . .'

'First step,' Carlos confirmed.

'First step,' Bout echoed.

Carlos thrust out a hand to him. 'Alejandro.'

'Alejandro,' Smulian echoed, thrusting out a hand himself.

'Alejandro, deal!' Carlos declared. He and Bout shook hands, and there were smiles all around.

Carlos pulled out his phone. He could hardly believe it, but it was time. He needed to call Wim, to greenlight the takedown. The DEA agents would be in their operations room just a few doors away, and they would be here in seconds. He made the excuse that he was calling Snow, to ask him to meet in the bar for a celebratory drink.

But Carlos didn't quite get the response that he was expecting from Agent Brown. The entire operation had been kept a strict secret from all in the Sofitel, in case anyone thought to tip-off the targets. As a result, the DEA hadn't been able to find out from the hotel staff which conference suite the meeting was taking place in.

Carlos didn't know their room number, either. He hadn't arranged the booking. That had been Snow's responsibility. He just had to hope that Wim would use his initiative and call The Bear. In the meantime, he was somehow going to have to stall things, while the agents and the Thai police tracked them down.

He killed the call.

He sensed Ricardo getting to his feet, in preparation for what he believed was the takedown team bursting through the door. Quick as a flash, Carlos reached over and pulled the Colombian back into his seat. Ricardo shot Carlos a look: had he completely lost his mind? Carlos had to push him back into his chair for a second time, as he tried to get up once again.

Across the way, Bout was busy packing his briefcase. If he and Smulian headed for the door, there was no way that Carlos and Ricardo could tackle both of them, not to mention the body-guard, Belozerovsky. In any case, they had no legal right to do so: it was the Thai police who had to make the arrests.

Carlos racked his brains for something to say that would delay everyone's departure, but without alerting them to the coming raid.

'Okay, okay, he's going to be downstairs,' he began, as if he was referring to Snow. 'That way, uh, we change, uhm ... He go ... he go with me and his friends ...'

The words petered out. Carlos' head was spinning. He could sense the others staring at him: what the hell was all of that supposed to mean?

'Okay ...' Smulian ventured.

'And uhm ... uhm, thank you,' Carlos started again, in desperation. 'Thank you very much. Let's ...'

Bout glanced searchingly from Carlos to Ricardo and back again. 'We have same ... objective ...' he announced, in a reassuring tone. 'Uh, so we also have ... what do you call it? Ideology. Uh, idea of building ... a Latin communism.' Bout made an expansive gesture and glanced at Carlos and Ricardo.

The two of them forced a laugh. Of course, by now Ricardo knew that something was badly wrong.

'Okay ... Okay. Thank you ...' Carlos repeated, playing for time. *Madre de Dios* – mother of God – *how had this all become so screwed up so quickly?*

Smulian glanced at Bout, checking if he was ready. The Russian went to grab the notepad on which he'd itemized all the weaponry.

Carlos felt as if he were about to have a heart attack: where the hell were the DEA, plus the Thai Police takedown team?

CHAPTER TWENTY-SEVEN

BANGKOK, THAILAND, MARCH 2008

A dozen sets of boots thundered down the corridor on the twenty-seventh floor of the Bangkok Sofitel. Finally, the Thai Police and DEA agents had been given a room number where the conference suite – and the targets – were supposedly situated.

The phalanx of armed men turned a corner, heading for what they hoped was the correct location. Everyone on the takedown team was dressed in civvies, so as to blend in, but that didn't fool Belozerosky for long. As they charged towards the conference suite, the big Russian tried to use his bulk to block the doorway.

Belozerosky was almost twice the size of Taksin Sathon, the commander of the elite Thai Police unit, but that didn't deter Wim and Zach. Both former military, they dropped their shoulders and barged the bodyguard out of the way. Officer Sathon charged through the space so created, as figures surged in after him, guns drawn.

'Hands up! Hands up!' Commander Sathon screamed. He swept the room with his Glock. 'EVERYBODY!'

Carlos and Ricardo backed towards the wall, arms raised above their heads. All Carlos could think was: *thank God they've made it at last.* But his relief quickly turned to consternation. He watched in horrified fascination as Bout tried to carry on as normal – as if the raid couldn't be happening, let alone be anything to do with him – reaching into his briefcase, presumably to check on something.

Commander Sathon pinned Bout in the sights of his Glock, his finger tight on the trigger. 'You are under arrest!' he screamed.

Still the Russian didn't seem to register or respond. Carlos felt his blood run cold. He could see the killer look blazingly in the Thai police officer's eyes. For all Commander Sathon knew, Bout might be reaching for a concealed weapon.

Commander Sathon dashed forwards, until his weapon was right in the Russian's face. '*Everybody*, hands up! HANDS UP!'

Carlos tried to shrink back further against the wall, to shield himself from the bullets, convinced that the shooting was about to start. Neither he nor Ricardo wanted to risk being caught in the crossfire.

DEA Supervising Agent Lou Milione had also gone in on the raid. He stared at the scene, aghast. He simply could not believe that they had come so far with Operation Relentless, only for the target to get himself riddled with bullets during the takedown.

Finally, Bout seemed to realize the mortal danger that he was in. He slid his hand out of the briefcase, then raised both slowly above his head. A phalanx of Thai police officers grabbed him and shoved him back against the wall.

Everyone – Carlos, Ricardo, Smulian and now Bout – was manhandled into the same position; faces to the wall, legs spread and hands above their heads, as the Thai police proceeded to frisk them.

Commander Sathon pointed at Bout, who was standing next

to Smulian: 'Handcuff him first!' he barked, placing a hand on Bout's shoulder. 'Cuff him first!'

Thai police swarmed around the Russian, who towered head and shoulders above them, slapping on the handcuffs. With the main target finally secured, Wim swept his gaze across the conference table. He noted Bout's briefcase, plus the Sofitel notepad lying nearby. He made a beeline for the jotter, casting an eye down it. Chock-full of weapons specifications:

AA = 100 + 700-800
AK47 10–20 m
SVD – 250 (100 Miras Nucturas)
F1 – 20,000; ZIP
7.62 X 54 = 10,000,000
60mm – 500
82mm – 200
120mm – 40
(c) – plastic – 5
RPG-7, AG-17-40, RPG-22.

Wim flipped over the page, and noticed the scribbled diagram of some kind of aircraft, with the letters 'UAV' written beside it. He scooped up the jotter and stuffed it in his pocket. Crucial evidence.

He turned to Carlos and gestured urgently for any notes that he might have. It was vital to prevent the targets from noticing any collusion between the 'FARC' and the DEA team, but as Smulian and Bout had their faces to the wall, the risk seemed worth taking.

Furtively, Carlos slipped Wim the handwritten notes that he'd made during the meeting. The DEA agent also grabbed Carlos' precious recording devices – his watch and key-fob – and the audio-evidence that they should contain, before doing the same with Ricardo. Yet more crucial evidence.

The DEA's regional director in Bangkok, Tom Pasquarello, had also gone in on the takedown. He moved over to Bout, introduced himself, and asked if the Russian understood what was happening to him.

Bout seemed preternaturally calm and collected. 'The game is over,' he remarked, simply.

Pasquarello wasn't sure exactly what Bout might mean: did he mean his own career, the charade by the 'FARC' team, or something else entirely? Pasquarello just couldn't tell. But most of all, he was flummoxed by Bout's response. He'd seen many people in similar situations. Some got angry; some tried to struggle; some turned emotional.

But Bout – he just seemed so totally *relaxed*.

Pasquarello had little chance to question Bout any further. Moments later the Russian was frogmarched out of the room. He was on his way to the RTP's local headquarters, where a scrum of press reporters and photographers awaited his arrival. Somehow, word of Operation Relentless had leaked out to the Thai and international media, including that a high profile target had been arrested.

Meanwhile, Carlos and Ricardo were having words with Wim and Zach. They had everything they needed evidentially, but Carlos and Ricardo would still need to get dragged to the Thai police station in cuffs, just as Bout had been.

'Why the fuck do we have to go to the station?' Carlos objected. 'We need to get to the airport and get the hell out of here.'

As Carlos had stressed, the moment immediately after the takedown was the most dangerous in any operation, particularly for the undercover operators. Taking Carlos and Ricardo to the Thai police station made no sense. It would expose them to the glare of publicity, not to mention danger.

A fierce argument ensued. Apparently, the Thai police had set the ground rules: everyone had to head to the police station immediately following the takedown. Reluctantly, Carlos and Ricardo allowed themselves to be paraded through the hotel and manhandled into a Thai police car. Inside, they discovered none other than Bout's bodyguard, Belozerosky.

As the vehicle pulled into the traffic, siren blaring, Carlos's mind was racing. This was the most risky stage of any case. The bad guys had been busted, but the undercovers were still present on the ground. It was time to run. To the USA. To safety. So why the hell were they getting their faces exposed to all and sundry? Carlos was pissed off as hell.

Ricardo had far less experience of undercover operations, yet even he was troubled by the way things were going. But it was Bout's bodyguard who had taken things the worst of all: Belozerosky was in tears. He kept complaining that the cuffs were cutting into his wrists and hurting him. Carlos and Ricardo had zero sympathy. They ignored him completely.

Mike, meanwhile, was still in his hotel room, oblivious to all that had happened. He took a call from Agent Zach. 'We've got him! Just thought you'd want to know.'

Mike couldn't believe it. The speed of Bout's arrest was testimony to the quality of the planning and execution of this stage of the operation. But it begged a vital question: what was The Bear supposed to do now? Carlos' words of a few days earlier flashed through his mind: when the sting went down, all the undercovers could do was run . . .

Agent Zach told him they needed to clap him in handcuffs, and lead him through the Thai police station, so Bout could get a good eyeful. All part of the subterfuge and the theatre.

Mike wasn't happy. 'I don't do handcuffs. Period. So that ain't happening.'

Zach tried to persuade Mike otherwise, but he was adamant: other arrangements would have to be made to get The Bear out of there.

Of the five men arrested, Smulian was steered in an entirely different direction to the others. He was handed over to the DEA agents and frogmarched to his hotel room. There, the Englishman was cuffed to a chair, as the DEA team rifled through his possessions, seizing his laptop, his mobile phones and his camera.

Agent Zach proceeded to unleash on Smulian with both barrels, outlining just what a nightmare he was facing. Every single meeting that he had ever had on the deal had been secretly recorded, starting with Curaçao. Every word Smulian had uttered had been caught on tape. His phone calls had been intercepted, his text messages captured and his emails logged. The DEA had everything they could wish for on Andrew Michael Smulian.

Among other things, he faced charges of 'conspiracy to kill United States nationals'. That alone carried a twenty-five-year life sentence, and in the US Federal justice system there was zero parole. Right now Smulian faced two choices: either he agreed to accompany the DEA team to the USA, or he would rot in a Thai gaol.

No one needed to explain to Smulian the ramifications of incarceration in a Thai prison. Smulian was sixty-seven years old.

He was basically penniless, so had few funds with which to hire a lawyer. By anyone's reckoning, his chances of survival were slim. Smulian – in deep shock and traumatized by what had happened – understood this much: to stay in Thailand was tantamount to a death sentence.

But the alternative was to head for the USA, which would mean cooperating with the DEA in their case against Viktor Bout. Right now, as he sat cuffed to his chair, Smulian felt too shocked to make any kind of a rational decision. His mind was reeling. One moment he had been poised to strike the deal of a lifetime; the next, he was staring into the abyss.

In fact, Smulian was in such deep shock that it didn't even register with him that Zach was noting down all his answers.

Wim, meanwhile, was processing all that had been seized – scribbled notes, hardware, recording devices – into evidence. There was an utterly heart-stopping moment when he went to check the recordings of the conference suite meeting, and El Comandante's device turned out to be blank.

As far as Wim could tell, Ricardo had failed to switch it on properly. Thankfully, Carlos' professionalism had saved the day: his watch and key-fob had been properly activated, and they had captured the hours of discussions perfectly.

With his mind frozen in shock, Smulian was bundled into a vehicle and driven to the same Thai police station as the others. That journey seemed to have a sobering effect upon him. It brought Smulian to his senses. By the time they reached their destination, Smulian had made his decision: he agreed to accompany Agents Brown and Zachariasiewicz to the USA.

At the police station, Belozerosky had just been given his marching orders. He'd been handed a fistful of Thai baht, and ordered to leave the country and never to return. Bout, meanwhile, sat quietly in a Thai police interview room, as the wheels of Bangkok justice began to turn, and press photographers tried to sneak shots through doorway and window.

Wim and Zach made their way towards that room. It was time to give Bout a similar ultimatum to the one they'd delivered to Smulian. They found the Russian bear seated in a chair, his legs outstretched, his cuffed hands folded in his lap, lips pursed thoughtfully.

'Mr Bout, I think it's only fair I explain to you that the entire meeting was recorded and it came out crystal clear,' Zach told him.

Bout put his head down for a good few seconds, as he tried to digest what he'd just heard. Then he glanced at the DEA agents. 'If everything is recorded, then you have everything.' Bout's manner was quiet and reserved. 'You have all the cards on the table.'

The agents outlined Bout's options: either rot in a Thai gaol while awaiting extradition, or accompany the DEA team to the USA. Bout considered this for a short time, before giving his answer.

'I think I need speak to attorney.'

Bout was duly fingerprinted, documented and processed into Bangkok's Bangkwang Central Prison.

When Wim and Zach left the Thai police station, they had with them Bout's black file containing all of his FARC research. They also had the Insight Travel Map that Bout had used during the conference suite meeting. It covered a good chunk of South America, and there were handwritten notes and scribbles over the Colombia section. More corroborating evidence.

From Bout's hotel room the Thai police had seized his ASUS

laptop, zip drives, a Canon camera and his Colombia guide-book. One of the FBI's Bangkok team – a computer expert – was allowed to make a 'mirror-image' of Bout's hard-drive, creating an exact duplicate of its contents. In due course DEA computer forensics experts would have a field day with the data.

Already, the takedown was making headlines around the world, and especially on US networks. CNN ran with the leads – 'Fifteen-year odyssey of tracking Viktor Bout', and '"Most-wanted" arms dealer arrested in Thailand.' *USA Today* trumpeted 'Russian "Merchant of Death" detained'. The *Los Angeles Times* ran with the relatively sober headline 'Long-sought global arms dealer arrested'. The *Washington Post* reported 'Reputed Global Arms Dealer Arrested', while *Mother Jones* magazine ran with '"Merchant of Death" Viktor Bout is Arrested in Thailand'.

In the UK, the *Guardian* splashed the headline '"Lord of War" arms trafficker arrested.' The *Daily Telegraph* announced '"Merchant of Death" arrested in Thailand', while the BBC reported 'Thailand holds "top arms dealer"'. The international media ran similar stories, while INTERPOL lauded the success of the oper-ation, praising the 'international cooperation behind the arrest of suspected international arms dealer by Thai Police'.

But in Russia, the media reports sounded a noticeably different note. Reportage of the arrest portrayed Bout as an 'alleged' or 'suspected' arms dealer, and as variously a 'businessman', 'Russian army officer', or even an 'ordinary citizen who found himself in difficult conditions abroad'. Russian officials were quick to raise their objections to Bout's arrest, describing it as 'suspicious' and 'sheer murkiness' and even 'illegal'.

It was all complicated by the fact that neither Russia nor Thailand listed FARC as a 'terrorist organization'.

The night of the arrest the DEA team gathered at a hole-in-the-wall bar near their hotel. The decades-long pursuit of Viktor Bout had been brought to an apparent end, which called for a beer or two. Mike was there: he'd slipped out of the Sofitel via the rear-entrance into an underground car park, a shadowy figure from the US embassy serving as his escort. Carlos and Ricardo were also in attendance – fresh out of the Thai police cells.

DEA Agent Pasquarello passed Mike the key-fob to Bout's room – it was his, as a keepsake, he declared. A memento of Operation Relentless. Without Mike Snow, none of this would have been possible. He was also introduced to the US prosecutor, Preet Bharara, who'd flown in to oversee this stage of Operation Relentless from the legal side.

People kept dropping in to congratulate the team. There was lots of backslapping and, 'Well done, Bear.' But the atmosphere proved strangely downbeat. Somehow, everyone seemed more bewildered than exultant. There was no big shootout to recover from. Instead, there was the knowledge that while Bout might be in custody, a long extradition process now loomed.

In a sense the journey was only just beginning, and many hurdles lay ahead. Already the Russian government was raising its strongest possible objections to Viktor Bout's arrest.

The highlight for Mike was when a baby elephant was led into the bar. The Bear was given some sugarcane and invited to feed the animal. He'd never been this close to a baby elephant before. Of course, he'd now been very close to a Russian bear: indeed, the entire Relentless team had. But whether they'd actually nailed Viktor Bout remained to be seen.

Shortly after midnight Andrew Smulian caught a flight to New York, in the company of DEA agents. On the drive to the airport he asked whether Snow worked for the DEA in some way. Snow's stubbornness was coming back to haunt him: if he'd allowed himself to be cuffed and arrested, along with the others, such suspicions were far less likely to have arisen so quickly.

Agent Zach countered Smulian's question with a question: 'Why, should he?'

'He's a very intelligent man who's done some exceptional things,' Smulian replied.

Agent Zach remained poker-faced. 'Okay. Noted.'

The fewer pieces Smulian could put together, the better. They needed him scared and confused and ready to drop his pants, as they say in law-enforcement circles, which was pretty much exactly where they had him right then.

A little later that night Margaret Snow took a call from DEA Agent Zach. 'You need to get out of there,' he warned her – meaning out of Africa. 'We'll have someone meet you upon arrival in the US. Just get yourself to New York.'

Bout, it was feared, had a long reach, and anyone connected to Operation Relentless – however tangentially and no matter where in the world they might be – was seen as being in danger. Margaret Snow confirmed she would do as instructed.

Early on the morning of 7 March Mike Snow left for New York. As the aircraft lifted off from Bangkok's airport, he decided Carlos Sagastume had just earned himself a new nickname: Die Voorbok. In South Africa, they use a goat to lead sheep to the slaughterhouse. The goat – a seasoned performer – knows it will emerge unscathed, and the sheep follow, innocent and unwitting to the last. The goat was called Die Voorbok. Right then, it seemed like the perfect name for Carlos.

The key players in Operation Relentless were fleeing for safety as fast as they could. But Carlos and Ricardo – doubtless the two team members under greatest threat – were stuck in Thailand. All flights to the US were booked solid for the next forty-eight hours. With news breaking on the hour about the fallout from Bout's arrest, this was the absolutely most dangerous time to still be in the country.

Smulian was arrested almost as soon as his flight touched down in New York. He was assigned a lawyer, who briefed the Englishman on what lay ahead, leaving him in little doubt as to how dire was his situation. He faced charges on multiple counts, including 'conspiracy to kill United States citizens', 'conspiracy to provide anti-aircraft missiles', and 'conspiracy to provide material support to a terrorist organization.'

He would very quickly enter into a series of 'proffer sessions', at which he could attempt to negotiate some kind of a deal with the DEA. If those 'proffer sessions' bore fruit, he might in turn strike a 'cooperation agreement' with the US government. If he stuck to the letter of that agreement, turning evidence against Viktor Bout, he might get away with 'time served'.

Smulian's argument was that he was simply the little guy in the deal. He'd only driven the car to the bank; he hadn't intended to play any role in the robbery. The DEA negotiators didn't much care: all they were interested in were the terms of the deal, and the kind of evidence Smulian could provide on the stand.

By 9 March 2008 all of the Operation Relentless team were safely back in the USA. Mike Snow and his wife would rendezvous in New York, where they would enter into a witness protection programme. Along with Carlos and Ricardo, they now faced the long haul of getting themselves and the evidence shipshape for trial – that's if Bout's extradition to the USA went ahead.

The US Grand Jury indictment, which would be used to argue for Bout's extradition, charged him with multiple crimes. Describing him as an 'international weapons trafficker', it outlined how 'to carry out his weapons-trafficking business, VIKTOR BOUT . . . assembled a fleet of cargo airplanes capable of transporting weapons and military equipment to various parts of the world, including Africa, South America and the Middle East.'

The indictment went on: 'To provide cover for his illicit arms transactions, BOUT developed an international network of front companies, and used his cargo airplanes to deliver lawful goods, such as food and medical supplies, in addition to arms.'

On Count One, the Conspiracy to Kill United States Nationals, the indictment charged Bout 'and others' – chiefly Smulian – with agreeing 'to provide the FARC with millions of dollars' worth of weapons to be used, amongst other things, to kill nationals of the United States in Colombia'. It then listed the meetings in Curaçao, Moscow, Copenhagen, Bucharest and Bangkok, and the key events therein, including Bout agreeing to sell the 'FARC' hundreds of surface-to-air missiles, and affirming that the US was 'his enemy'.

Count Two was broadly similar to count one: 'Conspiracy to Kill Officers and Employees of the United States.' It simply extended the reach of Count One. Count Three was self-explanatory: 'Conspiracy to Acquire and Use Anti-Aircraft Missiles.' In the charge, Bout and his co-conspirator were accused of agreeing to 'export surface-to-air missile systems to enable the FARC to attack United States aircraft in Colombia'.

Count Four accused Bout and his co-conspirator, Smulian, of

'Conspiracy to Provide Material Support to a Terrorist Organization.' In the charge, the two were accused of agreeing 'to provide the FARC with millions of dollars' worth of weapons for the FARC to use to protect their cocaine trafficking business and to attack United States interests in Colombia, knowing that the FARC . . . was engaging in terrorist activity'.

With Bout languishing in a Bangkok gaol, the Operation Relentless team had got their man. The charge sheet appeared damning, as did the wealth of evidence ranged against him. But whether Bout would face justice or not was an entirely different matter.

After several weeks' incarceration, Viktor Bout's apparent composure seemed to crack. He was filmed by the media yelling out his objections to his imprisonment, from behind the bars of his cell. 'I am addressing the President of Russia, Vladimir Putin: I have been in Thai prison for more than a month on charges fabricated by the Americans. I am asking you to find out why I have been arrested, and to force the Thai government to return me home.'

Bout was not returned home to Russia.

It would take more than two years – and bitter accusations of dark dealings by both the American, Russian and Thai administrations – before eventually he was extradited to the USA. In what the press hailed as 'the trial of the century', held in a Manhattan courtroom, Carlos and Ricardo, plus Agent Brown, provided powerful evidence for the prosecution.

But it was Andrew Michael Smulian who arguably gave the most compelling testimony. Indeed, a *New York Times* article hailed him thus: 'Conduit to Arms Sting, a Star Witness.' Dressed in a blue blazer and with his signature shock of white hair, Smulian – who had spent three years in gaol already – proved remarkably solid on the stand, even under a fierce cross-examination in which Bout's lawyer tried to argue that he might be losing his memory.

Sadly, between Bout's arrest and trial, Mike Snow had been diagnosed with an apparently terminal form of cancer. He played no role in Viktor Bout's prosecution.

Bout himself did not offer a word in his own defence, which meant that the jury never got to hear from him directly. Bout's lawyer, Albert Dayan, argued that it was the prosecution's responsibility to prove his client's guilt – as opposed to Bout needing to prove his innocence – and it was better if the Russian remained silent.

In October 2011 Viktor Bout was found guilty by the jury on all four counts as charged. In April 2012 he was sentenced to serve twenty-five years in a US penitentiary. Since then he has appealed his sentence on several occasions.

None of those appeals has been successful.

EPILOGUE

The trial of Viktor Bout – and the subsequent appeals – is worthy of a book in itself, but lies outside the scope of this narrative. It took two years to extradite Viktor Bout from Thailand. Upon his arrival in the US, Preet Bharara, the US Attorney overseeing the case, told the press: 'Today . . . accused arms dealer Viktor Bout begins to face American justice. The so-called Merchant of Death is now a Federal inmate.' He faced charges 'for his alleged agreement to supply an arsenal of military grade weapons to men he believed one, represented the Colombian terrorist group known as the FARC, and two, were bent on killing Americans.'

At the subsequent trial Viktor Bout's defence seemed to be predicated on the claim that he was never a seller, a broker or a trafficker of arms. He was only ever a carrier of weaponry. His was simply an airborne taxi service. Bout's lawyer attempted to mount the argument that Viktor Bout and Andrew Smulian's negotiations with the FARC were actually an elaborate sting operation concocted by them. It had been a two-way con game. Bout was a cash-strapped former arms dealer; 'a broke conman conning buyers to sell planes'.

In the defence case, Bout and Smulian had somehow 'tricked' Carlos Sagastume and Ricardo Jardeno into meeting in Thailand, via the promise of an arms deal, but with the actual intention of selling them aircraft that would be used to deliver arms. Bout's avowedly anti-American comments were all part of the con: he was baiting the FARC, just as they were baiting him.

The defence failed on several counts. One, the vast body of evidence painstakingly complied by the DEA – the transcripts, wiretaps, recordings and witness testimonies – did not support such an argument. Two, there was no credible explanation given as to just who Bout – and Smulian – believed Carlos Sagastume and Ricardo Jardeno to be, if not the FARC.

But more than anything, Andrew Smulian's testimony powerfully disavowed such an argument. In both the prosecution and defence case, Smulian was accepted as Bout's co-conspirator. The difference centred around whether he was a co-conspirator in what each man believed to be a genuine deal with the FARC, or a co-conspirator in some shadowy plot to con two persons unknown out of millions of euros, by flogging them some Russian cargo planes.

At trial, Smulian clearly and consistently argued that it was the former. If he was lying, as the defence tried to argue, then he was doing so repeatedly under oath in a US court of law. Moreover, as part of his plea-bargain with the US Government he would also have had to lie repeatedly over the past two years, and that, frankly, beggared belief.

Bout's lawyer attempted to argue that Smulian's memory was failing and that he was plagued by forgetfulness. If anything, Smulian's forthright performance at trial proved the otherwise.

He was also accused of being willing to lie under oath, to secure a shorter gaol sentence. Again, Smulian's rebuttal of such an argument was clear and credible.

The prosecution called six witnesses in addition to Smulian. Agent Brown gave evidence, as did confidential sources Carlos Sagastume and Ricardo Jardeno, plus DEA computer forensics expert Stephen Marx, among others.

In his summing up, the US Assistant Attorney, Brendan R. McGuire, outlined why Operation Relentless had been necessary. 'It is no mystery . . . why the DEA investigated Viktor Bout. This is a man who had the experience, the will, the relationships, to arm conflicts. You heard how he had done it before, in the Congo . . . in Angola and in East Africa . . . This is a man who had been sanctioned by the United Nations, and also by the United States . . . As Viktor Bout said himself, he had been at war with the US for ten to fifteen years.'

At 1.20 p.m. the day after the hearings came to an end, the twelve-strong jury delivered its verdict: guilty as charged on all counts. Bout was sentenced in April 2012. Before Judge Shira Scheindlin announced her sentence, she asked if he had anything he wanted to say to the court.

'I am innocent,' Bout declared. 'I don't commit any crime. There is no crime to sit and talk. If you gonna apply the same standards to me, then you're gonna gaol all those arms dealers in America who selling the arms that end up killing Americans . . . It's a double standard. It's a hypocrisy. I want to go home. I don't commit any crime. I am innocent.'

Judge Scheindlin imposed the twenty-five-year mandatory sentence, but in doing so she aired a note of caution, possibly even regret. 'But for the approach made through this determined sting operation, there is no reason to believe Bout would ever have committed the charged crimes.'

'Viktor was extremely lucky with the judge assigned to his case,' says American author Gerald Posner, who became a personal confidant to Bout after his extradition. 'He got a judge who was independent, extremely bright and was not someone who would simply rubber stamp the prosecution's case . . . the fact that he emerged from the trial without a mandatory life sentence in the country's most oppressive maximum security facility is largely down to her.'

Upon her retirement from the judiciary, Judge Scheindlin voiced further reservations. 'I'm not defending him,' she told the *New York Times* of Bout, 'but he's a businessman. He was in the business of selling arms.' He was not a fighter or a terrorist from Al Qaeda, 'who lives to blow up civilians in a supermarket . . . They reeled this guy in. They offered him a lot of money . . . I gave the lowest sentence I could possibly give.'

In the process of writing this book, I have wondered how a man of Bout's experience, intellect and cunning could have allowed himself to go down at trial seemingly without a fight. Over time, I have wondered if this really was as much of a mistake as it at first appears. Did Bout really blow it, or did he somehow *allow* his defence to flounder, as the least worst option open to him at the time?

Matt Potter – Russian expert, Bout aficionado and author of the excellent book *Outlaws Inc.* – suggested to me this might well be the case. 'I'm not sure I really think he blew it at all. On the contrary, maybe – just maybe – he played his hand rather smartly. Maybe going down with a whimper . . . was the best of all options. It meant he didn't have to talk about any of the other work he's done; it meant he didn't have to talk about Africa, or Afghanistan, or any of the covert deliveries he's been making . . .

'This was the one scenario everyone could afford. Except of course, Viktor. He's in for twenty-five years. Or is he?' Potter concluded that, 'The hand Bout played is careful indeed. It's about the long game: talk in court in the US in an attempt to get off, or to cut a deal, and you might succeed; but you'll probably fail anyway, and messily, having played all of your cards and sold out all of your contacts . . . Fail on purpose, however – brief your attorney poorly, insist he witters on about US hypocrisy, blithely miss all the hints a deal may be on the cards – and you'll go down . . . Like a mobster who keeps *schtum* in gaol . . .'

In other words, did Viktor Bout realize that the risks were too great either to cut a deal with the US prosecutors, or to take the stand and ask others to do so in his defence? Under cross-examination by the prosecution attorneys, who knows what Bout and associates might have been forced to reveal? What inconvenient truths might have emerged at trial? And what then were his prospects of ever returning to the mother country? Pretty near zero.

In short, did Bout allow himself to be the fall guy, because all other options were infinitely less preferable?

In speaking to Mark Galeotti – Russian expert and Senior Researcher at the Institute of International Relations, Prague – I got a sense this might be the case. 'Bout took the hit at trial. The trial felt more like a POW situation: name, rank and serial number and that was it. Nothing else. There was no real defence, but actually that was Bout's fault. It was his choice what he did at trial. And that created a narrative – that he was somehow an innocent let down by an incompetent defence.

'In truth, he'd have been a hostage to fortune if he'd tried to mount a proper defence, because that may well have revealed inconvenient secrets. The Igla missiles are not things you pick up at Costco. It would have been very hard to mount a proper defence . . . without revealing secrets. In fact, how Bout presented himself at trial was pretty much how a professional intel officer comports himself in hostile territory. It's a no-comment situation.'

As Galeotti points out, 'US intel has no doubts that Bout was a Russian intel asset. There is a grudging respect within that community as to how he took the hit and went down and stayed silent.'

Galeotti goes one step further. He posits the intriguing scenario that since the fall of the Soviet Union, the Russian state has used organized crime networks as a global intelligence conduit, working through 'individuals who are part-time assets within those networks. In Bout's case he was acting as an agent of Moscow, and by offering arms deals to all he was aiding the Russian state's struggle to keep its arms manufacturing industries turning a profit. Moving substantial military kit requires logistical capacity and Bout provided that. He was also a very useful asset in terms of intel gathering.

'The US was not so concerned perhaps about closing down Bout's operations,' Galeotti maintains. 'It was more a case . . . of once they had him, who knew what Bout might be able to tell them. That was why the Russian state tried so hard to prevent Bout's extradition, and then to influence the trial and after to get him returned to Russia.'

Viktor Bout's arrest and conviction proved controversial at the time and continues to do so. World opinion seemed split between those who believed Bout was the incarnation of all evil and deserved all he got, and those who claimed he was a victim of a US-led witch-hunt – Russians somehow making a convenient 'bad guy' target.

'It has become hyper-partisan,' Matt Potter told me. 'But in truth there are shades of grey; the world is made up of shades of grey, and there must always be an appeal to truth and common sense. Bout himself did things in which he was fundamentally and wilfully blind to the consequences . . . You wear the hat, you have to obey the rules, and at the time you start to deal in attack helicopters you have to accept responsibility for doing so, and that those who enforce the law will come after you.'

Mark Galeotti argues that Bout's case was 'driven in part by how you feel about the US and its will and capacity to use its muscle abroad. That's what has informed a lot of people's opinion that somehow this is "poor Viktor Bout facing a frame-up". His defence seemed to promote the idea that he was some kind of political prisoner. The Russia propaganda channels – Russia Today, etc. – were pushing the story that Viktor Bout was a busi-nessman and the nasty USA hunted him down for unknown/shadowy reasons.

'Viktor Bout was an arms dealer and a GRU officer,' Galeotti concludes. 'He was caught on tape extolling the virtues of selling weapons to narcoterrorists to kill Americans. But it's become one of the cases via which global anti-Americanism can be articulated.'

'The line between who's employed as an asset formally, or who's simply an asset because of what they do has become totally blurred,' Potter points out. The West should have foreseen 'the entire Russian information war', he argues. 'In a sense the Soviet Union didn't break, it just bent and metamorphosed. The difference is, via the means the Russians use today to exert power and influence you don't even see it coming, as it's no longer tanks and military. In Bout's case, his status as to whether he's a cast-iron GRU asset or just a genuine "good lad" is fluid.'

Some have argued that Bout's conviction did little to stop the flow of illicit arms to conflict-torn areas of the world. Certainly, he was not – and is not – the only arms dealer in the world. At the time of his arrest and conviction, there were many others plying this shadowy trade.

As Mark Galeotti remarks: 'There are more small-time operators, and I wonder how long it is before one or two of them fill the vacuum . . . Viktor Bout did not create the market. He was able very effectively to capitalize on it, but he didn't create it, and where there's a market there will be other suppliers.'

'The government agents played Bout perfectly,' Gerald Posner told me. 'They wanted him very badly for a long time, because of his former arms sales . . . If you listen to Viktor Bout's side, he believes they went for him because he made arms sales to rebels and governments that the US was trying to block. But when the US puts an embargo on one side of a conflict getting arms, that increases the price that side is willing to pay, and the profit margins for someone who can get them the weaponry. Someone like Viktor – a businessman first and foremost – will sell to whoever pays the highest price. That's just business.'

Some years after Bout's arrest, the US-based Conflict Awareness Project issued a report entitled 'Viktor Bout's Gunrunning Successors: A Lethal Game of Catch Me If You Can'. The report stresses that the capture and prosecution of Viktor Bout served a purpose: it sent a powerful message that arms traffickers would face stringent penalties if brought to book for their criminal activities.

Former British minister, now Lord Hain, agrees: 'Some seem to have argued that focusing on one individual has done little to stop the arms trade or to address the wider issues. I disagree and believe that you need headline prosecutions as a deterrent to others. Just because you cannot prosecute everyone doesn't mean you should prosecute no one.'

The conclusion of the Conflict Awareness Project report is that 'international arms brokers remain uniquely unregulated'. It outlines how the successors to Viktor Bout – former colleagues of his, and mostly Russian – are rebuilding his network. They use the same excuses for their activities as he did, 'insisting that they are just in the transport business'. The lax legal controls on the arms trade continue to 'make a mockery of UN resolutions and sanctions regimes'.

Recent UN estimates suggest there are approximately 875 million small arms in circulation, manufactured by one thousand different companies located in close to one hundred countries. Clearly, there is much work to be done.

WHERE ARE THEY ALL NOW?

RÓMULO RAMIREZ: Ramirez, the Venezuelan drugs-cartel's European fixer and money launderer, was subsequently busted by the DEA, and much of the wider Venezuelan cartel was brought to justice. Aircraft procured by DEA sources had been inserted into the Cartel's dope-running fleet, to track and trace their network.

RICHARD CHICHAKLI: in January 2013 Richard Chichakli – the man wanted for acting as Bout's US fixer – was arrested in Australia. He was subsequently sentenced in a US court to five years in gaol, and to forfeit $1.7 million. He was found guilty of having tried to purchase two aircraft illegally to transport weapons into war zones, among other charges. Noting how Chichakli was 'involved with Viktor Bout, a notorious arms dealer', judge William H Pauley described him as having 'a warped sense of right and wrong . . . It is hard to figure out how he keeps up with all the fictions he created in this case.'

ANDREW SMULIAN: Smulian received a five-year gaol sentence for his part in the FARC arms-dealing conspiracy. He told the courts: 'I categorically accept full responsibility for my conduct,' and apologized unreservedly for his crimes. As his sentence included time served he was released from prison in early 2013, aged seventy-two, and was offered a witness protection programme. He'd used his time in prison to try to reform himself, studying Latin and Hebrew and reading hundreds of books, including those by Lincoln, Mandela, Gandhi and the complete works of Shakespeare.

VIKTOR BOUT: under Viktor Bout's sentence of twenty-five years without parole, he will be released in 2037, when he will be approaching seventy years of age.

PIERRE VILLARD: Frenchman Villard continues to deal in aircraft and double as a DEA source when required.

RICARDO JARDENO: after a number of further DEA missions, Jardeno returned to Central America, to invest his newfound wealth in business there. He has since largely dropped off the radar.

CARLOS SAGASTUME: the King of Sting remains active as a DEA undercover source, and is at the present time the most experienced and successful DEA undercover operator of all time.

MIKE SNOW: The Bear survived his cancer, proving him right, he believes, in the conviction that 'thoughts become things'. His illness is now in remission.

THE OPERATION RELENTLESS TEAM: following the successful conclusion of Operation Relentless and the sentencing of Bout, each of the DEA undercovers was given a substantial reward, running into millions of dollars. Team Relentless re-formed to carry out one or two further DEA missions, but that is another story.

SUGGESTED FURTHER READING

For those interested in reading more about this story or the wider issues, or watching more on the same, these sources are well worth looking at:

Merchant Of Death: Money, Guns, Planes and the Man Who Makes War Possible, by Douglas Farah and Stephen Braun (John Wiley & Sons, 2007)

The Shadow World: Inside the Global Arms Trade, by Andrew Feinstein (Penguin Books, 2012)

Outside In, by Peter Hain (Biteback Publishing, 2012)

The Infiltrator: Undercover in the World of Drug Barons and Dirty Banks, by Robert Mazur (Little Brown, 2009)

Escape From Kandahar, by Alexander Petrovich Mishchenko (Cultural Information Bank, 2001) [only available in Russian]

Outlaws Inc., by Matt Potter (Pan Macmillan, 2012)

Zero, Zero, Zero, by Roberto Saviano (Allen Lane, 2013)

War On The Mind: The Military Uses and Abuses of Psychology, by Peter Watson (Hutchinson and Co., 1978)

The Notorious Mr. Bout, a film by Tony Gerber and Maxi Pozdorovkin

The book *Operation Mayhem* (Orion, 2015), by Steve Heaney and myself, tells the full story of the Pathfinders' deployment to Sierra Leone, on Operation Palliser, and their defence of Lungi Lol.